»In Search of the ›Great American Op

D1540623

Populäre Kultur und Musik

Herausgegeben von Michael Fischer
im Auftrag des Zentrums für Populäre Kultur und Musik
der Universität Freiburg
und Nils Grosch im Auftrag der Universität Salzburg

Band 17

Frédéric Döhl
Gregor Herzfeld
(Hrsg.)

»In Search of the ›Great American Opera‹«

Tendenzen des amerikanischen
Musiktheaters

Waxmann 2016
Münster · New York

Gedruckt mit freundlicher Unterstützung des SFB 626 *Ästhetische Erfahrung im Zeichen der Entgrenzung der Künste* aus Mitteln der Deutschen Forschungsgemeinschaft.

Sonderforschungsbereich 626
Ästhetische Erfahrung im Zeichen
der Entgrenzung der Künste
Freie Universität Berlin

Deutsche
Forschungsgemeinschaft
DFG

Bibliografische Informationen der Deutschen Nationalbibliothek

Die Deutsche Nationalbibliothek verzeichnet diese Publikation in der Deutschen Nationalbibliografie; detaillierte bibliografische Daten sind im Internet über http://dnb.d-nb.de abrufbar.

Populäre Kultur und Musik, Bd. 17

Print-ISBN 978-3-8309-3124-9
E-Book-ISBN 978-3-8309-8124-4
ISSN 1869-8417

© Waxmann Verlag GmbH, Münster 2016

www.waxmann.com
info@waxmann.com

Umschlaggestaltung: Pleßmann Design, Ascheberg
Druck: Hubert & Co., Göttingen
Gedruckt auf alterungsbeständigem Papier, säurefrei gemäß ISO 9706

MIX
Papier aus verantwor-
tungsvollen Quellen
FSC® C016439

Printed in Germany

Inhalt

Vorwort.. 7

Gregor Herzfeld

Größe als Erhabenheit.
Einführende Gedanken zu Bernard Herrmann... 9

Aaron Ziegel

Crafting the Soundworld of American Opera, 1910–1912 19

Marcus Gräser

»Recognizably American«. Aaron Coplands *The Second Hurricane*
(1936/37) als musikalische Theatralisierung des Politischen im *New Deal*.............. 45

Christopher Lynch

Operatic Conventions on Broadway, 1935–1960.. 65

Micah Wittmer

Toward an American Folk Opera. Performing Primitivism and
Negro Folk Culture in Hall Johnson's *Run, Little Chillun!* (1933) 81

Nils Grosch

Oper als Strategie der kompositorischen Selbstinszenierung und Wertbegriff:
Street Scene (1946) und *West Side Story* (1957)... 101

Marie Louise Herzfeld-Schild

The Sound of Music (1959) – »A Great American Opera«?........................ 113

Mauro Fosco Bertola

Glass *avec* Fukuyama oder Philip Glass' *The Voyage* (1992)
und das Ende der Geschichte 131

Frédéric Döhl

About the Task of Adapting a Movie Classic for the Opera Stage:
On André Previn's *A Streetcar Named Desire* (1998) and
Brief Encounter (2009) 147

John Link

Sense and Sensibility: Music on Stage in *What Next?* 177

Sharon Mirchandani

Libby Larsen's *Barnum's Bird*. The »Great American Opera« 199

Amy Bauer

»The Mysteries of Selma, Alabama«. Re-telling and Remembrance
in David Lang's *The Difficulty of Crossing a Field* 219

Autorinnen und Autoren / Authors 235

Vorwort

Groß, amerikanisch, Oper?

Was macht eine Oper »groß«, was macht sie »amerikanisch«? Zwei problematische Begriffe prägen die Rede von einer »Great American Opera« und machen sie in mehrfacher Hinsicht verdächtig: Ein gängiges Modell von Geschichtsschreibung verortet das 20. Jahrhundert, zumindest den – in sich nicht weniger problematischen – Bereich der vermeintlichen »Kunstmusik«, in kritischer Distanz zum Großen. Das Große, das Monumentale, das Überwältigende, das im langen 19. Jahrhundert seine Konjunktur hatte, gerät im Zeitalter der demagogischen Massenverführung und systematischen Massenvernichtung zur suspekten Dimension. Und dies gilt insbesondere dann, wenn es mit dem Attribut einer nationalen Zugehörigkeit gepaart wird. War es nicht eben jener bürgerliche Nationalismus, der direkt zu den Extremismen der beiden Weltkriege geführt hat? Beim Amerikanismus kommt hinzu, dass es selbst unter den Vorzeichen eines ausgeprägten Nationalismus und seines Hangs zur Klischeebildung schwierig sein dürfte, genau auszumachen, was eigentlich als »amerikanisch« zu gelten hat, insbesondere im lange Zeit von europäischen Genremodellen geprägten Kultur- und Musikbereich.

Und dennoch: Die »große amerikanische Oper« war und ist Gegenstand diverser Diskurse analog zur Diskussion um »The Great American Novel«. Die Verlockung, den »großen amerikanischen Roman« aufzuspüren, der gleichsam das Wesen seines Herkunftslandes zum Ausdruck bringe, scheint derart mächtig, dass bis heute mit Werken von Herman Melville bis Philip Roth stets neue Kandidaten angeführt werden. Bereits 1925 übertrug Benjamin Morris Steigman das Konzept auf die Musik und nannte Werke wie Horatio Parkers *Mona* (1912) oder Reginald de Kovens *Rip van Winkle* (1919) erste Versuche, eine »Great American Opera« zu kreieren. Im akademischen Kontext verwendete zuletzt etwa Lawrence Kramer 2007 den Terminus, um Opern wie André Previns *A Streetcar Named Desire* (1998) oder John Adams' *The Death of Klinghoffer* (1991) zu charakterisieren. Zwischen diesen Werken liegen etliche Jahrzehnte, die ihrerseits Zeugen einer äußerst produktiven Herstellung von Musiktheater in den USA waren, die mit unterschiedlicher Intensität auf die Herausforderungen der »Oper«, des »Großen« und des »Amerikanischen« reagierten. Der vorliegende Band möchte die gesamte Palette der amerikanischen Musiktheaterwelt im 20. Jahrhundert ungeachtet möglicher Labels wie »kritisches« oder »avantgardistisches« Komponieren in den Blick nehmen und dabei schlaglichthaft fragen, ob und, wenn ja, in welcher Form es eine Annäherung an eine »Great American Opera« gab und gibt und was die Suche danach motiviert. Allgemeine Voraussetzungen und Begleitumstände der Kulturgeschichte sind dabei ebenso Thema, wie es darum geht, detaillierte analytische Einlassungen vorzunehmen. Hier werden insbesondere die oftmals nicht genug gewürdigten Unterschiede zwischen ästhetischen Herangehensweisen, wie sie im europäischen Raum und speziell in der BRD der Jahrzehnte nach dem Zweiten Weltkrieg gepflegt und propagiert wurden, und solchen, die jenseits des Atlantiks vor dem Hintergrund davon abweichender historischer Erfahrungen sich herausbilden konnten, zu beachten sein. Denn mit der Idee des Erhabenen im Rücken, wie sie im nordamerikanischen Terrain quasi ohne Bruch und Lücke bis heute Geltung beanspruchen kann, wird die affirmative Zuwendung zu »großen« Sujets, die nicht auch selten Sujets des Großen sind, erst verständlich.

Die deutschsprachigen Beiträge dieses Bandes gehen auf Vorträge zurück, die am 6. Dezember 2013 im Rahmen eines Workshops des SFB 626 an der Freien Universität Berlin mit der großzügigen Unterstützung der Deutschen Forschungsgemeinschaft gehalten wurden. Allen Autoren sei gedankt für die gelungenen Verwandlungen ihrer Wort- in Schriftbeiträge! Die Herausgeber freuen sich auch besonders, die Einsendungen eines Call for Articles im englischsprachigen Bereich veröffentlichen zu können, ohne die das etwas seltsame Konstrukt entstanden wäre, dass sich eine Handvoll deutschsprachiger Wissenschaftlerinnen und Wissenschaftler über Phänomene der amerikanischen Kulturgeschichte beugt, ohne in den Austausch mit ihren in dieser Kultur tätigen und beheimateten Kolleginnen und Kollegen zu treten. So sind wir froh, dass das Verhältnis ausgewogen ist und dadurch ein von »außen« und »innen« balancierter Blick entstehen konnte. Christel Frazer hat dankenswerterweise die Redaktion der englischsprachigen Texte ausgeführt. Schließlich danken wir der DFG, deren finanzieller Zuschuss die Drucklegung ermöglicht hat, sowie dem Waxmann Verlag für die Veröffentlichung und Daniela Langer für die zuvorkommende Betreuung des Veröffentlichungsprozesses und das sehr engagierte Lektorat.

Frédéric Döhl und Gregor Herzfeld

Gregor Herzfeld

Größe als Erhabenheit
Einführende Gedanken zu Bernard Herrmann

Das Paradigma *Moby-Dick*

Herman Melvilles Roman *Moby-Dick* (1854) erfreut sich bei Publikum und Künstlern aller Medien anhaltender Beliebtheit und kann als konstante Auseinandersetzung mit der Möglichkeit einer eigenen Traditionsbildung im kulturellen Bereich der USA über die Jahrhunderte hinweg gelesen werden.

Mit seinem *Moby-Dick* schrieb Melville zur Mitte des 19. Jahrhunderts den exemplarischen Romanbeitrag zum amerikanischen Erhabenheitsdiskurs. Im Unterschied zu den europäischen Modellen, die sich von Edmund Burkes Darstellung des Erhabenen in seinem *Philosophical Enquiry* (1759) über Immanuel Kants Analyse in der *Kritik der Urteilskraft* (1790) bis zu den poetischen Konzepten der britischen Lake Poets William Wordsworth und Samuel Taylor Coleridge (um 1800) reichen, transformiert Melville das Erhabene zu einer Dimension des schlechthin Großen, das nicht mehr bloß unser Vorstellungsvermögen übersteige und aus der Ferne bloß genossen werden könne. Der Schrecken, der in europäischen Konzepten insofern noch positiv rückgekoppelt wird, als das erschreckte Subjekt sich seiner eigenen Kräfte versichert, führt bei Melville in direkter Konfrontation mit dem Schrecklichen, ganz wörtlich, zu nichts, d.h. es findet keine Überhebung des Subjekts über sich selbst statt. Im Gegenteil wird die gefürchtete Existenzbedrohung erschreckend real bis zur Vernichtung. Die Seereise der Pequod im *Moby-Dick* ist eine Reise in die Welt des Erhabenen in diesem skizzierten Sinne. Auf zwei Bestandteile dieser Welt ist besondere Aufmerksamkeit zu lenken: die Natur und der Charakter (in modernerer Terminologie: Bewusstsein). Die Natur war »das einzige, womit Amerika sich im Vergleich zu Europa auf geradezu unvorstellbare Weise gesegnet findet..., ein Landschaftsraum von unermeßlicher Weite und Vielfältigkeit.« (Poenicke, 1972, S. 18) Jene »vastness« der Natur, die Element jeder Erhabenheitsvorstellung ist, verlegt Melville im *Moby-Dick* auf das Meer. Das Meer als natürliche Umgebung der Walfänger ist ebenso Sinnbild für die menschliche Freiheit abseits der gesellschaftlichen Vereinbarungen an Land wie für die Leere als Gefahr, die diese Freiheit birgt. Im unermesslichen, weiten und abgründigen Meer droht der Mensch zu versinken, zu ertrinken, seine Psyche steht in der Gefahr zu vereinsamen und in der Isolation jeglichen Halt, ja sich selbst zu verlieren, wie es im Roman der Schiffsjunge Pip erlebt, der beim Walfang über Bord gespült wird, eine Nacht allein im offenen

Meer verbringen muss und nach seiner Rettung vor Erhabenheitsangst den Verstand verloren hat. Dies bringt den Naiven seinem Gegenpol, dem erfahrenen Alten, sehr nahe: Captain Ahab, der nach dem Vorfall eine Art Seelenverwandtschaft zu Pip verspürt. Beide teilen eine extreme Form der Erhabenheitserfahrung, denn Ahab ist seit seiner Begegnung mit dem überdurchschnittlich großen und scheinbar unbesiegbaren Weißen Wal, die ihn ein Bein gekostet hat, besessen von der Idee, den Wal erneut zu stellen und zu töten. Für ihn kondensiert alle Erhabenheit der Welt, ihre Ungerechtigkeit, ihre Boshaftigkeit, ihre Unerreichbarkeit, die die absolute Grenze des menschlichen Fassungsvermögen zu sein scheint, in genau diesem Tier und seine intime Hoffnung ist es, mit seiner Tötung diese Grenze, die Mauer, die ihn selbst sublimal, also darunter befindlich sein lässt, zu durchbrechen. Er träumt also von der Transzendierung seiner selbst als einer Art Selbsterlösung aus der schlechten Welt. All dies gerinnt nun zur wahrhaft existenziellen Jagd nach Moby-Dick; in der Figur Ahabs manifestiert sich daher die Kombination zweier literarischer Motive: erstens der Quest als »zielgerichteter Reise«, als »Suchwanderung«, die nicht nur in die erhabene Außenwelt vorstößt, sondern auch die Abgründe des Innenlebens beleuchtet; sowie zweitens, und mit der Seelenerforschung verbunden, die Monomanie als psychopathologisches Moment der krankhaften Fixierung auf das eine Ziel, dessen äußerliche Größe im Falle Moby-Dicks mit geradezu gigantischen Ausmaßen an Bedeutung für die besessene Seele korrespondiert. Im Kern allerdings – und dies kann als die Paradoxie des »American Sublime« angesehen werden – ist und bleibt Moby-Dick – trotz aller Versuche, ihn zu beschreiben, zu lokalisieren, zu kategorisieren, weiß, d.h. unbestimmt, unerkannt, unergründlich. Dies thematisiert Melville in dem zentralen Kapitel »The Whiteness of the Whale«, wo die Weiße als »heartless voids and immensities of the universe«, »not so much a color as the visible absence of color, and at the same time the concrete of all colors« (Melville, 1952, S. 193) angesprochen wird – ein Symbol für das Erhabene also, dessen Überfrachtung an Bestimmungen einen Umschlag in Bestimmungslosigkeit bedingt.

Erhabene Musik in Bernard Herrmanns *Moby-Dick* (1938)

Moby-Dick fand dementsprechend große Resonanz im Konzertsaal, im Film (mit einem entsprechenden Soundtrack versehen) und auf der Bühne. Sie reicht von Bernard Herrmanns sinfonischer Kantate von 1938 über die ikonische Verfilmung von Ray Bradbury und John Huston mit Gregory Peck (1956) bis hin zu Jack Heggies und Gene Sheers Oper von 2010, die auch außerhalb des Orts ihrer Uraufführung (Dallas Opera) große Erfolge feiert. Wie nun transportiert etwa ein Komponist wie Herrmann, Hitchcocks Herrmann, die Größe seiner Vorlage in einen Klang?

Der 1911 in New York City geborene Bernard Herrmann gehört zur Generation Elliott Carters, Samuel Barbers, John Cages, Benjamin Brittens u.a. Demnach war er erst 26 Jahre alt, als er den Plan fasste, sich des gewaltigen Stoffs des Romans in Form einer Oper anzunehmen. Erfahrungen hatte er zu diesem Zeitpunkt insbesondere als Dirigent gesammelt, da er seit 1934 dem Team der Orchesterleiter beim Columbia Broadcasting System angehörte, wo er binnen 9 Jahren zum Chefdirigent aufsteigen sollte. Beim CBS lernte er zwei wichtige Menschen kennen: Orson Welles und Lucille Fletcher. Für Ersteren schrieb er zunächst Rundfunk-, dann Filmmusik (ihre erste gemeinsame Arbeit war *Citizen Kane* von 1941, laut American Film Institute »the greatest American picture of all time«), Letztere wurde seine erste Ehefrau und schrieb das Libretto seiner einzigen Oper *Wuthering Heights* nach Emily Brontë – auch dieses Stück ist, der englischen Vorlage zum Trotz, ein geeigneter Kandidat für eine »Great American Opera«.

Bei aller Vielseitigkeit, die das Werk Herrmanns, sei es nun für das Radio, den Film, die Bühne oder den Konzertsaal, auszeichnet, gibt es doch gewisse Konstanten. Darunter ist erstens das Interesse an extremen, rätselhaften, vielschichtigen, psychisch abnormalen Charakteren zu zählen, heißen sie nun Norman Bates, Max Cady (aus *Cape Fear*), Marnie, Madeleine bzw. Carlotta, Travis Bickle (aus *Taxi Driver*) oder eben Captain Ahab und Heathcliff (aus *Wuthering Heights*). Zweitens, im Wesentlichen um diese Charaktere und die von ihnen ausgehenden Handlungen emotional-atmosphärisch umzusetzen, fällt eine sehr aufmerksame Behandlung orchestraler Klänge auf, die so einprägsam und bisweilen quälend erscheinen, dass sie emblematische Qualitäten annehmen, wie das legendäre Streichermotiv aus *Psycho*.

Moby-Dick war Herrmanns erstes großes Stück Konzertmusik. Der ursprüngliche Plan, aus dem Roman eine Oper zu machen, wurde fallengelassen, was in Anbetracht der Machart der Vorlage als vernünftige Entscheidung erscheint: Die dramatischen Anteile der Erzählung beschränken sich grob gesagt auf den Beginn und das fulminante Ende sowie einige wenige Passagen dazwischen. Sie stellen aber nur eine der vielfältigen Gestaltungsweisen dar, welche Melville ganz bewusst nebeneinander stellt, um einen gewissermaßen vielchörigen Klang der Stimmen des Erzählers zu erzielen. Den fraglos ungeheuer packenden Szenen, wie Ishmael, der Ich-Erzähler, den Harpunier und Kannibalen Queequeg kennenlernt und zum Blutsbruder gewinnt, wie Captain Ahab nach vierzig Tagen Seereise erstmals auf Deck der Pequod erscheint und bald seine eigentliche Mission, die Jagd auf den Weißen Wal, propagiert, wie diverse Walfänge ablaufen und schließlich, wie ganz am Ende (nach ca. 750 Seiten) endlich Moby-Dick gesichtet wird und nach einer dreitägigen Hetzjagd schließlich das Schiff zerstört und seine gesamte Besatzung – den Erzähler ausgenommen – in den Tod stürzt, diesen dramatischen Geschehnissen stehen unzählige Einschübe und Abschweifungen gegenüber, in denen Melville seinen Narrator alles das zum besten geben lässt, was 1850 über Walfang und -verarbeitung, Seefahrt, Geographie, Biologie (die sog. Cetologie), Naturgeschichte, Mythologie und Theologie des Wals zu erfahren war. Diese Digressionen, die einen Großteil des Buchs und damit auch seinen unverwechselbaren Charakter ausmachen, sind vom dramatischen Gesichtspunkt her unbrauchbar. Möglicherweise hätte Herrmann hier bereits ein filmisches Vorbild benötigt, um aus der epischen eine überzeugende dramatische Anlage zu machen. Doch John Hustons Film kam erst 1956 in die Kinos. Ihrer konnten sich dann Jake Heggie und Librettist Gene Sheer 2010 für ihre *Moby-Dick*-Oper bedienen, Herrmann hingegen bog mit der Hilfe eines Mitarbeiters bei der CBS, W. Clark Harrington, das Ganze noch zur Kantate ab, die allerdings nun recht dramatisch ausfiel. Vermutlich steckt in ihr ein Großteil der Erfahrung, die Herrmann bei der Komposition von Radio-Melodramen gesammelt hat. Sie stellt meines Erachtens einen entscheidenden Schritt zur großen Oper *Wuthering Heights* dar.

Größe erzeugt Herrmann hier in erster Linie durch die Verwendung eines großen Orchesters, das im Fall von *Moby-Dick* doppelte bis dreifache Holzbläser vorsieht (darunter ein Kontrafagott), drei- bis vierfaches Blech (darunter eine Tuba), einen Schlagzeugapparat, der vier Spieler verlangt, (darunter eine Donnertrommel, bei der durch Schütteln ein Donnergrollen ausgelöst wird) sowie Harfe und Streicher. Instrumentiert wird die Partitur so, dass nicht selten das gesamte Orchester zu hören ist, noch häufiger bedient sich Herrmann des satten Bläserklangs, um wie gleich zu Beginn Signale wie Fanfaren zu schmettern, die zusammen mit Paukenwirbeln den Topos der feierlichen, majestätischen Größe in der Musik zelebrieren (Henschtel, 2013). Zudem steigt am Anfang des Stücks der Männerchor blockartig, hymnisch, fast schon archaisch ein, um das biblische Motto aus Genesis 1,21 »And God created great whales«, ein wahrhaft großes Wort, das auch Melville dem Roman vorausschickt, zu intonieren.

Es können im Rahmen dieser Einleitung nicht alle Facetten der Umsetzung präsentiert werden; der Fokus soll auf dem Schluss der Kantate liegen, wo zwei Momente der Größe hörbar werden: natürlich die Besessenheit Ahabs bei der frenetischen Hetzjagd sowie die Stärke des »Leviathans« wie der Wal bei Melville oft genannt wird, aber auch die charakterliche, fast schon philosophische Größe Ahabs, welche sich in immer wieder interpolierten, melancholischen Besinnungen auf sein Schicksal, auf sein bevorstehendes Ende, auf seine Todesergebenheit äußern. Solche melancholischen Betrachtungen hatten den eher ruhigen und dem Topos des Lyrischen verpflichteten Teil der Kantate geprägt. Als dann der Wal gesichtet wird und Starbuck, der erste Steuermann, versucht, seinen Kapitän zu überreden, von dem Tier abzulassen, ist Ahab erst recht zum Angriff angestachelt, wie das militärische Trompetensignal kundtut. Im Verlauf seiner folgenden Hassrede auf den Wal verlässt Ahab immer häufiger den Modus des Singens, der sicherlich einen noch kontrollierten Eindruck vermittelt, und wechselt ins Sprechen, Rufen, Brüllen, was seine nicht zu bändigende Besessenheit ausdrückt. Ein retardierendes Moment bildet der langsamere, *piano* und wiederum gesungen vorzutragende Einschub Ahabs, wenn er wieder scheinbar im Besitz seiner Beherrschung sinnierend Abschied von der Weltoberfläche nimmt: »I turn my body from the sun. Oh, lonely death on lonely life!«. Der große Orchesterklang, der die große Passion des großen Charakters Ahab begleitet, sammelt sich effektvoll in einem extrem tiefen, alleine gelassenen Ton der Bassregister – den immensen Abgrund, der Ahab nun aufnehmen wird, verdeutlichend und Raum schaffend für seinen letzten Satz »Thus, I give up the spear!« –, bevor ein letztes Aufbäumen des vollen Orchesters Tod und Zerstörung von Crew und Schiff in überwiegend dreifachem *Forte* instrumental vermittelt. Dem Schlusssatz des Romans gesprochen von Ishmael »And I only am escaped alone to tell thee« – wiederum ein biblisches Zitat, diesmal aus dem Buch Hiob 1,16, wovon sich die sprichwörtliche Hiobsbotschaft herleitet –, diesem Wort genügt ein einsames, einfaches, freilich grauenvoll tiefes und knarrendes Kontra-C im Kontrafagott, also der tiefste Ton, der dem Orchester, ohne Herabstimmen der Kontrabässe, zur Verfügung steht.

Herrmanns *Wuthering Heights* (1951) als »Great American Opera«

In Emily Brontës *Wuthering Heights*, einem der großen britischen Romane der viktorianischen Zeit, jener »›Great tradition‹ of the English novelists« (Stoneman, 1996, S. 126ff.), die Vorlage für eine große amerikanische Oper im Zeichen des Erhabenheitsdiskurses zu erblicken, mag zunächst inkonsequent erscheinen. Doch war es schließlich die Rezeption im großen amerikanischen Film Hollywoods, welche Herrmann auf das Sujet brachte und in seiner Wahrnehmung beeinflusste. Auf den literarischen Brontë-Umkreis wurde er erstens durch die Verfilmung des Romans von 1939 aufmerksam, die William Wyler mit Lawrence Olivier und Merle Oberon sowie der Musik Alfred Newmans drehte und die eine Art »Durchbruch« des bis dato eher zurückhaltend rezipierten Texts bei einem größeren, amerikanischen Publikum bewirkte; zweitens durch seine eigene Arbeit an der Filmmusik zu *Jane Eyre* (von Robert Stevenson, mit Orson Welles). Für die Ausbildung gewisser narrativer Muster im Hollywood-Film – wie die tragische Dreiecksliebesgeschichte und die Konstellation der »Liebenden auf der einsamen Bergspitze gegen den Rest der Welt« – waren beide Filme im Fahrwasser von *Gone with the wind* (1939) auch in Abweichung von der ursprünglichen Darstellung in den Brontë-Vorlagen ein entscheidender Schritt und sie begegnen uns in der Oper wieder. Interessanterweise fand in den 1940er Jahren eine Annäherung in der Rezeption der beiden Romane der Schwestern Brontë durch Filme, Illustrationen oder Bühnenadaptationen statt: *Jane Eyre* wurde im Sinne von *Wutherings Heights* stimmungsmäßig verdüstert, aus *Wuthering Heights* hingegen wurde ein Drama der sozialen Klassen und einer wahren, aber unmöglichen Liebe, der rätselhafte Anti-Held Heathcliff konnte zum tragischen Helden der Ausgestoßenen mutieren (Stoneman, 1993, S. 16).

Deutlich wird die Orientierung Herrmanns und seiner Librettistin Fletchers an der Romanverfilmung auch daran, dass ihre Oper wie der Film (und mit ihnen die meisten Adaptationen) nur die erste Hälfte des Romans einschließen, also mit dem Tod der Catherine Earnshaw-Linton enden. Die gemäßigte, zu einem versöhnlicheren Zusammenleben fähige zweite Generation der Lintons und Earnshaws wurde gestrichen, was sicherlich nicht nur eine Frage des dramatischen Anliegens, sondern auch der zur Verfügung stehenden Dauer im anderen Medium war. Die Konzentration auf das verhinderte, tragische Liebespaar steht im Einklang mit der Vermittlung von »romance« durch die Hollywood-Akteure.

Zudem sind es genau die zwei bereits im Zusammenhang mit *Moby-Dick* angesprochenen Themen, Natur und Charakter, die im Roman eine herausragende Rolle spielen und durch ihre spezielle Behandlung in den amerikanischen Erhabenheitsdiskurs integriert werden konnten. Was im *Moby-Dick* das Meer war, ist in *Wuthering Heights* das Moor. Der Roman spielt in der Nähe eines kleinen Dorfs in Yorkshire mitten im Hochmoor und diese Landschaft prägt in all ihrer Schönheit (in Frühling und Sommer und dementsprechend in der Jugend der Protagonisten) und ihrer Erhabenheit (in Herbst und Winter und im Erwachsenenalter, das als Zeit des Leidens beschrieben wird) die gesamte Stimmung des Romans, den Charakter der Protagonisten und somit auch den Fortgang der Handlung. Insofern gibt es eine enge Korrespondenz zwischen der Erwähnung und Schilderung von natürlichen Gegebenheiten und Ereignissen und der Charakterisierung der Akteure im Roman. Mit der Literaturwissenschaftlerin Sydny M. Conger ist zu konstatieren:

> Nature provides her [E. Brontë] with a fund of analogies that help to describe the indescribable; namely, the irrational, magnetic attraction between Heathcliffe and Catherine (Conger, 1978, S. 1003).

Gerade für jenes Unbeschreibliche, kaum in Worte zu Fassende, das auch dem Autor des *Moby-Dick* alle erdenklichen literarischen Mühen abgerungen hat, stehen Bilder, Metaphern, Symbole aus der Natur, namentlich aus dem nordenglischen Hochmoor. Insbesondere die urwüchsige, dem Außenstehenden nicht zu vermittelnde, bisweilen dämonische Anziehungskraft, die Catherine und Heathcliff bis über den Tod Ersterer hinaus miteinander verbindet, sedimentiert sich in Naturbildern aus dem Moor, etwa in dessen Brise, die per Windstoß den Raum erfüllt, sobald ein Fenster geöffnet wird – so geschieht es, als Catherine stirbt oder wenn ihre ruhelose Seele Bewohner ihres alten Zimmers auf »Wuthering Heights« heimsucht. Der Name dieser Behausung, zu Deutsch »Sturmhöhe«, impliziert die Wind, Wetter und Landschaft ausgesetzte Lebensform ihrer Bewohner; und ebenfalls in Heathcliffs Namen, der »Heideklippe« bedeutet, offenbart sich die urwüchsige Naturverbundenheit seines Charakters. Analog zur rauen, unwirtlichen Natur Nordenglands sind die Charaktere kaum zu bändigen, daher auch eher als erhaben denn als schön zu bezeichnen. Dieser Zug ist dermaßen ausgeprägt, dass bei vielen zeitgenössischen, aber auch heutigen Lesern Verwirrung und eine ablehnende Haltung ausgelöst wird: Der Roman bietet schlicht keinerlei Möglichkeit zur (affirmativen) Identifikation mit einer seiner Figuren:

> It is Heathcliffe's and Catherine's enigmatic and often destructive impulses that are »sublime,« »threatening,« and, indeed, even sometimes »unspeakable« (Conger, 1978, S. 1003).

Emily Brontë nutzt die Technik einer extremen Kontrastbildung, um das Verstörende an *Wuthering Heights* zu vermitteln, einen Kontrast nämlich zwischen der bürgerlich viktorianischen Welt des Herrenhauses Thrushcross Grange, wo die Lintons residieren, und dem heruntergekommenen, eher bäuerlichen Anwesen Wuthering Heights, wo die Earnshaws hausen. Während das Herrenhaus mit Schönheit (Vernunft, Harmonie, kultivierte, gebändigte Natur) einhergeht, besticht Wuthering Heights durch seine erhabenen Züge (Gefahr, Zerstörung, Rätsel, Schauer):

> Everything associated with Wuthering Heights is akin to the sublime: the natural setting and the passion of Catherine and Heathcliff – dangerous, destructive, mysterious, awe-inspriring. All associated the the Grange, however, belongs to what these theorists [of eighteenth-century aesthetics of landscape] called beauty: rational harmony, cultivated, tamed nature (Williams, 1985, S. 125).

Herrmanns vieraktige Oper zeigt all diese Facetten des Romans, was vorzuführen leider den Rahmen dieser Einführung sprengen würde. Es sei aber wenigstens ein großer Moment der Oper hervorgehoben, namentlich das Finale des II. Aktes. »Großes« findet sich dort in der verschmelzenden Darstellung der erhabenen Natur, der von Hollywood geprägten großen »romance« und des unbändigen, grenzenlos-großen Charakterzugs der Protagonisten. Zur Situation der Handlung: Catherine und Heathcliff sind im fortgeschrittenen Teenageralter und sie hat gerade dem Heiratsantrag des bürgerlichen, angesehenen, aber eher normalen Edgar Linton von Thruscross Grange entsprochen, was sie ihrer Kinderfrau Nelly mitteilt. Durch kritisches Nachfragen Nellys gerät Catherine in die Lage, ihre Liebe zu Edgar mit einem Naturbild zu vergleichen, nämlich den Jahreszeiten und Wetter ausgesetzten Blättern eines Baumes. Ihre Liebe zu Heathcliff hingegen – dem Findelkind, mit dem sie wie mit einem Bruder aufgewachsen ist – sei wie die ewigen Felsen. Ihre Rede kulminiert in der Aussage »Nelly, I am Heathcliff!«, was die unverbrüchliche, kaum nicht einmal mehr als dialektische Einheit anzusehende Seelenidentität zwischen den beiden zum Ausdruck bringen soll. Heathcliff selbst, der unter der Missachtung, ja Misshandlung durch den älteren Bruder Cathys, Hindely, leidet, war bei diesem Gespräch im Raum ohne Cathys Wissen anwesend. Er ergreift die Flucht als Cathy äußert, sie könne Heathcliff niemals heiraten, weil dies sie degradieren würde. Ihre anschließende Liebeserklärung hat er also nicht mehr gehört. Nun bemerkt Cathy dieses Unglück. Ihre verzweifelten Rufe ins dunkle Moor hinaus, Heathcliff möge doch wiederkommen, greifen die Musik des I. Akts, und zwar die Musik ihrer »romance« auf, die wir hören, als die eher noch kindlichen Cathy und Heathcliff einen unbeschwerten, von gegenseitiger tiefer Zuneigung geprägten Tag im sommerlichen Moor verbringen. Mit dieser Musik der großen Leidenschaft zieht nun zugleich ein schweres Gewitter auf: ein erhabener Wetterumschwung, der den Umschwung der Liebeskonstellation anzeigt. Die zitierte Liebesmusik ist an den »Heathcliff«-Rufen einer fallenden Sekunde und einem jener hermannschen einprägsamen, emblematischen Klänge zu erkennen, nämlich einem b-Moll-Akkord mit großer Septime, die sich mit dem gesungenen fallenden Halbtonschritt zusammen zur Sexte erniedrigt. Als solcher Moll-Akkord mit Sixte ajoutée bleibt der Klang unaufgelöst und oftmals wiederholt stehen, und wirkt wie das subdominantische Bruchstück einer fragmentierten, unausgeführten Kadenz. Diese Liebesmusik nun wird immer engmaschiger mit solchen Klängen verwoben, die das heraufziehende Unwetter andeuten: Blitze und Donnergrollen (Z. 39, 1 vor Z. 40, Z. 41 etc.). Entsprechend assimiliert sich Cathy an die Natur und das Wetter, indem sie die Tür aufreißt, hinausruft und schließlich in das stürmische Moor hinausläuft, wohin auch Heathcliff verschwunden ist. Hier zeigt sich der Grenzen sowie häuslichen Schutz und Hülle ignorierende Wesenszug der beiden. Die grenzenlos Liebenden »verschmelzen«, voneinander getrennt, auf dem Höhepunkt ihrer unter negativen Vorzeichen gestellten Leidenschaft mit der sie umgebenden, lebensfeindlichen Natur. Orchestrales Signum dieses Vorgangs ist ein weiterer Klang (Z. 43), harmonisch betrachtet ein »harmloser« fis-Moll-Akkord, der aber so gewaltig instrumentiert ist, dass er geeignet ist, Schauer beim Hörer auszulösen. Außerdem bewegt sich der Spitzenton *fis* erst chromatisch zu *f*, dann zum Tritonus *c* fort, während fis-Moll in allen anderen Stimmen liegen bleibt und eine große Reibung erzeugt. Dieses Klanggebilde kennt der Hörer aus dem Prolog, wo der gealterte Heathcliff von Cathys ruheloser Seele vor dem bei Schneesturm geöffneten Fenster heimgesucht wird – also aus der einleitenden Präsentation der Verschmelzung von erhaben-schrecklicher Natur mit dem zum Gespenst mutierten, die ultimative Grenze zwischen Leben und Tod überschreitenden Charakter Cathys. Groß und effektvoll beendet eine instrumentalmusikalische Schilderung der Stürme in Natur und Seele schwer und aufgewühlt den Akt.

Die Oper verdient eine ausführlichere Behandlung als es diese Einführung leisten kann. Doch hoffe ich, dass einige Grundzüge dessen, was Herrmann zur Suche nach einer »Great American Opera« beiträgt, bereits deutlich geworden sind: zunächst ein großer, erhabener Stoff als Vorlage und dann eine musikalische Behandlung, die nicht etwa aus einem avantgardistischen Skrupel heraus darum bemüht wäre, allein dem »Fortschritt« des musikalischen Materials behilflich zu sein, sondern die nicht davor zurückschreckt, große Sujets und Leidenschaften darzustellen, um dadurch große Emotionen zu rühren und so ihren Vorlagen zu entsprechen. Über den Umweg des Films, dessen Gestaltungsweisen das Opern- und Konzertschaffen Herrmanns begleiten und füttern, wird damit an den vormals ureigenen Bereich des unterhaltenden, den Zuschauer einnehmenden Musiktheaters angeknüpft. Denn es sollte in Herrmanns leinwandlosem Komponieren nicht allein ein filmmusikalischer Zugriff festgestellt werden (was an der Oberfläche sehr einleuchtet), sondern umgekehrt auch ein Wiederaufgriff dessen, was der Film nicht nur in der Frühphase seiner Entwicklung von der Oper übernommen und gelernt hat[1]. Die nicht zu überhörende Ähnlichkeit von *Wuthering Heights* mit der Musiksprache Puccinis bezeugt dies auf assoziativer Ebene. Es stellt sich schließlich die Frage, ob und inwiefern dies ein Modell für spätere, ähnlich verfahrende Opern aus den USA geworden ist.

Nicht wegzudiskutieren ist allerdings die Tatsache, dass Herrmann bisher weder im bereich der Konzert- noch der Bühnenmusik ein großes, mit dem seiner filmischen Produktion annähernd vergleichbares Publikum erreicht hat. Überhaupt ist die amerikanische Oper, sofern sie nicht als Operette oder Musical produziert wird, keine Erscheinung, die sich durch den Umfang ihrer Rezeption auszeichnen würde. Dies ist auf vielfältige Faktoren zurückzuführen, von denen einige in der Dominanz des europäischen Repertoires auf dem Opernmarkt und einer historizistischen, quasi »musealen« Praxis der Spielplangestaltung zu suchen ist. In jüngerer Zeit allerdings begegnen einige aktuelle Projekte großer amerikanischer Opernhäuser diesem Missstand, indem sie Aufträge an solche Komponisten verteilen, die erstens die »großen« Stoffe amerikanischer Literatur aufgreifen (wie Werke von Edgar Allan Poe, Herman Melville, Louisa May Alcott, Mark Twain, F. Scott Fitzgerald, John Steinbeck, Theodore Dreiser, Arthur Miller etc.), die nicht selten auch mit großen Verfilmungen verknüpft sind, und sich zweitens damit an ein vergleichsweise großes Publikum wenden. Die marginale Bedeutung des Regietheaters in den USA und die im Vergleich zur lange Zeit in Europa vorherrschenden kritischen Avantgarde unverkrampfte Herangehensweise an das Thema Oper bereiten einen geradezu idealen Boden für eine Renaissance der »großen« Oper über das endlose Wiederaufnehmen von Repertoirestücken hinaus. Für denjenigen, der dieser Entwicklung mit Sympathie gegenüber steht, besteht also durchaus Grund zur Hoffnung…

Literatur

Conger, Syndy M. (1978). Nature in Wuthering Heights. *PMLA*, 93 (5), 1003-1004.

Hentschel, F. (2013). Feierlichkeit. Expressive Qualität und historische Semantik bei Beethoven. *Archiv für Musikwissenschaft*, 70 (3), 161-190.

Melville, H. (1952). *Moby-Dick, or, The Whale* (1851). L. S. Mansfield, H. P. Vincent (Hrsg.). New York: Hendricks House.

Poenicke, K. (1972). *Dark Sublime. Raum und Selbst in der amerikanischen Romantik* (= Jahrbuch für Amerikastudien. Beihefte, Bd. 36). Heidelberg: Winter.

---

1   Vgl. Kieler Beiträge zur Filmmusikforschung, Band 11, 2014, der sich auch mit solchen Verbindungen von Oper und Film beschäftigt (http://www.filmmusik.uni-kiel.de/KB11).

Stoneman, P. (1996). *Brontë transformations. The cultural dissemination of Jane Eyre and Wuthering Heights.* London: Prentice Hall.

Stoneman, P. (1993). Introduction. *Wuthering Heights.* London: Macmillan.

Williams, A. (1985). Natural Supernaturalism in »Wuthering Heights«. *Studies in Philology,* 82 (1), 104-127.

Aaron Ziegel

Crafting the Soundworld of American Opera, 1910–1912

Introduction

Long before opera composers in the United States could justifiably consider taking on the task of producing *the* »Great American Opera,« the practical matter of simply finding the opportunity to have one's opera performed or produced proved a much more relevant challenge. In the nineteenth century, the history of opera in the United States largely consists of usually short-lived opera companies, primarily touring organizations without permanent theaters to call home, and their efforts to bring the European-composed repertory to an American audience (see, e.g., Ahlquist, 1997; Ottenberg, 1994; Preston, 1993). The role of newly composed, native works is a marginal one, at best. While such repertory certainly does exist from that period, taken in total, the works seem more like a series of singularities, limited in terms of the audience's reach, in critical attention from the nation's press, and in influence upon later composers or the broader cultural scene. A new work might be mounted for a few nights in one city, and it might even be published in a piano-vocal score, but beyond those few attendees lucky enough to hear one of these performances, the impact of such a work essentially ended with the fall of the final act's curtain. Such a pattern could not result in the formation of a national school of operatic production here in the United States to rival those found in any of the principal European nations. A relatively small number of composers with the requisite training, a lack of stable opera companies with the financial means to create new works, and the general impression that opera, as a genre, was an exclusively European import all contributed to this situation. Operatic productivity in the United States began to increase toward the turn of the century, as all three of these factors developed in a positive direction. A greater number of trained composers, city-supported resident opera companies, and a burgeoning audience desiring to witness stage premieres led to a confluence of conditions necessary for the eventual emergence of a distinctively American style of operatic composition.

During the early 1910s, for the first time in the nation's history, new scores were composed, published, produced, discussed in the press, and viewed in multiple cities (and sometimes even heard in excerpts on recordings) in a great enough frequency that examples of the genre began to influence one another. Composers were aware of their colleagues' efforts. Critics could draw comparisons and assess trends. The audience's enthusiasm for a work sometimes led to subsequent revivals. One might say that the nation's musical culture had finally matured into the making of operatic history, rather than simply the receiving of it second-hand from Europe. From our point of view today, this period marks a turning point at which »American Opera« begins to seem like a tangible quantity—something that is uniquely definable, something that is searching for its own distinctive musical style. This search is the subject of this essay. Composers at the time were, in their own separate ways, all seeking to answer one key question: What should an American opera sound like? They shared a common goal to create works that could simultaneously coexist alongside the established European repertory while still striking listeners as a uniquely American-sounding contribution to the genre. In the analysis that follows, examples drawn from four operas first staged from 1910 to 1912 illustrate that, during this three-year period, there was indeed something of an emerging consensus regarding how composers can achieve a specifically American soundworld upon the operatic stage. The selected works and composers, along with the location and year of the staged premiere, is shown in the table below. (See the appendix for further production details and cast lists.)

Composer	Work Title	Premiere City and Year
Arthur Nevin (1871–1943)	Poia	Berlin, 1910; preceded by a concert performance in Pittsburgh, 1907
Victor Herbert (1859–1924)	Natoma	Philadelphia, 1911
Frederick Converse (1871–1940)	The Sacrifice	Boston, 1911
Mary Carr Moore (1873–1957)	Narcissa	Seattle, 1912

Table 1: Selected Repertory.

Taken as a group, this selection represents an exemplary cross-section of American operatic creation at the time. All of these works were fully staged, thus they had achieved a complete realization of their musical and dramatic potential. Unperformed or unproduced works are less likely to be representative of the period's understanding of what American opera should be. All were published in piano-vocal scores, thus music critics, professional musicians, other composers, and even amateurs at home could easily study these examples. Since the music was widely disseminated, rather than only hearable in live performance, the relative impact of a score upon the nation's broader musical scene and its potential for influence upon other composers was much greater. Indeed, each work could serve as a point of reference for those that followed. Furthermore, the musical press across the whole country eagerly followed this operatic history in the making. Finally, the librettos of each work provide an indigenous plot setting. As many commentators of the time observed, an authoritative »American« opera must surely be set in the New World.[1]

Early background

Americans had indeed been creating new operatic stage works from the earliest years of the nation's history. At the start of the nineteenth century, these resembled mostly spoken plays with songs more than true »grand operas.« Both *The Indian Princess*, an »operatic melodrame« with music by John Bray, produced in Philadelphia in 1808, and *The Enterprise*, an »operatic drama« with music by Arthur Clifton, produced in Baltimore in 1822, include an orchestral overture, songs, duets, and choruses with some additional instrumental music, but they employ spoken dialogue, rather than recitatives. The songs are generally brief, with simple diatonic melodies and occasionally strophic texts, more suited to singing actors than true operatic voices. Only once in each work do both composers demonstrate a grander musical ambition by writing a lengthy and virtuosic aria for their respective soprano protagonists. As operas from the European repertory became better known and more popular toward the middle of the century, American composers did occasionally attempt to contribute their own examples to the genre. Most notable are the three operas by William Henry Fry (1813–1864): *Aurelia the Vestal* (1841), *Leonora* (1845, revised 1858), and *Notre Dame of Paris* (1864). Fry's musical idiom in these works, however, remained close to that of his Italian and French contemporaries. Striving for a specifically American soundworld was not a significant part of his operatic agenda.

Toward the end of the century, the chorus of commentators calling for a truly »American« opera was growing. In 1895, a writer for *The Outlook*, for instance, seemed understandably troubled by the fact that »Many who have hoped that an American composer would someday satisfy their ambition for American [opera] have grown faint with long waiting« (»An American Opera,« 1895). Late nineteenth-century composers, such as Dudley Buck, Frederick Gleason, and Silas Pratt, while more systematic in their pursuit of operatic success, were hindered by the fact

---

1   For plot summaries of the selected examples, see Ziegel, 2011, pp. 354–61. Bibliographic details of scores and librettos are included at the start of the references section. This present essay complements my earlier article that explored how libretto writers at the time sought to construct an American idiom in their sung texts; see Ziegel, 2009.

that the majority of their works remained unperformed. Even the operatic efforts of more prestigious composers around the turn of the century met with little acceptance. Walter Damrosch's *The Scarlet Letter* (1896) was at least produced in Boston, but perhaps that had more to do with the fact that Damrosch himself was the director of the opera company. George Whitefield Chadwick's *Judith* (1901) and John Knowles Paine's *Azara* (1903) both had to settle for unstaged concert performances.

By 1905, the forecast for American opera looked especially bleak from Oscar Sonneck's point of view:

> [T]oday we are as far from American opera of artistic importance as we ever have been. Not that our composers lack the power to write dramatic music, but [...] [they] have almost stopped trying their hands at this sadly neglected branch of our art. The struggle against the apathy of the public, eternally in love with flimsy operettas [...] and on the other hand against the commercial cowardice and avarice of the managers, seems hopeless. Whether or not a change for the better will take place cannot be foretold. (Sonneck, 1905, p. 485)

Fortunately, Sonneck's pessimistic prediction turned out to be wide of the mark, for the public's demand for new American works, composers' increased productivity, and managements' willingness to stage the premieres were near at hand. Commentators in the early 1910s seemed thoroughly convinced that the opportune time for writing opera was now. By 1911, for instance, Lawrence Gilman beamed that »as for the generous and patriotic men who control the destinies of our opera-houses, they have opened wide the doors and there are hospitable words upon their lips« (Gilman, 1911, p. 751). Just three years later, he returned to the topic even more confidently and affirmed that

> there is not the slightest question that the production of operas by native composers set to texts in the vernacular is a highly desirable thing. No one who is interested in the growth of a native musical art but would rejoice to see operas by American composers, sung in the vernacular, established in the regular repertoire. (Gilman, 1914, p. 148)

Walter Pritchard Eaton likewise recognized that the conditions were right: »We have today at last men with the dramatic technique needed to build an effective libretto. We have plenty of native singers of operatic stature. [...] We have composers who know the tools of their trade« (Eaton, 1911, p. 675). Composers too seemed swept up in the enthusiasm for new operatic creation. Frederick Converse, for example, noted in a diary entry, dated 19 March 1910, his determination that »We are bound to write operas in America, just as we have built up great commercial enterprises—they can't stop us« (Garofalo, 1994, p. 39). Indeed, the nation's opera lovers felt that they were witnessing a key turning point in their musical history, as Littell McClung explained in 1910:

> [To those] who take a broader and more up-to-the-minute view of the great increase in the demand for grand opera in all parts of the country, the expression »American opera« means the dawn of a new artistic era in the United States. [...] When we shall hear a successful composition by an American composer sung in English, this country will have made a step that will undoubtedly mark a new period in the annals of music. (McClung, 1910, pp. 423–424)

This »dawn of a new artistic era« was heralded in no small part by a changing attitude at New York's Metropolitan Opera (Met), ushered in by its general manager Giulio Gatti-Casazza, whose tenure at the Met spanned from 1908 to 1935. Following the lead of popular opinion, he made a concerted effort to bring new American works to the stage. As the manager recalled, »When the request that this should be done became reasonably general and representative, I took steps at once to procure« an American score, noting that »it was an obvious duty to find out what [American operas] there were.« After an initial foray with three performances of Frederick Converse's *The Pipe of Desire* in March of 1910, the Met announced a $10,000 prize competition for a newly composed work. Gatti-Casazza explained that his motivation grew from a wish »to probe more deeply into the dark, unfathomed caves and to explore for blushing flowers, unpublished and unseen« (Brenon, 1913, p. 377). The prize eventually went to Horatio Parker's *Mona*. This work was shown four times in March and April of 1912, and seemed at first glance to be a perfect candidate for a project such as this. However, its dramatization of the conflict between the Druids of ancient Britain and their Roman occupiers suggests that achieving Americanness was not one of Parker's key priorities. An unnamed music critic, writing for *The Nation* shortly after the premiere, complained that while the »score consists of substantial, serious, scholarly music [...] one listens in vain for a note distinctively American.« The writer concludes that, rather than constructing a uniquely indigenous soundworld, Parker's idiom simply made »use of phrases that have long been the common property of all composers« (»Professor Parker's Prize Opera,« 1912, p. 296). This is not to suggest that the work is without merits, but it does explain the exclusion of *Mona* from the present sample.[2]

---

2   The preceding text is of course a highly selective summary. For an exceptionally thorough overview of American-composed operas, see Kirk (2001). For a comprehensive survey of opera in the United States, but one that primarily focuses on the performance history of repertory imported from Europe, see Dizikes (1993). The most thorough examination of the American operas presented at the Met under Gatti-Casazza's management is from Guzski (2001).

Components of an American idiom

Returning now to the works by Nevin, Herbert, Converse, and Moore (see Table 1), the remainder of this article will document four distinctively American musical components that the composers chose to integrate with an inherited European tradition of opera writing. While not an exclusive list, the selected areas of emphasis include: (1) musical expressions of patriotic or heroic sentiments, (2) the use of characteristically American styles of choral writing, (3) the incorporation of American Indian melodies, and (4) the inclusion of sacred music materials. Given that any of these topics could easily support entire studies of their own, an overview of how such traits operate in conjunction with each other is presented below. In total, this provides a glimpse into how these composers sought to craft a soundworld for American opera.

In both *Natoma* and *The Sacrifice*, the principal male characters are American military officers. *Natoma*'s naval lieutenant, Paul Merrill (tenor), is serving as an envoy to Spanish-controlled California, while *The Sacrifice*'s army captain, Burton (baritone), is fighting in the Mexican-American War. The opera's plots are set in 1820 and 1846, respectively. As is typical in opera, both men are romantically drawn to women from exotic »other« ethnic groups. Paul's love interest is Barbara, the daughter of a Spanish nobleman, and Burton is attracted to Chonita, described in the libretto as »a young Mexican lady.« In each score, both men sing of their pride in the United States, especially their belief in the nation's superiority over the Spanish and Mexicans. The respective excerpts in which the characters articulate these sentiments employ a remarkably similar musical idiom.

In Act II of *Natoma*, Paul sings a passage variously referred to as the »Ode to Columbus« or »Paul's Address.« This heroic aria begins ostensibly as a tribute to Christopher Columbus, thereby showing respect to California's Spanish rulers (Example 1a), but midway through the number, Paul's focus shifts to »Columbia« rather than »Columbus« (Example 1b). Columbia, described in Paul's lyrics as both the »goddess of our liberty« and the »goddess of the free,« serves as a symbolic personification of all that is superior in the United States. While Paul might respect the original Spanish settlers of California, the American commitment to liberty is what truly receives his pledge of loyalty. Throughout, Herbert allows the tenor ample opportunity to sustain clarion high notes, while brass-led fanfare figures leave no doubt about the character's personal valor. An upward surging leitmotif, further reflecting Paul's heroism, undergirds much of the introductory recitative (not shown here) and reappears again in the orchestral accompaniment following the final vocal note (boxed in Example 1b).

Example 1a: Herbert, Natoma, Act II – Paul's »Ode to Columbus« (1911, p. 264).

Example 1b: Herbert, Natoma, Act II – Paul's »Ode to Columbus« (1911, p. 268).

Burton expresses related sentiments in the middle of a passage in which the character first openly declares his love to Chonita. She has come to Burton fearful of the danger posed by the ongoing military conflict and frightened that she will lose her own true beloved, a Mexican fighter named Bernal. Burton attempts to win her affection by arguing that American superiority offers her the best chance for safety and security (Example 2). In contrast to Herbert's tuneful vocal writing, Converse's text setting is more declamatory in style. It is the orchestral accompaniment instead that presents surging melodic lines, sustained high notes, and rising dotted leaps. The melodic writing in both examples conveys an aspirational sense of hope, matching each character's belief in their nation's destiny and greatness. It is a gestural embodiment of American heroism in musical terms.

Example 2: Converse, The Sacrifice, Act I – Burton's Love Declaration (1910, p. 52).

Despite these various signifiers of patriotism, one searches in vain for an exclusively »American« sound in these passages. The above-mentioned musical traits could just as easily appear in any operatic passage that is expressive of male heroism. The intentions here seem to be less about creating uniqueness and more about proving the suitability of these New-World archetypes for the operatic stage. The characters of Paul and Burton need to fit comfortably within the repertory's established line of heroes, not to stand apart from them. Listeners must accept that Paul and Burton could comfortably take their places alongside all the Siegfrieds, Radamès, and Paminos of the opera world. Herbert, for one, recognized that a composer need not necessarily feel obliged to »Americanize« the soundworld of music for characters whose nationalist convictions were already at the forefront of their constructed personas. The composer explained:

> An American atmosphere is not obtained by pepper-casting the score with themes from patriotic songs. Puccini, in *Madama Butterfly*, makes use of ›The Star Spangled Banner,‹

for instance, and also of a few Japanese harmonies. Does that make his opera American, Japanese, or even a mixture of both? (Kaye, 1931, p. 213)

Ultimately, this particular ingredient of the soundworld becomes American through lyrics and context much more than through musical idiom.

However, if we recognize the specifically nationalist purpose to which this heroic musical idiom is applied, then it can also serve to reinforce the American credentials of a character who might otherwise seem an outsider. Such is the case with the title role in Nevin's *Poia*. The opera is a re-telling of a Blackfeet tribal legend that relates how Poia, cursed with a disfiguring facial scar from birth, journeys to the realm of the Sun God Natosi in order to beg for the curse's removal. While he is there, Poia rescues the Sun God's son from an attack by vicious eagles. To reward his bravery, Natosi heals Poia's scar and sends him back to the tribe as the Sun God's chosen prophet. Whereas Poia could have been an exotic, mystical, or fantastical type of character, Nevin instead composed heroic-sounding music for him, similar to what Herbert and Converse would later create for Paul and Burton. One representative passage occurs in the scene in which Poia (tenor) makes up his mind to undertake the dangerous journey to the realm of the Sun God (Example 3). While this excerpt also makes use of a quoted Blackfeet tribal melody (to be discussed below), Nevin's musical focus on the characterization of Poia's bravery suggests that he too, like Paul and Burton, can serve as an American role model. Even though Poia's lyrics do not explicitly articulate patriotic or nationalist sentiments, the stylistic idiom would seem to argue that audiences should accept Poia as a sort of proto-American.

Complementing these solo-voice acclamations of patriotic heroism, Moore's *Narcissa* includes a scene in which the chorus expresses a related message of New-World bravery. Here, the singers represent settlers immigrating to the Northwest Territory who have finally reached the end of their arduous journey across the Oregon Trail. They sing while waving an American flag (Example 4). Choruses are, of course, an expected ingredient in an opera score, one with a long-established precedent as a means to convey nationalist sentiments. However, in American operas of this period, the style of choral writing is often carefully designed to impart a uniquely American color to the proceedings. Nevin's chorus sings in praise of the Sun God Natosi (Example 5), Herbert presents a chorus of sailors (Example 6), and Converse offers a chorus of soldiers (Example 7).

Example 3: Nevon, Poia, Act I – Poia's War Song (1909, p. 48).

Example 4: Moore, Narcissa, Act III – Arrival of Immigrants (1912, p. 201).

Example 5: Nevin, Poia, Act II – Ceremonial Song (1909, p. 65).

Example 6: Herbert, Natoma, Act II – Sailors' Chorus (1911, p. 259).

Example 7: Converse, The Sacrifice, Act II – Soldiers' Chorus (1910, p. 99).

The idiom throughout Examples 4 through 7 is remarkably consistent. The homophonic texture, the generally close spacing of the voices, the relatively simple harmonic progressions, and the primarily diatonic melodic lines work together to achieve a strong sense of communal expression. This results in a direct and accessible style, far removed from the chromatic complexities and heightened dramatic expression found in much operatic writing from the 1910s, including substantial proportions of these four scores as well. Instead, the choruses here reveal an unmistakable kinship with the various participatory traditions of choral singing that were popular in the United States at the time, ranging from oratorio societies to college glee clubs. Herbert's soldiers and Converse's sailors even betray a hint of the barbershop style, most notably in Herbert's tightly knit harmonies, with two parallel descending tritones in the closing cadence of Example 6.

Any of these excerpts, particularly the soldiers' and sailors' choruses, could have been included simply to achieve dramatic contrast. The first audiences would surely have been familiar with analogous soldier/sailor scenes in works as diverse as Charles Gounod's *Faust*, Giuseppe Verdi's *Il Trovatore*, Richard Wagner's *Flying Dutchman*, or W. S. Gilbert and Arthur Sullivan's *H.M.S. Pinafore*, where such numbers are common stock components. On the one hand, these excerpts do fulfill dramatic functions related to what audiences were accustomed to seeing, but they also operate on a second and arguably more significant level. Moore's immigrants, Herbert's sailors, and Converse's soldiers act as the emblems of average, everyday Americans. Likewise, Nevin's Sun-God worshippers, via the consistent application of this shared choral idiom, seem less like exotic outsiders and more like members of the audience's own community. If the audience is to accept these staged portrayals as representatives of themselves, then what better way to characterize each group than through a musical style that the audience might recognize as their own.[3]

If heroic males are made to fit in with European operatic tradition, and choruses draw upon a familiar idiom, then this next component contributes a distinctively New-World atmosphere precisely because of its marked degree of difference. Of the various indigenous musical sources available, composers at this time most consistently turned to the music of American Indians as a means for creating a soundworld entirely removed from European traditions.[4] With all four plots set in the American West, it comes as no surprise that Indian characters might make an appearance on the operatic stage. Indeed, as late as 1925, Arthur Elson was still advocating for the types of plot subjects developed in all four operas selected for the present study. Elson wrote:

> As regards subjects for librettos, we have a great variety of the best. They include Indian legends, colonial adventures, pioneer events, and historical scenes of great power. [...] [I]t should not be hard for anyone with literary and dramatic taste to concoct a libretto that should be little inferior to the Wagnerian stories in stage effect. (Elson & Elson, 1925, pp. 379–80)

However, this decision proved to be one of the most widely debated aspects of these scores, with operatic Indians making up only one small facet of a much larger issue. Since the focus here is on musical style, only a brief examination is warranted. On the one hand, because of their uniquely New-World provenance, the inclusion of either quoted Indian melodies or new material composed in imitation of that style was seen as a guaranteed way to achieve a distinctively American soundworld. Composer and Indian music-collector Frederick Burton, for example, encouraged his contemporaries to make use of this source, writing that they »should be inspired by patriotic eagerness that our country should prove to be not behind others in melodic resources, but as richly endowed as any land that ever had boundaries« (Burton, 1909, p. 193). On the other hand, critics of the practice complained that Indian music was so far removed from the backgrounds of both composers and audience members that its inclusion resulted in something that was ultimately less American in nature. H. J. Whigham, editor of *Town & Country* magazine, for instance, pointed out that »Indian folk songs [...] are in no sense the heritage of American composers. [...] The Indians are an alien race and neither their language nor their music is ours« (Whigham, 1911, p. 24). The four operas selected here illustrate a more moderate stance. Collectively, they seem to follow the advice of Henry Finck

---

3   For further information on the standard performance repertory in the United States around the time of these operas' premieres, see Ziegel, 2011, pp. 345–51.

4   Note that I recognize the need for terminological sensitivity and tribal specificity when referring to diverse groups of Native Americans. My use here of the potentially pejorative »Indian« echoes what is found in the period sources themselves.

and Daniel Gregory Mason, who respectively encouraged the use of Indian materials »only as occasional spices« or »now and then for an artistic holiday« (Finck, 1906, p. 356; Mason, 1918, p. 251). Even in a score like *Poia*, that relies exclusively on the use of Indian characters, borrowed Indian musical materials make up only one facet of the overall soundworld. Within such an eclectic context, an appropriated Indian melody, when inserted into a traditionally late-Romantic idiom, does not necessarily remain recognizably Indian. Harmonization, orchestration, and operatic vocal production all obscure the origin to varying degrees.[5]

Two representative examples of quoted Indian melodies in *Poia* can be seen in Examples 3 and 5 above. Nevin, unlike some of his colleagues, did actually come into direct contact with live performances of Indian music in an authentic context. During two summer-long visits to the Blackfeet reservation in Montana in 1903 and 1904, he collected melodies that would eventually find their way into the opera (see Nevin, 1916). In Example 3, an »Indian War Song« appears in the orchestra beneath the tenor's declamatory melody. The persistent eighth notes carry an aggressive war-drum rhythm, while a falling chromatic bass motion leads the melody into unexpected harmonic terrain, moving from e minor through both b minor and f-sharp minor before a nonfunctional cadence returns to the tonic. The quoted melody itself, in the upper voice of the orchestral reduction, is pentatonic, repetitive, rhythmically strong in profile, and descending in overall contour. While listeners at the time would have recognized these traits as stereotypical signifiers, Nevin's Indianist passages are not always this explicit. Indeed, one of the defining features of his scores is the fluency with which he shifts from a colorfully exotic soundworld into a more conventional late-Romantic mainstream. The »Indian ceremonial song« quoted in Example 5 is a case in point. The four-part voice leading and strongly functional E-flat major tonality disguise the melody's origins despite its repetitive melodic shape and irregular phrases that expand beyond the confines of a triple meter.

Perhaps the most stereotypically Indianist number in all of American opera is Herbert's »Dagger Dance« (Example 8), an orchestral highlight that kept the name *Natoma* alive far longer than any other score of the time. As the scene unfolds, the villainous Castro has challenged Natoma to join him in an ancient ritual dance. Castro intends the dance to serve as a distraction while his master Alvarado attempts to abduct the beautiful Barbara. Natoma notices the deception and stabs Alvarado to death with her dagger. The drone open fifth, drum-rhythm bass, descending melodic outline, and sharp rhythmic accents are the most salient features. The melody is Herbert's attempt to »get the effect of Indian music without using the thing itself« (»Victor Herbert's First,« 1910). The static accompaniment reinforces the primitive

---

5   The most comprehensive study of Indianism in music can be found in Pisani (2005). For a
     more detailed analysis of the critical debates surrounding Indianism in American operas
     specifically, see Ziegel (2011).

feel of the music, while the harmonic dissonances foreshadow the ferocity of which Natoma will soon prove capable. For all this Indianist atmosphere, however, the dance also serves a much more traditionally operatic plot function by providing a backdrop for the plot's key turning point. Critics were quick to point out the obvious kinship between the »Dagger Dance« and *Salome*'s »Dance of the Seven Veils,« something American audiences had only recently become acquainted with.

Example 8: Herbert, Natoma, Act II – Dagger Dance (1911, p. 284).

Indian music is less prominent, but nonetheless present in both *The Sacrifice* and *Narcissa*. While only an infrequent occurrence in Converse's score, the composer does make the unusual decision to incorporate a melody ostensibly unchanged from its source. A minor character named Pablo (baritone) sings a quoted melody with its original vocables intact (Example 9). Converse uses this style here precisely for its strangeness, a quality emphasized in his distinctive harmonization of the tune. In the plot, the passage functions as an offstage warning to the Mexican fighter Bernal, which interrupts his love duet with Chonita. She is so startled that she asks, »What is that weird music?« The »weirdness« of the music, rather than its Americanness, is the most striking feature, especially when coming from the voice of a character allied with the enemy. Moore too incorporates Indian music as a means to separate characters as outsiders. In one scene, the prophetess Waskema (mezzo-soprano) realizes that the arrival of so many immigrant settlers will inevitably result in the end of her way of life (Example 10). The music is again harmonically static and rhythmically repetitive. By foregrounding Indianist musical traits, the threat of how the tribes might respond becomes all the more ominous. Yet despite the overtly stereotyped presentation, Seattle's music critic, Paul Hedrick, still praised Moore for »faithfully and accurately« incorporating Indian music »during which the ear of the trained musician is gratefully conscious of something absolutely new and very well done« (Hedrick, »Narcissa Approved,« 1912). Paradoxically, Indian music could simultaneously be both indigenously American, thereby contributing to the formation of a national idiom, and uniquely exotic, thereby satisfying an audience desire for adventurous displays of »local color.«

Example 9: Converse, The Sacrifice, Act I – Pablo's Indian Song (1910, p. 92).

Example 10: Moore, Narcissa, Act II – Waskema's Prophecy (1912, p. 82).

One final ingredient deserving attention here is the way in which these composers incorporate passages of sacred music into their overall dramaturgical design. This includes both solo prayers and choral singing. Again, these are fairly common ingredients in operas from the European canon—from Wagner's *Tannhäuser* and *Parsifal* to Gounod's *Faust* or Verdi's *Il Trovatore* and *Otello*, among many others— yet the American approach strikes out in several new directions. First, when present, the sacred music passages are always specifically Christian in outlook, rather than generically spiritual, and thus the chorus from *Poia* praising the Sun God Natosi must be excluded here. Despite the often difficult, if not outright antagonistic, relationship between American Protestants and Catholics at the time, these operas pursue a more ecumenical outlook, incorporating materials, as appropriate, to the plot, setting, and time period. Secondly, the sacred music ingredients often serve an expressly symbolic function—either working to win audience sympathy for a character's actions or serving as a sort of divine endorsement for the ultimate resolution of an opera plot. In all cases, the presence of Christian faith comingles with the notion of American progress and exceptionalism.

In *The Sacrifice*, Converse includes a prayer aria for his heroine Chonita (soprano). His Boston audience would likely have been familiar with similar operatic prayers, including scenes for Desdemona in Verdi's *Otello* and Elisabeth in Wagner's *Tannhäuser*; yet in *The Sacrifice*, Converse must accomplish a more complicated task than that presented in either precedent. Unlike Desdemona or Elisabeth, Chonita is an outsider figure. Burton's longing for her crosses the divide of nationality, ethnicity, and class, thus Converse must musically prove that she is worthy of his devotion. The passage known as »Chonita's Prayer« accomplishes this task admirably (Example 10). Chonita erroneously believes that her beloved Bernal has been killed in the previous night's skirmish. Tired of resisting Burton's advances, she turns to prayer, kneeling before the cross at a mission church altar, and begs for the strength to persevere. Rather than exoticising the character, Converse's subtle harmonic sense, natural text declamation, chromatic inner voices, and richly expressive melodic line duly capture the supplicatory devotion of Chonita's attitude. By witnessing this prayerful expression of her personally held faith, an audience is much more willing to accept the »sacrifice« of the opera's title. Ultimately, Burton forfeits his own life in order to allow Chonita and Bernal to escape to safety and freedom. Without this demonstration of Chonita's ability to enter into the realm of sacred music, she might otherwise seem unworthy of Burton's sacrificial love. Her spirituality is what substantiates the patriotism of the American's actions.

In *Narcissa*, Moore likewise reveals her characters' devout faith through musical means. In this work, however, the balance between sacred music and standard operatic ingredients is fundamentally realigned. Indeed, Christian observances and their accompanying sacred music become the centerpiece of her score. Here, not only does faithfulness function as a symbol of patriotism, but sacred music also provides a consistent backdrop to the unfolding events of the plot. Throughout the opera, Moore incorporates hymn singing at times of great conflict or personal significance, as one might expect in a plot based upon the lives of two real-life nineteenth-century missionaries. Aside from a passing quotation of OLD HUNDRED, Moore's five other hymns are newly composed. In each case, their texts speak directly to the plot situation at hand, as the characters seek consolation, sing praises to God, or ask for strength to combat the challenges they are facing. Her re-creation of the idiom of nineteenth-century Protestant hymnody is, of course, distinctively American in nature. Sung prayer also plays a significant role in reflecting Narcissa's inner feelings. In the third act, for instance, she is overcome by the stress of missionary life and the rigors of the frontier. She turns to prayer, seeking reaffirmation of her mission, asking God to »prosper us in work for Thee. Bless us, nerve our hearts, our hands, in thine employ.« (See the opening phrase of this soprano prayer aria in Example 12.) By emphasizing Narcissa's spiritual strength, Moore seems to assert the link between the character's faithfulness and the patriotic role that she plays in enabling westward territorial expansion.

Example 11: Converse, The Sacrifice, Act II – Chonita's Prayer (1910, p. 165).

Example 12: Moore, Narcissa, Act III – Prayer Scene (1912, p. 143).

Even if *Narcissa* could almost deserve the generic appellation of »sacred opera,« it is not the period's only example that explores the theme of divinely justified territorial expansion. Indeed, the conviction that it was the providential destiny of the United States to extend its territory across the entire continent, although this was a securely established geographic reality by the early 1910s, clearly offered much dramatic potential for composers and librettists at the time. Perhaps Moore's later development of this topic was inspired by one of the most remarkable applications of sacred music in all of American opera: the final scene of Herbert's *Natoma*. Here, the work of nation building is in fact accomplished through sacred music. In an ambitious, compositional choice, the three principal characters cease to sing and instead assume the role of silent actors, while the musical accompaniment becomes exclusively sacred and choral in content. Natoma, having killed Alvarado as described above, has sought sanctuary in a church mission. The scene begins with organ music that soon accompanies a double male chorus singing a seventeenth-century Latin hymn text. Next, the nuns of the convent enter, softly singing the »Sanctus« to a simple accompaniment of muted violins (Example 13a). Finally, the full chorus and orchestra join together for a climactic, *grandioso* reprise of the »Sanctus« theme (Example 13b).

Example 13a: Herbert, Natoma, Act III – Chorale Finale (1911, p. 325).

Example 13b: Herbert, Natoma, Act III – Chorale Finale (1911, p. 330).

While this music plays, the action that unfolds on stage provides a metaphor for manifest destiny itself. The mission nuns welcome Natoma into their community as a new convert. Paul and Barbara clasp hands and kneel before the altar. The priest offers a benediction, and Natoma departs to the convent as the curtain falls. As an Indian with first rights to the territory, Natoma symbolically relinquishes her claim by joining the convent. Likewise, through Paul's union to the Spaniard Barbara, the American now becomes the rightful inheritor of the California territory. Sacred music makes explicit that the plot's outcome, symbolic of national progress, has indeed been divinely guided.

The perpetual state of »not yet«

Taken in total, these four operas yield a remarkably consistent approach to the genre. Given the shared stylistic idiom and cohesive sense of accomplishment in these scores from the early 1910s, one must surely recognize that American opera had at last become a uniquely definable quantity. With similar musical components serving related dramatic and symbolic purposes, the genre of opera had indeed coalesced into a distinctive, indigenous variant. Yet these and other contemporaneous works seemed unable to satisfy music critics' expectations of what form »American« opera should ultimately take. Throughout the period's critical commentary, one finds a consistent strand of argument that insists the genre was »not yet« acceptably American enough, regardless of how many new works composers continued to create. In June 1911, just after the premieres of both *Natoma* and *The Sacrifice*, Clarence E. Le Massena was quoted in the magazine *Current Literature,* worrying that »Probably we shall never witness the establishment of American opera in our day and generation. We may [only] live to see its inception« (»Outlook for American Opera,« 1911, p. 654). Herbert F. Small, writing for *Musical Quarterly*, was still echoing the same concerns seven years later: »American Opera is not yet, but [...] the time is ripe for it, and we must have it« (Small, 1918, p. 37). As late as 1927, William Saunders, also writing for *Musical Quarterly*, expressed dismay that despite the »decided urge in the United States towards the creation of a distinctively national type of opera [...] nothing of a highly outstanding character has yet emerged.« He wondered if it remained »too early yet [to expect] a genuine national genius« who could »found a national system of opera« (Saunders, 1927, p. 82). Even Edward Hipsher, who, as the author of the groundbreaking *American Opera and Its Composers*, was arguably the most committed advocate for new native repertoire, conceded that »›The Great American Opera‹ is yet to be written« (Hipsher, 1934, p. 448). There was perhaps some consolation for those remained hopeful. An unnamed writer in *The Independent* noted that »If, as many believe, the great American novel has not yet been written, it is hardly to be wondered at that in the realm of operatic composition, which is so much younger an art than the writing of fiction, so little that is worthwhile has been done in this country« (»An American Opera in Boston,« 1911, p. 658).

Ultimately, this yearning for one, single »great« American operatic exemplar created a situation in which the anticipation for any premiere was so overwhelming that the burden of expectations was virtually impossible to meet. Henry Krehbiel, the nation's most influential music critic at the time, recognized that the first performance of *Natoma* in Philadelphia »was obviously looked upon as a momentous event upon which hung everlasting things« (Krehbiel, 1919, p. 227). The production of *Poia* in Berlin was seen as »an epoch-making event because it marks the first substantial recognition ever accorded to transatlantic composers in the land where Beethoven and Wagner were born« (»Nevin's Work,« 1910). *The Sacrifice* was heralded as »the most notable endeavor in the field of grand opera attempted by an American musician,« while another critic exhorted »all reasonably-minded people [to] admit« that the premiere of *Narcissa* was indeed »an epoch-making event« (»Noted Tenor to Sing,« 1911; Hedrick, »Mrs. Moore's Opera,« 1912). Thus, as each subsequent candidate for the title of »Great American Opera« appeared, if a work instead turned out to be something more closely related to the European tradition or if it was not the blazing masterpiece that had been hyped in the pre-performance press, then the only possible conclusion for the genre's advocates was simply »not yet.«

Looking back on these years from the vantage point of 1932, Saunders recognized that 1910 »commenced what may, so far as opera is concerned, be regarded as the age of enlightenment,« even if the not-yet caveat still lingers:

> The effect of this is only now beginning to be felt, but the immediate results were decidedly happy, as the minds of many of the ablest of America's composers were gradually turned into what may be called operatic channels, and steady progress has since been made towards what must, sooner or later, emerge as a truly American national opera. (Saunders, 1932, p. 149)

Despite his admission that the nation is still waiting, Saunders was virtually alone among commentators from this period in detecting the threads of consistency that bind together the operas premiered during the early 1910s. He felt that other critics were to blame for having overlooked a primary unifying characteristic:

> It was clearly obvious to all who had taken the least trouble to study the scores and tendencies of these works, that there was, from beginning to end, a distinct and conscious urge towards the formation and evolution of a pronounced and distinctive American idiom. (Saunders, 1932, p. 150)

As the analysis here has tried to show, the presence of this »conscious urge« does indeed unite the works from this period into what deserves recognition as the nascent school of American opera. Even if acknowledged »greatness« in the genre would be somewhere in the not-too-distant future, the accomplishments and contributions of composers working during the 1910s must not be overlooked.

Appendix: Premiere Production Details

COMPOSER: Arthur Nevin
LIBRETTIST: Randolph Hartley (sung in Eugenie von Huhn's German translation)
TITLE: *Poia*
DATE: 23 April 1910
VENUE: Royal Opera House, Berlin
PRINCIPAL ROLES

Poia (tenor)	Walter Kirchoff
Natoya (soprano)	Mrs. Francis MacLennan (i.e., Florence Easton)
Sumatsi (baritone)	[?] Bischoff
Nenahu (contralto)	Margarete Ober
Natosi (bass)	Putnam Griswold

CONDUCTOR: Carl Muck
NOTES: Both Florence Easton and Putnam Griswold are Americans. Additionally, a third American singer, Lucy Gates, appeared in a minor role as the »Spirit of Winter.«
CAST LIST SOURCES: »Berlin Welcomes,« 1910; »America's First Assault,« 1910; Hipsher, 1934, p. 339

COMPOSER: Victor Herbert
LIBRETTIST: Joseph D. Redding
TITLE: *Natoma*
DATE: 25 February 1911
VENUE: Metropolitan Opera House, Philadelphia
PRINCIPAL ROLES

Natoma (soprano)	Mary Garden
Barbara de la Guerra (soprano)	Lillian Grenville
Lt. Paul Merrill (tenor)	John McCormack
Don Francisco de la Guerra (bass)	Gustave Huberdeau
Juan Bautista Alvarado (baritone)	Mario Sammarco
José Castro (baritone)	Frank Preisch
Father Peralta (bass)	Hector Dufranne

CONDUCTOR: Cleofante Campanini
NOTES: The published vocal score incorrectly gives the premiere date as 23 February 1911, which was in fact only a public dress rehearsal.
CAST LIST SOURCE: Hipsher, 1934, p. 261

COMPOSER: Frederick Shepherd Converse
LIBRETTIST: Converse, with lyrics by John Macy
TITLE: *The Sacrifice*
DATE: 3 March 1911
VENUE: Boston Opera House
PRINCIPAL ROLES

Chonita (soprano)	Alice Nielsen
Captain Burton (baritone)	Roman Blanchart
Bernal (tenor)	Florencio Constantino
Tomasa (contralto)	Maria Claessens
Magdelena (soprano)	Bernice Fisher
Corporal Tom Flynn (bass)	Howard White

CONDUCTOR: Wallace Goodrich
CAST LIST SOURCES: Hipsher, 1934, p. 135; »Critical Review,« 1911

COMPOSER: Mary Carr Moore
LIBRETTIST: Sarah Pratt Carr
TITLE: *Narcissa* (or *The Cost of Empire*)
DATE: 22 April 1912
VENUE: Moore Theater, Seattle, Washington
PRINCIPAL ROLES

Narcissa Whitman (soprano)	Luella Chilson Ohrman
Marcus Whitman (tenor)	Charles Hargreaves
Delaware Tom (baritone)	Charles Derbyshire
Waskema (mezzo-soprano)	Mme. Hesse-Sprotte [Anna Ruzena Sprotte]
Elijah (tenor)	Alfred A. Owens
Siskadee (contralto)	Romeyn Jansen
Chief Yellow Serpent (baritone)	Frederick Graham

CONDUCTOR: Mary Carr Moore
NOTES: *Narcissa* marks the first time in American history that a woman composer conducted her own opera in performance. The opera's librettist was the composer's mother.
CAST LIST SOURCE: »Mrs. Moore's Opera,« 1912

Published Scores and Librettos

Carr, S. P. (1912). *The Cost of Empire: Libretto for the Opera Narcissa*. Seattle, WA: The Stuff Printing Concern.

Converse, F. S. (1910). *The Sacrifice, Op. 27* [vocal score]. New York: H.W. Gray.

Converse, F. S. & Macy, J. (1911). *The Sacrifice: An Opera in Three Acts* [libretto]. New York: H. W. Gray.

Herbert, V. (1911). *Natoma* [vocal score]. New York: Schirmer.

Moore, M. C. (1912). *Narcissa* [vocal score]. New York: Witmark.

Nevin's Work Taken for Kaiser's Opera (1910). *New York Times*, 20 June.

Noted Tenor to Sing in *Lakme* (1911). *Boston Globe*, 1 March.

Redding, J. D. (1911). *Natoma: An Opera in Three Acts* [libretto]. New York: Schirmer.

References

(1895). An American Opera. *The Outlook*, 12 January, 70.

(1910). America's First Assault upon Berlin. *Current Literature*, 48, 659–660.

(1910). Berlin Welcomes the First Serious American Opera. *New York Times*, April 10.

(1910). Victor Herbert's First Serious Opera. *New York Times*, 10 October.

(1911). An American Opera in Boston. *The Independent*, 70, 658–659.

(1911). Critical Review of the Opera's Music and Story. *Boston Globe*, 4 March.

(1911). The Outlook for American Opera. *Current Literature*, 50, 653–654.

Anonymous (1912). Mrs. Moore's Opera to Be Given This Evening. *Seattle Daily Times*, 22 April.

(1912). Professor Parker's Prize Opera. *The Nation,* 94, 295–296.

Ahlquist, K. (1997). *Democracy at the Opera: Music, Theater, and Culture in New York City, 1815-60*. Urbana: University of Illinois Press.

Brenon, A. S. J. (1913). Opera in New York: The Views of Mr. Gatti–Casazza. *The Century Magazine*, 85, 368–378.

Burton, F. R. (1909). *American Primitive Music*. New York: Moffat, Yard and Company.

Dizikes, J. (1993). *Opera in America: A Cultural History*. New Haven, MA: Yale University Press.

Eaton, W. P. (1911). Where We Stand in Opera. *The American Magazine*, 71, 665–675.

Elson, L. & Elson, A. (1925). *The History of American Music*. New York: Macmillan.

Finck, H. T. (1906). What is American Music? *The Etude*, 24, 356–357.

Garofalo, R. J. (1994). *Frederick Shepherd Converse (1871–1940): His Life and Music*. Metuchen, NJ: Scarecrow Press.

Gilman, L. (1911). Opera in English. *The North American Review*, 193, 744–751.

Gilman, L. (1914). *Nature in Music: and Other Studies in the Tone-Poetry of Today*. New York: John Lane Company.

Guzski, C. (2001). *American Opera at the Metropolitan, 1910–1935: A Contextual History and Critical Survey of Selected Works.* Ph.D. Dissertation, City University of New York.

Hedrick, P. C. (1912). Mrs. Moore's Opera to Be Given This Evening. *Seattle Daily Times,* 22 April.

Hedrick, P. C. (1912). Narcissa Approved by Large Local Audience. *Seattle Daily Times,* 23 April.

Hipsher, E. E. (1934). *American Opera and Its Composers.* Philadelphia, PA: Theodore Presser.

Kaye, J. (1931). *Victor Herbert: The Biography of America's Greatest Composer of Romantic Music.* New York: G. H. Watt.

Kirk, E. K. (2001). *American Opera.* Urbana: University of Illinois Press.

Krehbiel, H. E. (1919). *More Chapters of Opera.* New York: Henry Holt.

Mason, D. G. (1918). *Contemporary Composers.* New York: Macmillan.

McClung, L. (1910). The Dawn of American Opera. *Sunset: The Magazine of the Pacific,* 25, 423–429.

Nevin, A. (1909). *Poia* [vocal score]. Berlin: Adolf Fürstner.

Nevin, A. (1916). Two Summers with the Blackfeet Indians of Montana. *Musical Quarterly,* 2, 257–270.

Ottenberg, J. C. (1994). *Opera Odyssey: Toward a History of Opera in Nineteenth-Century America.* Westport, CT: Greenwood Press.

Pisani, M. V. (2005). *Imagining Native America in Music.* New Haven, CT: Yale University Press.

Preston, K. K. (1993). *Opera on the Road: Traveling Opera Troupes in the United States, 1825–60.* Urbana: University of Illinois Press.

Saunders, W. (1927). National Opera, Comparatively Considered. *Musical Quarterly,* 13, 72–84.

Saunders, W. (1932). The American Opera: Has It Arrived? *Music and Letters,* 13, 147–155.

Small, H. F. (1918). On Opera. *Musical Quarterly,* 4, 37–49.

Sonneck, O. G. (1905). Early American Operas. *Sammelbände der Internationalen Musikgesellschaft,* 6, 428–495.

Whigham, H. J. (1911). Echoes of the Stage. *Town and Country,* 4 March, 24.

Ziegel, A. (2009). Enacting the Nation on Stage: Style, Subjects and Themes in American Opera Librettos of the 1910s. *The Opera Journal,* 42, 3–21.

Ziegel, A. (2011). *Making America Operatic: Six Composers' Attempts at an American Opera, 1910–1918.* Ph.D. Dissertation, University of Illinois at Urbana-Champaign.

Marcus Gräser

»Recognizably American«
Aaron Coplands *The Second Hurricane* (1936/37) als musikalische Theatralisierung des Politischen im *New Deal*

Für Jörg Nagler zum 24.11.2015

Die Suche nach dem ›Amerikanischen‹ in der Musik, die spätestens mit Horatio C. Kings 1876 veröffentlichtem Diktum »The Great American Opera is still unwritten« begonnen hatte (King, 1876, S. 192), unterlag in den folgenden Jahrzehnten Konjunkturen. Regelrecht dringlich wurde die Suche im Rahmen des nationalen Selbstdeutungsprozesses während der Großen Depression in den 1930er Jahren. Erstmals wurde der amerikanische Staat in der Reformpolitik des *New Deal* durch Arbeitsbeschaffungsmaßnahmen zu einem Akteur im Feld der ›Ermöglichung‹ von Musik: Das »Federal Music Project« beschäftigte im Rahmen der öffentlichen Arbeitsbeschaffung (Works Progress Administration, WPA) in den Jahren zwischen 1935 und 1938 rund 15 000 stellungslose Musiker aller Richtungen. Unzweideutig war der Zusammenhang zwischen jener »government-subsidized proliferation of orchestras administered by the WPA« und der wachsenden Zahl neuer Symphonien (Taruskin, 2010, S. 647).[1] Unter den Komponisten gab es eine Nachfrage nach dem ›Staat‹ – nicht nur als arbeitschaffender, sondern auch als musikpolitischer Instanz: 1938 debattierte der Kongress, auch auf Drängen vieler Komponisten, über die Einrichtung eines »Permanent Bureau of Fine Arts«, freilich ohne greifbares Ergebnis (vgl. Tischler, 1986, S. 136–156). Und im ›Staat‹, d.h. unter den Protagonisten der Administration Franklin D. Roosevelts, gab es eine Nachfrage nach Musik (der unterschiedlichsten Art) im öffentlichen Raum: nicht nur, aber auch aus dem Motiv heraus, durch eine kulturnationalistische Mobilisierung zur Schaffung/Stabilisierung amerikanischer Identität(en) in der Krise beitragen zu können. Staat und Musik fanden aneinander Gefallen, was zu einer besonderen und in den USA bislang unbekannten Konstellation aus Musik und Politik führte. Nie zuvor hatte der amerikanische Staat in irgendeiner Weise in den freien Raum der Kunst und Kunstausübung eingegriffen – weder durch öffentliches Mäzenatentum noch durch

---

1 Vgl. zum Aufschwung der Werkgattung Symphonie auch Tawa, 2009, vor allem S. 12–30. – Für die freundliche Hilfe bei der Recherche des Quellenmaterials danke ich Universitätsassistent Thilo Neidhöfer herzlich.

eine Lust an gesetzlicher Regulierung. Nie zuvor hatten die Künste in den USA zu den bevorzugten Repräsentations- und Präsentationsformen der Politik gezählt. Als sich dies in den 1930er Jahren zu ändern begann, war die Bereitschaft vieler Komponisten zur Partizipation in einer Schnittmenge aus Kunst und Politik groß: »Selten ist in einer Demokratie die Mehrheit der Künstler so stark auf die damals grassierenden politischen wie künstlerischen Ideologien eingeschworen gewesen (sozialer Realismus, Regionalismus)« (Beyme, 2005, S. 820).

Die alte Parole um eine »Great American Opera«, die King 1876 in Anknüpfung an die noch ältere Suche nach der »Great American Novel« (DeForest, 1868, S. 27) ausgegeben hatte, fand in der kulturnationalistischen Stimmung der 1930er Jahre jedoch keine rechte Fortsetzung – jedenfalls nicht unter diesem Begriff. Lassen sich dafür Ursachen benennen? Längst hatte sich unter Komponisten und Musikkritikern ein Bündel an Erklärungen dafür angesammelt, warum es eine *amerikanische* Oper so schwer habe: »The trouble lies«, so schrieb George Antheil 1934 in der Zeitschrift »Modern Music«, »in our national and instinctive feeling against opera. We are a musical nation reared upon the German symphony orchestra. Our esthetic is the esthetic of the abstract. When we go to the opera, we want to hear it in a foreign language!« (Antheil, 1934, S. 89). Die lange vorherrschende anti-theatralische Färbung der amerikanischen Kultur hatte ein nur mäßig interessiertes Publikum heranwachsen lassen, das, wie B. M. Steigman einige Jahre zuvor (unter der eher spöttisch gemeinten Überschrift »The Great American Opera«) in »Music and Letters« kritisiert hatte, damit zufrieden war, »the most lavish patrons in the world of operatic art« zu sein: »that is why we must put up with all sorts of outlandish music and librettos, sung in every language but our own« (Steigman, 1925, S. 359). Auf dem Schauplatz des Ringens um die »Great American Opera« wurde der Abstand zu Europa als dem kulturell maßstabsetzenden Kontinent verhandelt: Die »Great American Opera« hätte eine synthetische Leistung sein müssen: so ›europäisch‹ wie nötig, um in den Mutterländern der Oper Anerkennung zu finden, aber so ›amerikanisch‹ wie möglich, um eben den Abstand zu Europa eigenständig markieren zu können. Dieser paradoxe, quasi kaum einlösbare Zuschnitt hat die »Great American Opera« zu einem Ideal werden lassen, das um seiner dauernden Funktion im Diskurs willen gar nicht ›wahr‹ werden durfte.[2]

Ohnehin war in den 1930er Jahren viel von einer »operatic crisis« die Rede (Sessions, 1938, S. 146), die die Aufmerksamkeit vom Musiktheater in seiner traditio-

---

2 Die Parole scheint immer noch eine Funktion zu erfüllen: vgl. etwa Kramer, 2008. In der Literatur ist das Ringen um die »Great American Novel« wohl abgebrochen worden: »The rewards are too few, the fame too fleeting, the terrain too parceled out in neat subdivisions of distinct minorities. No one talks anymore of ›the great American novel‹.« (White, 2013, S. 30)

nellen Form eher abzog.[3] Nicht erloschen aber war »the question of musical nationalism« (Sessions, 1941, S. 211),[4] die keinen besseren Theoretiker finden konnte als den Komponisten Roger Sessions, der in den 1930er Jahren im Leitmedium der amerikanischen Komponisten, in der von Minna Lederman herausgebenen Zeitschrift »Modern Music«, zahlreiche Artikel und Aufsätze veröffentlichte, die den Stand der avancierten Musik jüngerer Komponisten reflektierten. In seinem 1941 veröffentlichten Aufsatz »American Music and the Crisis« resümierte Sessions die Debatten der 1930er Jahre und hielt fest, dass die Suche nach dem genuin ›Amerikanischen‹ in der Musik ebenso sehr eine Frage der Musiksprache wie der Herstellung einer »community of tastes between composer and public« sei (ebd., S. 214). Diese Herstellung aber könne nur gelingen, wenn die Musik »experience« speichere und »the authentic accents and gestures of American individuals« wiedergebe (ebd., S. 217). Die »question of musical nationalism« war in den 1930er Jahren tatsächlich weniger eine Frage des musikalischen Stils, sondern eher eine der Anerkennung des Komponisten durch die Öffentlichkeit. Nahezu alle in der Generation von Sessions waren regelrecht besessen von der »duty of the composer to write for a public« und einem – selbstgestellten, aber durch das innenpolitische Klima des *New Deal* beförderten – Auftrag zur öffentlichen Wirksamkeit und zum öffentlichen Gebrauch der Musik. Gleichwohl ging es dabei nicht um »art as function of the political state« (Sessions, 1933, S. 12), sondern eher um eine Selbstermächtigung der Künstler in einer Situation, in der auch in der Gesellschaft die Nachfrage nach einer politisch deutbaren Kunst wuchs.[5]

Dieses Spannungsfeld zwischen künstlerischer Produktion und (ersehnter) öffentlicher Wirksamkeit ließ eine politische Ästhetik zu, die im Folgenden an einem gemeinhin wenig beachteten Werk Aaron Coplands, der Schuloper *The Second Hurricane* (1936/37), untersucht werden soll. Copland war in der Durchsetzung des »Americanism« in der Musik zeitweise ein enger Verbündeter, Freund und Kollege

---

3   Erstaunlicherweise spielte der Film in den Debatten um neue Formen des Musiktheaters, soweit sie sich in »Modern Music« abspielten, kaum eine Rolle. Es blieb Kurt Weill vorbehalten, die Vermutung zu äußern, dass »the new musical art work« in den USA »may after all develop from the medium of the movies« (Weill, 1937, S. 188).

4   Zu einem materialreichen Rückblick auf die Geschichte des »Americanism« in der amerikanischen Musik aus der Perspektive der 1930er Jahre vgl. Rosenfeld, 1940.

5   Deutlicher noch als in den USA fiel der öffentliche Gebrauch der Musik in Lateinamerika, vor allem in Mexico und Brasilien, aus: Auch hier entstand eine kulturnationalistische Situation, die Komponisten wie Carlos Chávez (in Mexico) und Heitor Villa-Lobos (in Brasilien) in die Nähe eines politischen Funktionärstums brachte, zugleich aber auch der zeitgenössischen Musik einen bis dahin unbekannten Stellenwert im öffentlichen Raum verschaffte, der in den USA nicht ohne stille Bewunderung blieb (vgl. Goebel Labastille, 1937, sowie zum Phänomen des Musical Pan Americanism Hess, 2013. Zu Villa-Lobos in diesem Zusammenhang vgl. Negwer, 2008, S. 167–215).

von Sessions[6] und galt schon in der Zeit, aber stärker noch im Rückblick als ›der‹ genuine Repräsentant einer kulturnationalistischen Kehre in der zeitgenössischen amerikanischen Musik: Für ihn war die »question of musical nationalism« aber ohne die Suche nach einem musikalischen Idiom, nach einer »obviously indigenous expression« (Copland, 1952, S. 95), nicht zu beantworten. Damit war für Copland ein Werkverständnis im Spannungsfeld von Kunst, Politik und Gesellschaft zwangsläufig; Arthur Berger, Coplands erster Biograph, schrieb 1953 rückblickend:

> Liberal thinking has often accompanied the humanism and the idealistic outlook of creative individuals, as we may observe without any difficulty if we look back upon the history of the master in all artistic fields. The directions in which their aspirations turned did not always prove, in the end, to be conducive to the realization of these hopes ... But an artist looks for something on which to fasten these aspirations, and for Copland's generation, in the thirties, the New Deal provided it. The vein of optimism and patriotic sentiment, formerly confined to Rotarians and conservative artists, became *the thing* in the ranks of the *avantgarde*, and even composers who were unaware of the sociological origins fell in line, responding to what they thought was a purely creative trend. In their cries of »America I love you«, beating their breasts, they sometimes outdid the Rotarians. (Berger, 1953, S. 29)[7]

In den Charles Eliot Norton Lectures, die Copland 1951/52 an der Harvard University hielt, beschrieb er als wichtigste Bedingung für die Schaffung einer »indigenous music of universal significance« die Übereinstimmung zwischen Komponist und einer sich ihrer selbst bewussten Nation: »the composer must be part of a nation that has a profile of its own« (Copland, 1952, S. 79). Mit diesem Bekenntnis zu einem progressiven Kulturnationalismus einher ging auch eine Tendenz zur Affirmation – des Bestehenden, oder doch zumindest der Tradition, in der sich Gesellschaft und Komponist bewegten: »You cannot make art out of fear and suspicion; you can make it only out of affirmative beliefs. ... The artist should feel himself affirmed and buoyed up by his community« (ebd., S. 111). Auch wenn Copland hier – zur Zeit des beginnenden Kalten Kriegs – eher zurückhaltend und codiert schreibt,[8] ist die Besinnung auf die Jahre des *New Deal* und des Zweiten Weltkriegs deutlich zu spü-

---

6   Zum Verhältnis von Copland und Sessions vgl. Pollack, 1999, S. 165ff.
7   Hervorhebungen im Original. – Zur Bedeutung der Depression für die Abkehr vom »ironic mood« und vom »postwar hedonism« in der Musiksprache vgl. Taruskin, 2010, S. 637.
8   1953 erhielt Copland eine Vorladung vor das von Senator Joseph McCarthy geleitete Senate Permanent Subcommittee on Investigations, das ihn auf seine Verbindungen zum Kommunismus hin befragte (vgl. Crist, 2005a, S. 199, zum Verhalten Coplands vor dem committee vgl. Crist, 2005b, S. 297ff.).

ren: Nie zuvor waren Künstler und Gesellschaft in ihrer wechselseitigen Affirmation einander so nahe gewesen wie in diesen Jahren.[9]

Ob und wie Coplands *The Second Hurricane* als repräsentativ für die politische Ästhetik der 1930er Jahre eingeschätzt werden kann, hängt nicht davon ab, ob das Werk unter den Zeitgenossen oder rückblickenden Betrachtern (und Hörern) als prominent wahrgenommen wurde und wird. Auch die künstlerische Qualität des Werks ist nicht ausschlaggebend; ohnehin steht im Folgenden nicht der Notentext und das Klangereignis, sondern die ›Geschichte‹, die in der Oper erzählt wird, im Mittelpunkt: Sie verbindet das musikalische Werk am sichtbarsten mit den politischen, kulturellen und ideologischen Ereignissen und Diskursen der Zeit – zumal dann, wenn, wie in Coplands Schuloper, das pädagogische Exemplum und der Zuschnitt als »Gebrauchsmusik« vorrangig ist. Reinhart Kosellecks Hypothese: »was zu einer bestimmten Zeit sagbar war und in derselben Zeit komponierbar war, das wird … nicht völlig zusammenhanglos sein können« (Koselleck, 2006, S. 155) gewinnt mit Blick auf die Fallstudie zu einer Oper und die Absicht einer politischen Kulturgeschichte[10] eine doppelte Bedeutung: Sie behandelt einerseits den (hier nicht weiter thematisierten) Zusammenhang zwischen Libretto, Dramaturgie und musikalischem Material, andererseits postuliert sie einen Nexus zwischen dem musikali-

---

9   Die Tendenz zur Affirmation erklärt dann auch, warum »political radicalism … conservative results in the arts« zur Folge haben konnte (Copland & Perlis, 1984, S. 217. Zur Gefahr der Konformität in der Re-Konstruktion eines »American way« vgl. auch Susman, 2003, S. 164).

10 Die Forschung zur politischen Kulturgeschichte hat in der deutschsprachigen Geschichtswissenschaft der letzten zwanzig Jahre enorme Fortschritte erfahren (vgl. aus der reichhaltigen Literatur nur Hardtwig & Wehler, 1996 und Hardtwig, 2011), wenngleich auch die politische Geschichte der Kunst(werke) ihren Platz im Rahmen einer politischen Kulturgeschichte noch nicht gefunden zu haben scheint. (In den USA ist das anders. Dort hat Michael Kammen in zahlreichen Arbeiten die politische Dimension einer Kulturgeschichte der Kunst ausgelotet, vgl. etwa Kammen, 2004.) Die Schwierigkeiten einer politischen Deutung der Kunst sind allerdings auch nicht zu unterschätzen: »Diese konstitutive Unbegrifflichkeit und Mehrdeutigkeit bzw. relative Deutungsoffenheit des Ästhetischen, die aus seiner sinnlichen Präsenz resultiert, macht es für die Sozial- und Geschichtswissenschaften zu einer schwierigen Dimension aller Quellen. Aber die Unbegrifflichkeit des Ästhetischen bedeutet nicht, dass seine Bedeutung völlig unparaphrasierbar wäre« (Braungart, 2012, S. 100). Die prinzipielle Autonomie des Kunstwerks steht in einer politischen Kulturgeschichte nicht zur Disposition (vgl. Müller & Osterhammel, 2012, S. 20), die »künstlerische Verdichtungsleistung« aber stellt eine Erkenntnisquelle dar: »Wenn das Werk in der Erzeugung seiner fiktionalen gesellschaftlichen Wirksamkeit eine unbezweifelbare Stimmigkeit aufweist, dann drückt es zwingend, auch und gerade als fiktionale Handlungswirklichkeit, ein die empirische praktische Wirklichkeit strukturierendes Modell bzw. eine diese strukturierende Gesetzlichkeit aus, so dass deren werkimmanente Rekonstruktion uns erlaubt, jene Erkenntnis gesellschaftlicher Realität zu heben, die als triftige künstlerische Erkenntnis im Werk selbst schon vorliegt.« (Oevermann, 1997, S. 276, 335).

schen Werk und dem allgemein ›Sagbaren‹ – also auch dem Feld der Politik. ›Aufgehoben‹ in diesem Nexus ist das Ästhetische:

> »Es bedeutet einerseits immer etwas, was sich auch sagen läßt, und andererseits, kraft seiner ästhetischen Präsenz und Präsentativität, immer mehr, als sich sagen läßt. Daraus entstehen auch besondere Spielräume für die Ästhetik des Politischen« – wobei in der Analyse freilich zwischen »einem diskursiv beschreibbaren und einem ästhetischen, annäherungsweise paraphrasierbaren Aspekt der symbolischen Dimension von Kommunikation« unterschieden werden muß. (Braungart, 2012, S. 98, 103)

Coplands Schuloper – Virgil Thomson sprach von einer »high-school cantata« (Thomson, 1937, S. 235) – handelt von einer Gruppe von *High-School*-Schülern im Alter zwischen 14 und 17 Jahren, die sich einem Flugzeugpiloten, der einen Rettungseinsatz in einer Flutkatastrophe im Mittleren Westen koordiniert, als Helfer zur Verfügung stellen. Der Pilot muss jedoch mit einem Maschinenschaden alsbald landen und setzt die Jugendlichen ab, um dann mit dem, um die Last der Passagiere und der mitgebrachten Lebensmittelvorräte erleichterten, Flugzeug zu einem Reparaturplatz zu fliegen. Die gestrandeten Jugendlichen versammeln sich auf einem Hügel, geraten in Streit, und als ein verirrtes schwarzes Kind zu ihnen stößt, kommt es zu rassistischen Bemerkungen und einem Konflikt über die Verteilung der für die Flutopfer gedachten Lebensmittel. Im Augenblick der erneuten Gefahr – als ein zweiter »Hurricane« die Flut steigen lässt – findet die Gruppe aus sich selbst heraus den Weg zu einer stabilen Gemeinschaft, in die auch das schwarze Kind inkludiert ist. Nachdem alle im Absingen eines Liedes aus der Amerikanischen Revolution – »The Capture of Burgoyne« – vereint sind, naht Rettung in Gestalt eines Flugzeugs.

Das Geschehen wird von Chören Erwachsener und Schüler kommentiert – die deutlichste formale Anlehnung an die »Lehrstück«-Varianten in der deutschen Musiklandschaft der 1920er und frühen 1930er Jahre. Copland und sein Librettist Edward Denby waren mit dem deutschen Musiktheater der Zeit bestens vertraut – Denby hatte Jahre in Deutschland verbracht und Copland war mehrfach zu Festivals in Deutschland gewesen, u.a. 1927 bei der »Deutschen Kammermusik Baden-Baden« (in der Nachfolge der Donaueschinger Kammermusiktage), wo Hindemiths Oper *Hin und Zurück* und Kurt Weills *Mahagonny Songspiel* zur Aufführung gelangten. Copland hatte zur Mitte der 1930er Jahre einen Job als ›music teacher‹ an der Henry Street Settlement ›music school‹ in New York City angenommen und dort waren in einer Produktion mit Jugendlichen Kurt Weills und Bertolt Brechts *Der Jasager* und Paul Hindemiths *Wir bauen eine Stadt* aufgeführt worden (Citkowitz, 1933). Das Henry Street Settlement gab schließlich auch Coplands *Hurricane* in Auftrag (Copland & Perlis, 1984, S. 251).

Das Echo auf Coplands Schuloper war (und ist) gespalten. Nach der Uraufführung im Henry Street Settlement Playhouse am 21. April 1937 – mit dem jungen Orson Welles als Regisseur und Joseph Cotten in der Rolle des Piloten, der Rest des Ensembles bestand aus Laien – kam es nicht zu vielen Wiederholungen; erst im Krieg fand das Stück Verwendung in einigen Schulaufführungen. Unter den Zeitgenossen gab es durchaus Zustimmung, Virgil Thomson schrieb in »Modern Music«, dass die Uraufführung ein »cardinal event in the American musical theater« gewesen sei, er lobte die »idiomatic simplicity« der Musik und bescheinigte Denby, dass er »linguistically … the finest English libretto in some years« geliefert habe (Thomson, 1937, 235). Ganz frei ohne ›Spitzen‹ sind solche Aussagen von Thomson sicher nicht gewesen[11], aber seine Begeisterung für die Schuloper wird so authentisch gewesen sein, wie es sich für einen Widmungsträger der Oper gehörte. Ganz anders fiel die Kritik des Schriftstellers Thornton Wilder aus, der schrieb: »all the worst features of the Sunday school, the Boy Scout movement and those radio serials where Fred aged twelve helps the FBI clean up a nest of counterfeiters« (zit. nach Pollack, 1999, S. 310). Für Arthur Berger hingegen nahm die Schuloper einen zentralen Platz in der Herausbildung von Coplands »new style« in der Mitte der 1930er Jahre ein. Unter den Werken, die auf der Basis von broad American folk sources … the interest of a wider audience« zu stimulieren suchten, zählte *The Second Hurricane* als »the one that thoroughly convinced him the new style was worth pursuing further« (Berger, 1953, S. 30). Copland wollte, wie er selbst es formulierte, »›Gebrauchsmusik‹ with a difference« schreiben; diese sollte ambitionierter sein als es in den bekannten Beispielen aus der deutschen Musik der Fall gewesen war. So sehr Copland mit der Idee einer »more useful, relevant form of serious music« (Crist, 2005a, S. 75) sympathisierte, so sehr missfiel ihm, insonderheit bei Weill, der Drang nach Verständlichkeit durch den Gebrauch von »pseudo-popular songs in the jazz manner« (Copland, 1960, S. 185). Coplands Mitstreiter Marc Blitzstein war noch härter in seiner Kritik an Pseudopopularität: »Look at the style of music it brought forth!«, schrieb er in einem Artikel in der Zeitschrift »Modern Music« 1934, »Music which abjectly copied what the mob had already learned to like« (Blitzstein, 1933, S. 101). Was sollte an die Stelle einer solchen, im Moment der Aufführung schon abgenutzt wirkenden Musiksprache treten? Copland verzichtete in seiner Musik zusehends auf jeden Anklang an Unterhaltungsmusik und schrieb in einem Stil, den er selbst als »imposed simplicity« kennzeichnete; im Rückblick präzisierte er seine Aufgabe: »The musical challenge was to see how simple I could be without loosing my musical identity« (zit. nach Copland & Perils, 1984, S. 261).

Nach dem Krieg aber geriet der *Hurricane* fast in Vergessenheit. Erst Leonard Bernstein – ein bewährter Mitstreiter Coplands in der Propagierung amerikanischer Musik – wagte einen Rettungsversuch und richtete die Oper 1960 für eine Fernsehauf-

---

11 Copland ›rächte‹ sich in seinen Harvard-Vorlesungen 1951/52 (»Music and Imagination«), indem er die Musik von Thomson nun seinerseits als »midwestern pseudo primitivism« charakterisierte und ihm und Gleichgesinnten maliziös bescheinigte: »the frank acceptance of so limited a musical vocabulary is a gesture of faith in their own heritage« (Copland, 1952, S. 94).

zeichnung ein; eine gekürzte Version (in der der Chor durch Bernstein als *narrator* ersetzt wurde) erschien auf Schallplatte. Aber der Zeitgeist der frühen 1960er Jahre war von der Mentalität der »Thirties« weit entfernt; die Bernstein-Einspielung nutzte der (namentlich nicht genannte) Musikkritiker des »Harper's Magazine« für einen Verriss: »What militates against its success is a combination of factors – a rather embarrassing libretto, and an equally embarrassing writing-down on the composer's part. *The Second Hurricane* is far too Rover-Boyish to rank high as a work of art, and it is one of it's composers few real mistakes.« (Copland Now, 1961, S. 110) Gelegentliche Aufführungen seither haben am ambivalenten Eindruck der Kritiker nichts geändert: Neben der Bereitschaft, »vivacity and charm of the work« gelten zu lassen (Rhein, 2000), steht nach wie vor die Kritik an einem »wafer-thin narrative [that] takes an awfully long time to reach its flat and unsuspenseful conclusion« (Rockwell, 1985).

Den bislang prononciertesten Deutungsversuch des *Hurricane* hat Elizabeth Crist vorgenommen, die Copland in den 1930er Jahren als »firmly aligned with the cultural politics and ideologies of the Popular Front« sieht (Crist, 2005a, S. 73) und folglich auch Coplands Schuloper als Ausdruck der lose um die Kommunistische Partei der USA und ihre Vorfeldorganisationen herum gebauten »Cultural Front«[12] deuten möchte. Die Belege dafür sieht Crist sowohl in der Musik als auch in der *story* der Oper: in einer Musik, die, wie im *Hurricane*, für ein High-School-Orchester gedacht war, böten »triadic harmonies and diatonic melodies« die Voraussetzung dafür, dass »audible rhetoric over structural logic« die Oberhand behalte (vgl. Crist, 2005a, S. 5). Hinzu trat die Annäherung an den *folk song*: Ein *song* – »The Capture of Burgoyne«, ein Lied aus dem *revolutionary war* (1776/81), das die Gefangennahme eines englischen Generals schildert – kam vor, ohne dass sein Ton auf das allgemeine Idiom der Musik der Schuloper übertragen wurde.[13] Allein das Zitat eines *folk songs* aber reicht Crist schon aus, um einen Kurzschluss zu ziehen: »Copland's appropriation of a traditional tune is indicative of a growing interest in folk song among leftist composers in the mid-thirties and can be correlated to changes in Soviet aesthetic policy« (ebd., S. 86).[14] In der *story* der Schuloper ist es vor allem die Figur des jungen Afroamerikaners Jeff, die als Beleg für die kommunistische *Tendenz* des Werks gesehen wird: Analog zur kommunistischen Kinderliteratur und Pädagogik werde Jeff in der Oper als transformative Figur eingebaut, die den latenten Rassismus der anderen Jugendlichen erst weckt und schließlich überwinden hilft. Die Feier der

---

12   Zur »Cultural Front« vgl. Denning, 1996.

13   Zu »Burgoyne« und der Platzierung des *songs* in der Oper vgl. Levy, 2012, S. 318.

14   In der Nutzung von *folk songs* mag man die musikalische Variante jener Tendenz zur »documentary expression« sehen, die in der amerikanischen Kultur der 1930er Jahre eine wichtige Rolle spielte, vgl. Stott, 1973. Dickstein weist freilich in seiner politischen Kulturgeschichte der Depression klar nach, dass der Rekurs auf *folk songs* schon in den 1920er Jahren en vogue zu werden begann (Dickstein, 2009, S. 452).

Solidarität in der Schuloper »bespeaks«, so Crist, »a Popular Front commitment to creating an integrated community of black and white, rural and urban, impoverished and middle class« (ebd., S. 85).

Auch wenn außer Frage steht, dass Copland Sympathien für das politische Spektrum links des *New Deal* besaß und in Organisationen und Gremien der »Popular Front« und ihrer kultur- und musikpolitischen Vorfeldorganisationen mitwirkte[15], so bleiben doch Zweifel, ob der *Hurricane* so einfach über den Leisten einer kommunistischen Ästhetik geschlagen werden kann. Warren Susman hat schon vor mehr als dreissig Jahren in seinem epochemachenden Aufsatz über »The Culture of the Thirties« bemerkt, dass in diesem Jahrzehnt ein »deep interest in communitarian ventures« präsent gewesen sei, »that smacks more of the America of Brook Farm[16] than of the USSR of Five-Year Plans« (Susman, 2003, S. 153).[17] Tatsächlich verweisen viele Spuren in Coplands *Hurricane* wie auch in anderen seiner Werke aus den 1930er Jahren auf ältere Traditionen in der amerikanischen Kultur, die nun von den Strategen der »Cultural Front« neu synthetisiert wurden – die »Popular Front« favorisierte einen kulturellen Nationalismus und wollte den Kommunismus als Amerikanismus pur verkaufen. Fast könnte man Blitzsteins Bemerkung über die Gebrauchsmusik spöttisch paraphrasieren: die »Cultural Front« übernahm jene Bestandteile der amerikanischen Tradition, die ohnehin wohlgelitten waren. Das aber hieß, dass ein Komponist, der bewusst an der »Cultural Front« partizipieren wollte, sich durchaus in traditionellen Bahnen bewegen durfte – und andererseits: Wer sich in (thematisch) traditionellen Bahnen bewegte, konnte unversehens in die Nähe der »Cultural Front« geraten.

Die Gemengelage war also etwas unübersichtlich, fraglich aber ist, ob Copland und sein Librettist Denby mit dem *Hurricane* wirklich ein kommunistisches Lehrstück, ein »pedagogical tool« der »Popular Front« (Haas, 2008, S. 18), abliefern wollten.[18] Crist scheint sich selbst nicht ganz sicher zu sein und weist durchaus auf andere Traditionen hin (vor allem jene der *Settlement*-Bewegung), die für die *story* der Schuloper einen Rahmen geben konnten. Gleichwohl neigt sie dazu, Ambivalenzen in den Quellen im Korsett ihrer Argumentation verschwinden zu lassen. In einem

---

15   Den besten Überblick zu Coplands politischer Haltung und Aktivität bei Copland & Perlis, 1984, S. 218–230. Die Zeit als »fellow traveller« wird hier auf die »early thirties« begrenzt (ebd., S. 218); vgl. auch Taruskin, 2010, S. 671, der die Argumentation von Crist stützt.

16   Brook Farm, in der Nähe von Boston gelegen, war das berühmte kommunitäre Experiment der *New England Transcendentalists*, das von Nathaniel Hawthorne in seinem Roman *The Blithedale Romance* beschrieben wurde (vgl. Gura, 2007, S. 150–178).

17   Vgl. auch Dickstein, 2009, S. 447: »the turn toward populism, especially after 1935, was part of a wider development that went far beyond the new cultural policy of the Communist Party.«

18   In Michael Dennings umfassender Gesamtdarstellung der »Cultural Front« spielt Copland maximal eine Nebenrolle (Dennings, 1996, S. 283–295).

undatierten Brief von Denby an Copland aus der Entstehungszeit der Oper, aus dem Crist zitiert, findet sich folgende Bemerkung – im Anschluss an eine Debatte über die Arie der Queenie, einer Protagonistin der Oper: »It must express the job of being united, which I think is the root of society – it's post-revolutionary ideology … – it's not ›Forward‹ it's ›We *are* together and we like it.‹ At the same time it has to be represented as Future in Queenie's mind« (zit. nach Crist, 2005a, S. 85). Dieses durch das »We are together and we like it« charakterisierte *sentiment* der urwüchsigen Solidarität unterscheidet sich diametral von der Konstruktion des »Einverständnisses« in Bertolt Brechts und Kurt Weills Lehrstück »Der Jasager«, das im Henry Street Settlement zuvor schon zur Aufführung gelangt war. In diesem »Lehrstück« stehen nicht Solidarität und Rettung, sondern die Unterordnung eines Heranwachsenden unter ein abstraktes Ziel und schließlich die freiwillige Selbstaufgabe (durch Selbstmord) im Vordergrund. Crist sieht diesen Unterschied (vgl. ebd., S. 78), der Schluss daraus aber kann nur – gegen ihre Argumentation – darin liegen, genau an diesem Abstand ›ums Ganze‹ zwischen den beiden Werken auch den Abstand des *Hurricane* zu einer tatsächlich dogmatisch verstandenen kommunistischen Lehrstücktradition (und Ästhetik) zu messen. Vor allem aber kommt in dieser Briefstelle die Überflüssigkeit der »Revolution« zum Ausdruck – sie hat in den USA ja schon stattgefunden (woran natürlich auch der Burgoyne-*song* erinnert) und bildet offenbar einen Rahmen, in dem die Solidarität des »We are together« Praxis werden kann; die Zukunft kann sich hier auf die Reproduktion des Rahmens verlassen und ist insofern immer schon »post-revolutionary«.

Man kann diese Briefstelle mit einiger Anstrengung in der Argumentation auf die Propaganda der »Popular Front« rückbeziehen, die in ihrem unbedingten Willen zur ›Normalisierung‹ des Kommunismus im amerikanischen Alltag Wladimir Lenin und George Washington gleichberechtigt nebeneinander stehen ließ (vgl. Susman, 2003, S. 80). Naheliegender aber ist es, *The Second Hurricane* deutlich in anderen Traditionen verwurzelt zu sehen, mindestens sind multiple Lesarten zulässig – was dem Publikum der ersten Aufführungen 1937 deutlich bewusst war, deutlicher jedenfalls als Crist, die nur mit Verwunderung das Publikum beschreibt:

> *The Second Hurricane* was premiered before a distinguished audience … On the list of sponsors were composers (Carlos Chávez, George Gershwin), artists and intellectuals (Lincoln Kirstein, Carleton Sprague Smith, Paul Rosenfeld, Carl Van Vechten), as well as women patrons married to prominent men (Mrs. Alfred Knopf, Mrs. Rita W. Morgenthau, Mrs. Leopold Stokowski). (Crist, 2005a, S. 90f.)

Copland selbst sah im Premierenpublikum überwiegend gut situierte Angehörige des »carriage trade« (ebd., S. 91). Crist zieht ein mit Blick auf ihre prinzipielle Argumentation überraschendes Fazit: »it seems likely that the values espoused in *The Second Hurricane* – that values of charity, tolerance, compassion, and equality – were purposefully directed to this elite assemblage« (ebd.). Wurde hier eine subversive Botschaft unter ein Park-Avenue-Publikum ›geschmuggelt‹? Ergab sich das »carriage trade« einer sowjetischen Ästhetik in amerikanischer Verkleidung? Tatsächlich boten die angesprochenen *values* noch nicht einmal Gelegenheit zu *radical chic* – ganz im Gegensatz etwa zu Blitzsteins ›musical play‹ *The Cradle Will Rock*, das im selben Jahr uraufgeführt wurde und in einem industriellen Szenario veritablen Klassenkampf auf die Bühne brachte. Im Vergleich damit war *The Second Hurricane* harmlos, nichts im Libretto ging über die akzeptierte Emphase eines demokratischen Miteinanders und einer kooperativen Mentalität hinaus[19] – die »elite assemblage« konnte sich eher bestätigt als herausgefordert fühlen. Coplands Schuloper kam nicht von ungefähr in der ›music school‹ des Henry Street Settlement zur Uraufführung: *Settlements* waren privat finanzierte Zentren der Fürsorge und Bildung, die seit dem Ende des 19. Jahrhunderts in den Einwanderervierteln der amerikanischen Großstädte entstanden. Betrieben wurden die *Settlements* von bürgerlichen Sozialreformern, oft von Frauen, die – jedenfalls in der ersten Generation der *settlement residents* – das *Settlement* nicht als Arbeitsplatz, sondern als kommunitäre Lebensform schufen. Ihre Form der sozialen Arbeit half ihnen in ihrer eigenen Selbstbestimmung als *middle class*: Soziale Arbeit vermittelte durch die Interaktion von *Middle-Class*-Reformern und Armen zwischen den Klassen der Gesellschaft, ja, sie stellte durch die Permanenz der Erfahrung ›Gesellschaft‹ überhaupt erst her (Gräser, 2009, S. 181–186). »Erfahrung« gehörte zu den Schlüsselbegriffen der *Settlement*-Praxis (und -ideologie), die vor allem von der ersten Generation von *residents* in einer Fülle von Büchern und Schriften erläutert und ausgearbeitet worden waren.

Der inhärent pädagogische Duktus führte in den prominenten *Settlements* – und dazu zählte neben dem von Jane Addams 1889 in Chicago begründeten Hull House unbedingt auch das 1893 von Lillian Wald gegründete Henry Street Settlement auf der Lower East Side von Manhattan – zum Aufbau separater Musikschulen und Theaterensembles; die musische Erziehung, die alle Beteiligten zur Interaktion des Einander-Zuhörens zwang, figurierte prominent im Erziehungsideal der *Settlements*. Sessions Aufsatz »New Vistas in Musical Education« griff auf dieses Ideal zurück:

---

19   Benjamin D. Haas hält es für »typical of left-wing recruitment« efforts in the later 1930s«, dass auf revolutionäre Rhetorik »in favor of more inclusive language« verzichtet wurde (Haas, 2008, S. 40). Das macht es freilich schwer, dann noch zu unterscheiden, ob die »inclusive language« so gemeint war oder nur eine Camouflage darstellte. Vielleicht sollte man einfach die »inclusive language« im »Hurricane« für bare Münze nehmen. Signifikant ist auch die (oben zitierte) beißende Kritik von Thornton Wilder, der – jeder Verwicklung in die »Cultural Front« abhold – gar nicht auf die Idee kam, den von ihm abgelehnten Stück eine kommunistische Tendenz zu unterstellen.

Education is, in any real sense, nothing more or less than experience, and teaching, purely and simply the directing of experience with the object of saving the student from as many waste motions and as many blind alleys as possible. The teacher of music, therefore, has the unique function, not of retailing abstractions, but of *bringing the student into contact with facts* – facts of a demonstrable and fundamentally inexorable nature. (Sessions, 1934, S. 117, Hervorhebung im Original)

Der sozialreformerische und pädagogische Anspruch der *Settlements* wie der *musical education* ruhte (auch) auf dem theoretischen Fundament, das der Philosoph und Pädagoge John Dewey gelegt hatte: Er lehrte von 1894 bis 1904 an der University of Chicago und von 1904 bis 1930 an der Columbia University in New York und nahm in beiden Städten regen Anteil an der *Settlement*-Praxis (Westbrook, 1991, S. 167). Für Dewey stand die Erziehung im Mittelpunkt jedweden Fortschritts in der Gesellschaft: »A chief end of education is to see the defects in the existing social arrangements and to take an active part in bettering them« (zit. nach Haas, 2008, S. 37). Deweys Pädagogik und die soziale Praxis der *Settlements* waren komplementär: »Community, communication, and consensus were the ›sacred trinity‹ upon which Jane Addams's and John Dewey's democracy was based« (Lissak, 1989, S. 15). *The Second Hurricane* mag als ein ›pedagogical tool‹ gedacht gewesen sein (Haas 2008, S. 18) – aber nicht für die »Popular Front«, sondern viel deutlicher für die avancierte *Settlement*-Praxis. Auch die Figur des schwarzen Jugendlichen Jeff, die Crist als Transfer aus der kommunistischen Kinderliteratur der 1930er Jahre deutet (Crist, 2005a, S. 85), kann ihren Ursprung ebenso gut aus den *Settlements* der gleichen Zeit genommen haben, in denen man allmählich dazu überging, schwarze und weiße Jugendliche gemeinsam zu erziehen (vgl. die photographische Evidenz in Johnson, 1989, S. 52f.). Die Protagonisten des *Hurricane* absolvierten einen Lernprozess, der sie am Ende zu einem perfekten *Settlement*-Jugendclub werden ließ. Es bedurfte keiner Revolution, da die wünschenswerten Institutionen längst vorhanden waren.

Mit dem Ausleuchten der Nähe zwischen *Settlement*-Pädagogik und Coplands *Hurricane* ist die unmittelbare politische Relevanz der Schuloper freilich noch gar nicht angesprochen. Tatsächlich ist eine Lesart möglich, die in diesem Werk eine Zustimmung zum Gesellschaftsbild und zum Politikmodell des *New Deal* sieht, eine Zustimmung, die nahe an der Affirmation ist und damit weit über die bloße Akzeptanz hinausging, die der *New Deal* – die Gesellschaftspolitik Franklin D. Roosevelts, die den »rugged individualism« durch Institutionen kollektiver Sicherheit zu ersetzen suchte – in den Kreisen der »Popular Front« erfuhr. Copland hatte schon 1935 eine kleine Chorkomposition veröffentlicht – *What Do We Plant* (nach einem Gedicht von Henry Abbey) –, die auf einfache Weise den gesellschaftlichen Nutzen der Bäume besang, und das zu einem Zeitpunkt, zu dem das »Civilian Conservation Corps«, das arbeitslose Jugendliche und junge Erwachsene u.a. mit dem Pflanzen von Bäumen und der Pflege von Nationalparks beschäftigte, zu einer der populären

Agenturen des *New Deal* herangewachsen war (Pollack, 2000, S. 303f.). Auch wenn man daraus nicht notwendig eine explizite Parteinahme für Roosevelt und die Politik des *New Deal* ableiten kann und Copland weder in dieser Komposition noch im *Hurricane* im staatlichen Auftrag oder als Teil des »Federal Music Projects« komponierte, so zeigt sich in dieser kleinen Komposition ebenso wie in der Schuloper doch eine Nähe zu den Symbolen und *sentiments* des *New Deal*, die deutlicher bemerkbar sind als die Anlehnung an kommunistische Rhetorik und eine »Cultural Front«-Attitüde. Auch die Herkunft des *Hurricane* aus der Pädagogik der *Settlements* und der Gedankenwelt Deweys weist auf eine Traditionslinie zum Reformismus des *New Deal* hin.[20]

Vor allem zwei *features* der Schuloper korrespondierten mit Diskurs und Praxis des *New Deal*:

(a) Die Natur wird zum Gegenstand von politischem Handeln: Den Hintergrund für das Bewährungsszenario in der Schuloper bildete die Flut in einem nicht näher präzisierten Ort im Mittleren Westen der USA – ausgelöst durch einen Hurricane.[21] Naturkatastrophen und Fluten hatten sich in den 1920er und 1930er Jahren gehäuft: Die Versteppung der Great Plains in Oklahoma und im Norden von Texas durch die Auspowerung des Bodens und die kontinuierlichen Sandstürme führte zur Depossedierung zahlreicher Farmer im *dust bowl*, die Pacht nicht mehr bezahlen und Schulden nicht mehr bedienen konnten; mehr als eine Million »Okies« zogen auf der Suche nach Arbeit nach Kalifornien (Worster, 2004). Die großen Flutkatastrophen im Mittleren Westen, am Mississippi und am Ohio zu Beginn des Jahres 1937 (Welky, 2011) waren mehr als nur Wiederholungen des Üblichen: Vor dem Hintergrund der durch die Depression dauerhaft angespannten wirtschaftlichen Lage erschienen Naturkatastrophen als Spiegelungen einer prinzipiell als katastrophenhaft empfundenen Situation – jedenfalls in der medialen *imagination* (Shindo, 1997).

Crist zitiert aus dem Chor, der den zweiten Akt abschließt – »Like a giant bomb that strikes to kill. With the force of a dynamite blast, the Hurricane struck at Two Willow Hill – the Hurricane struck and passed« (*The Second Hurricane*, 1938, S. 66f.) –, und schließt daraus, dass die Wahrnehmung der Naturkatastrophe in der Sprache des Krieges erfolgte (Crist, 2005a, S. 80). Auch darin jedoch liegt zunächst eher eine Korrespondenz zur politischen Sprache des *New Deal*, der in der Bekämpfung der Depression nicht nur auf Instrumente der Staatsintervention in die Wirtschaft während des Ersten Weltkriegs zurückgriff, sondern auch in der Rhetorik die Analogie zur Kriegssituation beschwor. Der Chor am Ende des zweiten Akts beschreibt

---

20   Die Nähe zum *New Deal* betonen auch Tick, 2000, S. 150 und Botstein 2005, 450.

21   Die New Yorker Intellektuellen Denby und Copland begingen dabei freilich einen kuriosen Irrtum – Hurricanes entstehen auf dem Meer und erreichen die Küsten, nicht aber den Mittleren Westen, der freilich Raum für Tornados bietet; dieser Fehler wurde in der Druckversion der Partitur und der weiteren Aufführungsgeschichte nie korrigiert.

gleichwohl eher die Stimmung eines Ausgeliefert-Seins, einer nicht von Menschen zu kontrollierenden Wirkung, die eine Naturkatastrophe ebenso kennzeichnet wie die wirtschaftliche Depression, deren Folgen auf den Einzelnen unkalkulierbar und vor allem losgelöst von individuellem Erfolg oder Versagen waren. Die Katastrophen in der Natur und in der Wirtschaft aber führten in den USA zu einer Gestaltveränderung des Staates – der seit dem Amtsantritt Roosevelts 1933 der Depression mit Interventionen in die Sphäre der Wirtschaft Herr zu werden suchte und zugleich auch zu einem Agenten der Naturbändigung wurde: Die *dust bowl*, deren Ursachen schnell erkannt waren, bot Anlass zu einer Politik der *soil conservation* und der Rationalisierung des landwirtschaftlichen Maschineneinsatzes; die Flutkatastrophen führten zu *flood control*: einer Regulierung der Flüsse und ihrer Zuströme. Daneben gab es die sozialpolitische Versorgung der Opfer – im Falle der »Okies« durch den Versuch einer Not-Vergemeinschaftung durch *camps* in Kalifornien, die vom Department of Agriculture eingerichtet und betrieben wurden und in denen die Vereinzelung im Kampf um die Arbeitsmöglichkeiten auf den Obstplantagen durch Bildungs- und Freizeitangebote (und den Appell an den kommunitären *spirit*) abgefedert werden sollte (Worster, 2004; Welky, 2010).

(b) Die Herausbildung einer Gemeinschaft unter den Jugendlichen – »feeling free and equal, feeling join'd together«, wie es im triumphierenden Schlusschor heißt (*The Second Hurricane*, 1938, S. 110) – bildet das Kernstück der Schuloper. Die Rettung der Flutopfer und dann auch der gestrandeten Jugendlichen hatte freilich mehr mit Technik und dem Willen zur Organisation zu tun. In gewisser Hinsicht ist der Pilot, Mr. MacLenahan, der den Hilfstrupp Jugendlicher zusammenstellt (und der in der ersten Produktion von Joseph Cotten verkörpert wurde), eine Schlüsselfigur – denn auch wenn er wegen Maschinenschadens landen muss, dann alleine weiterfliegt und die Jugendlichen auf »Two Willow Hill« zurücklassen muss, wo sie schließlich in den Hurricane geraten, so steht er doch für den Optimismus einer technischen Zivilisation (an der auch der Jugendliche Lawrie teilhat, der in seiner Klasse als Technik-*nerd* ein Außenseiter ist – »he wears glasses« –, aufgrund seiner Erfahrung im Umgang mit Radio und Funk aber von MacLenahan für den Rettungseinsatz ausgesucht wird). Auch die Rettung kommt aus der Luft, ob es MacLenahan ist, der die Jugendlichen wiederfindet, oder ein anderer Pilot, bleibt offen. Die Interaktion von Gemeinschaftsgeist und technischer Rationalität im *plot* der Schuloper spiegelte dabei die im *New Deal* neu geschaffene Balance aus Gesellschaft und einem Staat, der im *New Deal* (und im Erleben des einzelnen Bürgers) eine neue Qualität bekam und Eingriffsmöglichkeiten erhielt, die weit über das hinausgingen, was an ›Staatlichkeit‹ bis dahin zur Entfaltung gekommen war. Die Legitimation des staatlichen Eingriffs – in die Strukturen der Ökonomie, in die Lebenswelt der Bevölkerung durch den Aufbau eines (rudimentären) Wohlfahrtsstaates und die damit verbundene Minimierung lebensweltlicher Risiken (Arbeitslosigkeit, Alter etc.) – geschah durch das ›Versprechen‹ einer Rationalität und Effizienz, die allein durch gesellschaftliche Selbstorganisation nicht (mehr) zu gewährleisten war, *ohne* diese freilich auch nicht wirksam werden konnte. Wollte man in Coplands Werk auch eine Spiegelung der *Probleme* dieser neuen Justierung von Staat und Gesellschaft sehen, so böte sich der Hinweis darauf an, dass beide Sphären in der Schuloper ihre Eigenlogik haben und nicht recht zueinander finden: Der *aviator* muss die Jugendlichen zunächst ›im Stich‹ lassen, da er nur mit einer von der Last der Passagiere befreiten Maschine weiterfliegen kann – und die Rettung der Jugendlichen ist ein ›Zufall‹, weil ein Rettungsflugzeug ein Taschenlampensignal wahrnimmt. Thomson spottete in seiner Rezension der Uraufführung: »It was our old friend the *deus ex machina* that did the job« (Thomson, 1937, S. 235).

Über die Korrespondenzen zwischen Coplands *Hurricane* und den Symbolen und *sentiments* des *New Deal* hinaus aber existiert noch eine weitere Bedeutungsebene, die das Werk in ein Narrativ einbindet, das ›größer‹ ist als die Aktualitäten der 1930er Jahre: Copland und Denby siedelten das Geschehen im Mittleren Westen an – in der veröffentlichten Partitur konkretisiert als »in no definite locality, although vaguely in the southern Middle West« (*The Second Hurricane*, 1938, S. V). Der Mittlere Westen aber erinnerte an die *frontier*, die im Zuge der Inbesitznahme des amerikanischen Westens voranschreitende Besiedlungsgrenze, die nicht nur den ursprünglichen Bewährungsraum für den ›Amerikaner‹ darstellte, sondern – in Frederick Jackson Turners berühmter Interpretation – den ›Amerikaner‹ überhaupt erst schuf (Waechter, 1996).[22] Roger Sessions' Anspruch an eine genuin amerikanische Musik – »rooted in the soil, and in the deepest human impulses that spring from man's contact with the soil and with other human beings« (Sessions, 1933, S. 6) – war damit räumlich Genüge getan, ganz anders als es etwa in einem urbanen *setting* möglich gewesen wäre.[23] Der partielle Zusammenbruch der Zivilisation im Augenblick einer Naturkatastrophe reproduzierte die *frontier* und bot jene Chance zur individuellen und gemeinschaftlichen Bewährung, die in der Schuloper den dramaturgischen Rahmen abgab.[24] Dass Gemeinschaftsbildung und Rettung auf einem Hügel stattfanden – auf »Two Willow Hill« – evozierte darüber hinaus auch noch das vertraute Bild von der »city upon a hill«, mit dem die Puritaner im frühen 17. Jahrhundert die Utopie eines »neuen Jerusalems« in ihren neuen Siedlungsraum

---

22 Zum Schwenk der Komponisten hin zur »traditional mythology of the American West« vgl. auch Taruskin, 2010, S. 637.

23 Auf den Mittleren Westen kommt Copland dann auch in seiner einzigen ›richtigen‹ Oper – *The Tender Land* (1952/54) – als Schauplatz zurück, und auch hier spielt das Geschehen in der Depressionszeit der 1930er Jahre.

24 Bernard Herrmanns Kantate *Moby-Dick* und seine Oper *Wuthering Heights* gehen auch deshalb für die Protagonisten ›schlecht‹ aus, weil hier in beiden Fällen – wofür natürlich die literarische Vorlage die Verantwortung trägt – eine Art ›negative‹ *frontier* entscheidend ist: das Meer und das Moor. Beide ›Räume‹ sind ›negativ‹, weil sie dem Menschen, ganz im Gegensatz zur offenen Siedlungsgrenze im Westen, keinen Raum geben können.

einschrieben und einen der Kernsätze des *American exceptionalism* formulierten. Die *frontier* stellte darüber hinaus auch eine Sehnsuchtslandschaft dar, die, wie andere solche Landschaften (Mexiko, Südseeinseln[25]) – eine Alternative zur in die Krise geratenen städtisch-kapitalistischen Wirtschaftsform darstellte (darzustellen schien). Die Komplexitätsreduktion, die solchen (gedachten) Landschaften zugeschrieben wurde, erleichterte die Idealisierung einer Gemeinschaft, die unter komplexeren Verhältnissen stets unter Druck steht und zur Auflösung neigt.

Coplands *Hurricane* lässt sich als Parabel auf die Große Depression *und* die ›große Antwort‹: den *New Deal* verstehen. Die Naturkatastrophe spiegelte das Scheitern des *American Dream* in der Wirtschaftskrise, und die Bewährung der Gemeinschaft aus gestrandeten Jugendlichen signalisierte den Wiederaufstieg einer geläuterten Nation, die sich nun stärker als zuvor als nationale Solidargemeinschaft begreifen sollte. »Recognizably American«[26] war Copland in seiner in bescheidenem Format auftretenden Schuloper in jeder Hinsicht – und die hier erreichte Kongruenz zwischen dem Horizont der Oper und dem Diskurs der Politik lässt *The Second Hurricane* zu einem raren Beispiel einer politischen Ästhetik, einer musikalischen Theatralisierung des Politischen werden, in der das Komponierbare und das Sagbare denkbar nahe beieinander liegen.

Literatur

Antheil, G. (1934), Opera – A Way Out. *Modern Music*, 11, 89–94.

Berger, A. (1953). *Aaron Copland*. New York: Oxford University Press.

Beyme, K. v. (2005). *Das Zeitalter der Avantgarden. Kunst und Gesellschaft 1900–1955*. München: C. H. Beck.

Blitzstein, M. (1933). Popular Music – An Invasion: 1923–1933. *Modern Music*, 11, 96–102.

Braungart, W. (2012). Ästhetik der Politik, Ästhetik des Politischen. Ein Versuch in Thesen. Göttingen: Wallstein.

Chase, S. (1931). *Mexico. A Study of Two Americas*. New York: Literary Guild.

Citkowitz, I. (1933). Spring Finale in New York. *Modern Music*, 11, 197–199.

Copland, A. (1938). *The Second Hurricane. A Play Opera in Two Acts. Libretto by Edwin Denby: Music by Aaron Copland*. Boston: C. C. Birchard & Co.

Copland, A. (1952). *Music and Imagination*. Cambridge: Harvard University Press.

Copland, A. (1960). Baden-Baden 1927. In Ders., *Copland on Music* (S. 183–188). Garden City, NY: Doubleday.

---

25 Vgl. Chase, 1931; Geiger, 2007.

26 Vgl. Copland & Perlis, S. 119: »My aim was to write a work that would be recognizably American within a serious musical idiom«. »Recognizably American« wurde geradezu zu einem Schlagwort in der Copland-Literatur, vgl. nur Pollack, 1999, S. 165 und Crist, 2005, S. 45.

Copland, A. & Perlis, V. (1984). *Copland. 1900 Through 1942*. New York: St. Martin's.

Copland Now (1961). *Harper's Magazine*, 222, 109–112.

Crist, E. (2005a). *Music for the Common Man: Aaron Copland During the Depression and War*. New York: Oxford University Press.

Crist, E. (2005b). Copland and the Politics of Americanism. In C. Oja & J. Tick (Hrsg.), *Aaron Copland and His World* (S. 277–306). Princeton: Princeton University Press.

De Forest, J. W. (1868). The Great American Novel. *The Nation*, 6, 27ff.

Denning, M. (1996). *The Cultural Front. The Laboring of American Culture in the Twentieth Century*. New York: Verso.

Dickstein, M. (2009). *Dancing in the Dark: A Cultural History of the Great Depression*. New York: W. W. Norton & Company.

Geiger, J. (2007). *Facing the Pacific: Polynesia and the U. S. Imperial Imagination*. Honolulu: University of Hawai'i Press.

Goebel Labastille, I. (1937). Americanismo Musical. *Modern Music*, 14, 76–81.

Gräser, M. (2009). *Wohlfahrtsgesellschaft und Wohlfahrtsstaat. Bürgerliche Sozialreform und Welfare State Building in den USA und in Deutschland 1880–1940*. Göttingen: Vandenhoeck & Ruprecht.

Gura, P. (2007). *American Transcendentalism: A History*. New York: Hill & Wang.

Haas, B. (2008). *Singing Songs of Social Significance: Children's Music and Leftist Pedagogy in 1930s America*. http://digital.library.unt.edu/ark:/67531/metadc9777/m1/1/ (abgerufen am 21. August 2013).

Hardtwig, W. (2011). *Politische Kultur der Moderne. Ausgewählte Aufsätze*. Göttingen: Vandenhoeck & Ruprecht.

Hardtwig, W. & Wehler, H.-U. (Hrsg.). (1996), *Kulturgeschichte Heute* (Geschichte und Gesellschaft, Sonderheft 16). Göttingen: Vandenhoeck & Ruprecht.

Hess, C. (2013). *Representing the Good Neighbour: Music, Difference, and the Pan American Dream*. New York: Oxford University Press.

Johnson, M. (1989). *The Many Faces of Hull-House: The Photographs of Wallace Kirkland*. Urbana-Champaign, Ill: University of Illinois Press.

Kammen, M. (2004). *A Time to Every Purpose: The Four Seasons in American Culture*. Chapel Hill, NC: University of North Carolina Press.

King, H. C. (1876). An American Opera. *The Aldine*, 8, 192f.

Koselleck, R. (2006). Geist und Bildung. Zwei Begriffe kultureller Innovation zur Zeit Mozarts. In Ders., *Begriffsgeschichten. Studien zur Semantik und Pragmatik der politischen und sozialen Sprache* (S. 155–158). Frankfurt am Main: Suhrkamp.

Kramer, L. (2008). The Great American Opera: Klinghoffer, Streetcar, and the Exception. *The Opera Quarterly*, 23, 66–80.

Levine, L. (1993). American Culture and the Great Depression. In Ders., *The Unpredictable Past: Explorations in American Cultural History* (S. 206–230). New York: Oxford University Press.

Levy, B. (2012). *Frontier Figures: American Music and the Mythology of the American West*. Berkeley: University of California Press.

Lissak, R. (1989). *Pluralism and Progressives: Hull House and the New Immigrants, 1890–1919*. Chicago: University of Chicago Press.

Müller, S. O. & Osterhammel, J. (2012). Geschichtswissenschaft und Musik. *Geschichte und Gesellschaft*, 38, 5–20.

Negwer, M. (2008). *Villa-Lobos. Der Aufbruch der brasilianischen Musik*. Mainz: Schott Music.

Oevermann, U. (1997). Literarische Verdichtung als soziologische Erkenntnisquelle. Szenische Realisierung der Strukturlogik professionalisierten ärztlichen Verhaltens in Arthur Schnitzlers Professor Bernhardi. In M. Wicke (Hrsg.), *Konfigurationen lebensweltlicher Strukturphänomene. Soziologische Varianten phänomenologisch-hermeneutischer Welterschließung* (S. 276–335). Wiesbaden: VS Verlag für Sozialwissenschaften.

Pollack, H. (2000). *Aaron Copland: The Life and Work of an Uncommon Man*. London: Faber & Faber.

Rockwell, J. (1985). Copland's ›Second Hurricane‹. *The New York Times*. http://www.nytimes.com/1985/11/15/arts/opera-copland-s-secong-hurricane.html (abgerufen am 20. Juli 2015).

Rosenfeld, P. (1940). »Americanism« in American Music. *Modern Music*, 17, 226–232.

Sessions, R. (1933). Music and Nationalism: Some Notes on Dr. Göbbel's Letter to Furtwängler. *Modern Music*, 11, 3–12.

Sessions, R. (1934). New Vistas in Musical Education. *Modern Music*, 11, 115–120.

Sessions, R. (1938). To Revitalize Opera. *Modern Music*, 15, 145–152.

Sessions, R. (1941). American Music and the Crisis. *Modern Music*, 18, 211–217.

Shindo, C. (1997). *Dust Bowl Migrants in the American Imagination*. Lawrence, KS: University of Kansas Press.

Steigman, B. M. (1925). The Great American Opera. *Music and Letters*, 6, 359–367.

Stott, W. (1973). *Documentary Expression and Thirties America*. New York: Oxford University Press.

Susman, W. (2003). The Culture of the Thirties. In Ders., *Culture as History: The Transformation of American Society in the Twentieth Century* (S. 150–183, 301–308). Washington: Smithsonian Institution Press.

Taruskin, R. (2010). *Music in the Early Twentieth Century*. New York: Oxford University Press.

Tawa, N. (2009). *The Great American Symphony: Music, the Depression, and War*. Bloomington, IN: Indiana University Press.

Thomson, V. (1937). In the Theatre. *Modern Music*, 14, 233–237.

Tick, J. (2000). The Music of Aaron Copland. In L. Gail & J. Tick (Hrsg.), *Aaron Copland's America: A Cultural Perspective* (S. 128–164). New York: Watson-Guptill Publications.

Tischler, B. (1986). *An American Music: The Search for an American Musical Identity*. New York: Oxford University Press.

Von Rhein, J. (2000). Aaron Copland's ›The Second Hurricane‹ at the Francis W. Parker School. *Chicago Tribune*. http://articles.chicagotribune.com/2000-1112/news/001112034 7_1_aaron-copland-libretto-second-hurricane (abgerufen am 20. Juli 2015).

Waechter, M. (1996). *Die Erfindung des amerikanischen Westens. Die Geschichte der Frontier-Debatte*: Freiburg: Rombach.

Weill, K. (1937). The Future of Opera in America. *Modern Music*, 14, 183–188.

Welky, D. (2011). *The Thousand-Year Flood: The Ohio-Mississippi Disaster of 1937*. Chicago: University of Chicago Press

Westbrook, R. (1991). *John Dewey and American Democracy*. Ithaca, NY: Cornell University Press.

White, E. (2013). The Lost Novelist. *The New York Review of Books*, 15. August, 30–31.

Worster, D. (1979, 2004). *Dust Bowl: The Southern Plains in the 1930s*. New York: Oxford University Press.

Christopher Lynch

Operatic Conventions on Broadway, 1935–1960

The 1930s witnessed the expansion of the traditional musical comedy as authors of works like *Porgy and Bess* (1935) combined the genre's conventions with the procedures of grand opera. Most histories of the musical present the two-and-a-half decades of operatic experimentation that followed *Porgy and Bess* as part of a gradual but continual line of theatrical evolution. According to this historical narrative, early musical comedies like Charles Hoyt's *A Trip to Chinatown* (1891) consisted of a series of entertaining songs and dances that were at best loosely stitched together by a minimal plot. Each successive generation of Broadway authors experimented with more substantial plots and complex musical apparatuses, eventually resulting in works whose components were fully integrated in a musically and dramatically serious whole, like Frank Loesser's »operatic« *The Most Happy Fella* (1956). This type of historical narrative is detailed, for example, in theater historian Ethan Mordden's recent history of the genre, which he introduces by characterizing Loesser's show as »what the American musical had been working up to for some one hundred years« (Mordden, 2014, p. x). This chapter, however, presents a complementary view of the emergence of operatic conventions on Broadway. Considering these conventions in light of the popular perception of the Metropolitan Opera House, it is argued here that widespread ideas about opera, shaped by the Metropolitan, led to and informed the exploration of operatic conventions at other institutions beginning in the mid-1930s.

As the only institution that regularly presented grand opera in New York in the early twentieth century, the Metropolitan molded New Yorkers' conceptions of the genre as a whole. In the century's early decades, the company became deeply influenced by the works and theories of Richard Wagner, adopting what Lawrence Levine has referred to as »Wagner's distinction between ›serious‹ and ›frivolous‹ opera« (Levine, 1988, p. 102). Wagner differentiated between composers of serious opera, who felt that »the burden of responsibility fell to music when she took upon herself alone the aim of drama,« and frivolous composers, who »have turned their backs upon [drama] and [...] have given themselves over to an unmixed musical empiricism« (Wagner, 1995, p. 24). To Wagner, the latter group of composers employed musical structures and procedures—like the Rossinian »double aria«—regardless of the dramatic situation. In Wagner's theory, dramatic form *was* musical form, and the Metropolitan's management reflected the influence of these theories when they passed over number operas by Gioachino Rossini and Wolfgang

Amadeus Mozart in favor of more through-composed and serious works like those by Wagner himself, Giacomo Puccini, and the late operas of Giuseppe Verdi.

Music criticism from the first few decades of the twentieth century demonstrates the extent to which the popular conception of opera shared and was shaped by the Metropolitan's biases. For example, an article in *Musical America* suggested that the best qualities of opera are »ideally viewed […] in the lyrical dramas of Wagner« and critiqued the works of Rossini and Gaetano Donizetti. »Whether the text be comedy or tragedy,« the author wrote, Rossini's operas are »told in rippling rhythms and highly ornamental bravura melodies« (How to Appreciate Opera, 1909). Wagnerian dramaturgy was seen as more mature or more evolved, which is often implied in the reception of the relatively rare productions of earlier operas. For the 100th anniversary of its premiere in 1916, the Metropolitan produced Rossini's *Il Barbiere di Siviglia*, and *Musical America* noted, »Its bubbling humor, its lightsome gayety, its melodic sparkle have not staled, though the forms in which they are cast fell into desuetude long ago« (*Barber of Seville*, 1916). Since the number opera format was seen as out of date, management at the Metropolitan and critics treated the occasional performance of such works as unusual. For example, *Musical America* characterized the Metropolitan's premiere of Mozart's *Così fan tutte* in 1922 as one of »General Manager [Giulio] Gatti-Casazza's […] novelties […] for the season« (Restore Mozart, 1922). The popular perception of opera, therefore, increasingly held the genre as consisting of serious and through-composed musical dramas, and works that did not conform to this conception were appreciated only as rare novelties.

By the 1930s, the Metropolitan's failure to keep apace of advancements on Broadway also began to shape perceptions of opera, and the Metropolitan's failures in this regard were blamed for the company's financial struggles during the Great Depression. Responding to reports in newspapers like the *New York Times* that the Metropolitan was »faced with a financial crisis which threatens its future« and that »the situation is grave for the future of grand opera in New York« ($350,000 Deficit, 1933), composer Deems Taylor addressed the operatic institution's problems. »Generally speaking,« he wrote, »the opera lags, mechanically and histrionically, half a century or more behind the spoken theater« (Taylor, 1933, p. 68). He also blamed opera's struggles on »the fact that opera, as produced in this country, is sung in virtually every language except that of the inhabitants of this country« (Taylor, 1933, p. 7). Critic Irving Kolodin voiced similar opinions, ridiculing »the antique stage, the ugly and tasteless sets, the unimaginative lighting, [and] the vast spaces which discourage any but the most rudimentary dramatic effects« (Kolodin, 1933, p. 784). In sum, opera was seen as failing because it was antiquated, visually uninteresting, and theatrically incomprehensible to those who only spoke English.

The popular perception that opera was not theatrical is perhaps best viewed in the critical reviews of Broadway works that employed operatic conventions in the 1930s and 1940s. *Time* magazine's preview of the trial run of *Porgy and Bess* in Boston in 1935 exemplified the view that operatic actors did not look their part. Boasting that *Porgy and Bess*'s »audiences will at least see and hear something different,« the magazine joked that »irreverent opera-goers will always giggle to see fat, formal singers decked with feathers and emitting feeble whoops.« The preview also lambasted the »stiff« chorus in the Metropolitan's latest American offering, Howard Hanson's *Merry Mount*, speaking to the perception of poor acting and possibly of uninteresting stage direction at the old institution (Porgy into Opera, 1935, p. 55). This was certainly the perception of opera to which William Hawkins compared *Regina* in 1949, writing, »If opera even suggests awkward people, florid vocalizing and clumsy acting, then *Regina* certainly is not opera« (Hawkins, 1949).

Reviews also demonstrated the popular belief that serious music must be intertwined with the drama, thus creating a sort of »popular Wagnerism.« Louis Kronenberger, for example, claimed that *Carousel* »possesses [...] a very great deal of music—some of it [...] operatic in the sense that it advances and interprets the story« (Kronenberger, 1945). Owing in part to the proliferation of this popular Wagnerism, and in another sense to the Metropolitan's lack of emphasis on the visual aspects of operatic production, opera was seen as a *musical*, not as a theatrical genre. Reviewing Gian Carlo Menotti's *The Medium* in 1947, Brooks Atkinson deemed the work to be an opera, writing, »Between opera and the dramatic stage there is a difference in emphasis that keeps the two mediums fundamentally separate. [...] Mr. Menotti has packed the drama into the music. He is not much interested in the libretto, which is undistinguished in literary style« (Atkinson, 1947). But musicalizing the drama often meant slowing the action, something that was seen as antithetical to what the critic John Chapman called »the Broadway sense.« Arguing that some of Loesser's songs in *The Most Happy Fella* were not operatic, he wrote, »Instead of taking time out from the action, they are part of it« (Chapman, 1956).

Negative opinions of the Metropolitan were often exacerbated by the fact that the company's American opera program, which produced fifteen works by American composers between 1910 and 1937, had failed to produce a single lasting repertoire item. Indeed, these works only reinforced the popular opinion of opera, and critics sensed little other than dullness in their music and presentation. In one fell swoop, for example, the *New York Times* music critic Olin Downes dismissed the scores of the Metropolitan's American operas as »labored or lumpish« (Downes, 1934). Such opinions rendered the Metropolitan's American undertakings as unmemorable. Writing shortly after the final performance of Taylor's *Peter Ibbetson*, which was one of the company's most successful American works, Kurt Weill failed to acknowledge the opera's existence when he wrote about the language of operatic performances in America. The lack of such an acknowledgment in an article in which he complained that »operas are performed in foreign languages which almost no one understands« indicates that even the most successful American operas at the Metropolitan failed to make a lasting impression (Weill, 1936, p. 63).

The stage was set, so to speak, for the exploration of opera at new institutions that might reinvigorate the genre and make it relevant to contemporary Americans. As Kolodin wrote, »There is no question that it would be to the advantage of the situation in New York for the public to be Metropolitan Opera-less for a year or two; for in that way there would certainly be provided the impetus for a new and vigorous organization« (Kolodin, 1934, p. 772). Even Taylor himself felt that opera needed new institutions, calling for »American opera companies, run by Americans« that would hire »a master of the English language.« This »master« would create translations that have »the same literary and poetic distinction as the original, and fits the music just as well,« and these updated works would be produced in »a modern theater« (Taylor, 1933, pp. 66–67).

This is the context in which Broadway became a site for experimentation with operatic procedures. Interestingly, the perception of the failing Metropolitan simultaneously invigorated this exploration and made Broadway authors wary of turning off potential audience members who harbored negative opinions about the genre. Therefore, Broadway authors, as will be shown below, very carefully adopted certain conventions from the opera house. Influenced by the Metropolitan and popular Wagnerism, composers and critics continued to see opera as a musical genre—»opera […] aims to further [its] plot *through* the use of music,« as Leonard Bernstein put it (Bernstein, 1959, p. 153). But the specific operatic procedures that composers utilized—nontraditional forms, ensemble numbers, and recitative—were handled in ways that distanced Broadway productions from the Metropolitan's presentations that were seen as nontheatrical, labored, and lumpish.

While previous scholarship has emphasized the differences between these works, the present chapter will focus on the similarities. In the first book to investigate the components and development of the American musical, Lehman Engel established a taxonomy of Broadway shows that explored operatic conventions, differentiating between »Broadway Opera« and »Opera on Broadway« (Engel, 1967). Such an approach is useful since these works represent a diverse cross section of the American musical, as the list in Figure 1 demonstrates. More recently, musicologist Larry Stempel has argued that the differences between the works preclude them from belonging to a single movement, writing, »It would be difficult to speak of them as a movement since there were so few […] [and] each piece remained virtually one of a kind, with few shared sensibilities among those who created them« (Stempel, 2010, p. 371). In what follows, however, those »few shared sensibilities« will be dwelled upon by analyzing a representative selection from the diverse body of Broadway shows that used operatic conventions. Rather than classify works as Broadway operas or operas on Broadway, each section will explore a different operatic convention—»seriousness,« ensembles, and recitative—in order to demonstrate how their use on Broadway extended from anxieties about the popular perception of opera.

Title	Composer	Year of Premiere
Porgy and Bess	George Gershwin	1935 (revised in 1941)
Johnny Johnson	Kurt Weill	1936
The Cradle Will Rock	Marc Blitzstein	1937 (Broadway in 1938)
Lady in the Dark	Kurt Weill	1941
Oklahoma!	Richard Rodgers	1943
Carmen Jones	Georges Bizet	1943
Carousel	Richard Rodgers	1945
Street Scene	Kurt Weill	1947
The Telephone / The Medium	Gian Carlo Menotti	1947
South Pacific	Richard Rodgers	1949
Lost in the Stars	Kurt Weill	1949
Regina	Marc Blitzstein	1949
The Consul	Gian Carlo Menotti	1950
The Saint of Bleecker Street	Gian Carlo Menotti	1954
The Most Happy Fella	Frank Loesser	1956
Candide	Leonard Bernstein	1956
West Side Story	Leonard Bernstein	1957

Figure 1. Select List of Broadway Works that Utilize Operatic Conventions.

»Seriousness« in the Musical Comedy

In 1956, Leonard Bernstein identified two types of »seriousness« that had infiltrated musical comedy over the previous decades. The first was concerned with the plot: »The more a show gets away from pure diversion, the more it tries to engage the interest and emotion of the audience, the closer it slides toward opera.« The second dealt with the music: »And the more a show uses music to further its plot, the closer it moves toward the same pole« (Bernstein, 1959, p. 153). As popular Wagnerism proliferated, Broadway writers saw these two types of seriousness as intricately connected; serious music drama was seen to demand music that was interwoven with the narrative.

Since the 1910s, the majority of show tunes had been written in three standard 32-bar forms of four equal-length phrases—AABA, ABAB, and ABAC—and these forms were employed in all shows regardless of the narrative, much like the procedures of Rossinian opera. Much of the »operatic« music that commenced in the 1930s, however, was more through-composed to match and amplify the immediate dramatic circumstances. As Bernstein put it, »The songwriter found himself called upon to … [write] much more than just a thirty-two-bar tune. Light and serious music were coming closer together« (Bernstein, 1959, p. 173). By merging musical form with dramatic form, Broadway writers were also able to combat the perception of opera as nontheatrical. In this sense, such procedures simultaneously appealed to those who wanted to see these works as Wagnerian music dramas in an American style as well as those who shared the negative popular perception of opera. Hoping to further appeal to both camps, authors were also often certain to balance such music with procedures derived from traditional musical comedy. Aiming for such broad appeal, Gershwin claimed that with *Porgy and Bess* he had »created a new form, which combines opera with theatre« (Gershwin, 1935), and Weill argued that a »reestablishment of the true musical theatre is scheduled to take place inside of the enormous territory between the two genres« (Weill, 1936, p. 63). Like Weill, following *Porgy and Bess,* many Broadway authors infused musical comedy with serious narrative themes, which they often depicted in »serious« musical episodes.

In his public statements, Gershwin distanced the plot and music of *Porgy and Bess* from the operatic conventions with which his audience was familiar. Explaining why *Porgy and Bess* was not produced by »the usual sponsors of opera,« he wrote, »When I chose *Porgy and Bess*, a tale of Charleston Negroes, for a subject, I made sure that it would enable me to write light as well as serious music and that it would enable me to include humor as well as tragedy« (Gershwin, 1935). Set in the fictitious African American community of Catfish Row, the crippled beggar Porgy and the drug-addicted Bess fall in love after her former lover Crown kills a man and flees. Gershwin balanced the seriousness of the plot with lighter moments like Porgy's song »I Got Plenty O' Nuttin'.« Happily living with Bess, he rejoices that he has everything he needs: »I got my gal, got my song, got Hebben de whole day long.« Unlike »De folks wid plenty o' plenty,« he is happy to leave his door unlocked. This song, perhaps the lightest moment in the entire work, is in the most common popular song form, AA'BA".

More serious moments in the show utilize more elaborate musical forms that parallel the development of the drama. Just after Bess confirms Porgy's suspicions that she has been with Crown and that he will return for her, the two sing »I Loves You Porgy,« which begins with an 8-bar musical phrase (A) in which Bess reassures

Porgy that she wants to stay with him. In the following phrase, to new music (B), Bess tells him she will not be able to refuse Crown when he returns. Porgy then interjects, asking Bess in recitative, »If dere war'nt no Crown, Bess, If dere was only jus' you an' Porgy, what den?« Bess's first two phrases introduced the first two sections of a normal ABAB 32-bar song, but Porgy's interjection (C) interrupts this normal trajectory. Bess then sings another 8-bar phrase to the music of (A), pleading with Porgy to protect her from Crown, after which Porgy sings a new musical idea (D) as he reassures her that she will be safe with him. The piece ends with Bess singing the opening music (A'), slightly extended to accommodate Porgy's new countermelody. Bess reiterates that she wants him to protect her and Porgy again reassures her that he will. The unusual song form—ABCADA'—is determined by the theatrical circumstance, not a predetermined musical template. This is Wagnerian dramaturgy, but unlike opera as it was popularly imagined, it is a musical scene in which an important character and plot development occur.

Such grafting of serious elements borrowed from opera onto the musical comedy became commonplace. In Richard Rodgers and Oscar Hammerstein's *Oklahoma!*, for example, Curly saves his lover Laurey from the unwanted advances of Jud. Despite the happy ending, the story contains serious elements that were unconventional on the popular stage, most notably the confrontation between Curly and Jud and the ensuing struggle in which Jud falls on his own knife and dies. The show contains numerous lighthearted scenes, like when Curly and Laurey sing the flirtatious duet, »People Will Say We're In Love,« in which the young lovers play »hard to get« by telling each other not to do things like »throw bouquets at me« or »laugh at my jokes too much« because it might give people the impression that they are in love. Like »I Got Plenty O' Nuttin',« this duet draws on the conventions of musical comedy. The *moderato* tempo, cut time meter, and gently gliding off-beats of the foxtrot style are typical of love songs, and the phrases are organized into a traditional AABA' pattern.

Complementing this lighthearted music, however, is Jud's dark song, »Lonely Room.« As opposed to the lighthearted playfulness of »People Will Say We're In Love,« »Lonely Room« opens with a dissonant F#/G dyad that pulsates for nine measures. As Joseph P. Swain points out, only with the arrival of an F# chord in measure 10 is the key of B minor established (Swain, 2002, p. 94), creating a musical instability that is representative of Jud's psychological state. The musical form also captures Jud's instability, following his meandering thoughts as he contemplates his loneliness, disdain for Curly, desire for Laurey, and his aspiration to »git me a womern to call my own.« As in *Porgy and Bess*, basing the musical form on a developing dramatic situation results in an unconventional pattern, in this case ABBCAB'. The inclusion of such serious music and content alongside conventional elements of musical comedy is most certainly why Downes hailed the show as »Broadway's gift to the opera« (Downes, 1943).

Almost all shows that contained serious plot elements featured at least one »serious« solo number to complement more conventional musical comedy songs. Stempel has analyzed such numbers to illuminate the competition between Rodgers and Weill. Analyzing Rodgers' »Soliloquy« from *Carousel* and Weill's »aria« (as the composer labeled it), »Somehow I Never Could Believe,« from *Street Scene*, Stempel argues that Weill was »upping the musical ante« by making greater use of »the musical rhetoric associated with traditions of opera, operetta, and concert music in Europe« (Stempel, 1986, pp. 325f.). Despite their »stylistic« differences, both are extended musical numbers in serious dramas. *Carousel* concerns the marriage of Julie Jordan to Billy Bigelow, who dies trying to steal money to support his pregnant wife and future child. »Soliloquy« illustrates a pivotal moment for Billy; as he ponders his future life with his child, he vows to get money by any means possible. *Street Scene* concludes with a husband's discovery of his wife's affair and the brutal double murder of her and her lover. In act 1, »Somehow I Never Could Believe« sets up this action. Anna, the wife, reflects on how she came to be unhappily married and longs for a loving relationship.

The abundance of »serious« songs whose unusual forms resulted from uniting music and drama is indicative of the appeal of catering to popular Wagnerism in these years. This appeal undoubtedly stemmed from the belief that such an aesthetic might allow authors to please a broad audience, including both those who wanted to see operatic music drama and those who wanted musicals to be theatrical. In addition to resulting in unusual song forms, the need to please the commercial theater's audiences also influenced authors' handling of ensemble numbers, as they often— but not always—worked to inject them with as much action as possible.

Ensembles

Like other conventions recognized as operatic, ensemble numbers were frequently attacked by critics for obstructing the development of the plot. Occasionally, however, critics defended them. Reviewing *The Consul*, Downes opined that ensembles could slow the action: »One of the oldest devices of opera, and the one that composers of a former day were especially prone to abuse, is the ensemble number—the duet, trio, quartet, chorus coming in and too often stultifying the progress of the drama.« But he also suggested that »this same device of ensemble can promote dramatic tension and conflict in a way impossible to the playwright who can use only the spoken word,« ultimately praising Menotti's ensembles: »Mr. Menotti has brought this time-honored operatic procedure [up] to date, employing it with gripping intensity« (Downes, 1950). In *The Consul*'s ensembles, Menotti slows the unfolding of the plot for lyrical portrayals of the characters' feelings, but even though Downes' notes that such moments have the potential to be effective, many Broadway writers, like Loesser, decided not to risk offending the critics' theatrical sensibilities and packed their ensembles with action.

In *The Consul*'s act 1 trio, »Now, O Lips, Say Goodbye,« the dramatic momentum pauses as Magda, her husband John, and John's mother express their sadness at John's departure, which is necessitated by the pursuit of John by the state for his involvement with revolutionaries. Only in the most general sense does the trio prepare later action when the characters vow to keep hope that they will reunite across the border; overall, rather than push the narrative forward, this number depicts the characters' emotional response to what they have just experienced. More in line with Broadway sensibilities, Menotti balances such moments with action-filled sequences, such as the act 2 septet »Oh, What A Lovely Dance.« In a room at the consulate, where Magda waits to secure the proper paperwork to leave the country, a magician attempts to speed along the process of obtaining a visa by impressing the secretary. When presenting her with a bouquet of flowers and performing magic tricks proves unsuccessful, he hypnotizes the others in the waiting room and convinces them that they are at a ball. The septet commences as Magda and two others dance around the room singing »Oh, what a lovely dance!« while the terrified secretary yells at the magician, who clumsily searches in vain for his papers. Adding to the confusion, two foreigners hypnotically chant »Balla, balla e non pensare/Sonno e morte son con noi.« When the secretary still refuses to hurry along the magician's visa request, he breaks the hypnotic spell, bringing the septet to an end. Unlike the act 1 trio, this scene appears to have been intended to satisfy the Broadway audiences' appetite for both action and humor, for it provides a fun-filled break in the middle of this depressingly intense work. Following this scene, Magda fails to obtain her paperwork, both her child and John's mother die, the authorities arrest John, and she commits suicide by placing her head inside an oven.

Unlike Menotti, Loesser rarely slowed the action in *The Most Happy Fella*, which he surely anticipated would be perceived as operatic. Soon after the premiere, he adeptly publicized the show in a way that would allow willing audiences to regard it as operatic but that would also be inviting to audiences that did not care for opera. »I may give the impression this show has operatic tendencies,« he said in an interview; »If people feel that way—fine. Actually, all it has is a great frequency of songs« (Millstein, 1956). Moreover, Loesser likely infused his ensembles with action because he anticipated that critics like John McClain would find »operatic overtones« in the show's »trios and quartets, […] [and] many duets« (McClain, 1956). Based on Sidney Howard's play *They Knew What They Wanted*, Loesser's *The Most Happy Fella* relies on an abundance of music to tell the story of the unlikely couple Rosabella and Tony, their dishonesty with each other, and Rosabella's affair with Joe, who Tony vows to murder before changing his mind and agreeing to raise Rosabella's and Joe's child as his own. In the trio »Nobody's Ever Gonna Love You,« Tony's sister Marie attempts to persuade him to leave Rosabella because of her affair, and

Rosabella's friend Cleo points out that Marie is only looking out for herself because she depends on Tony. A physical altercation ensues as Marie takes Tony's cane to prevent him from going back to Rosabella, but this wrestling only strengthens Tony's resolve to return to her.

As mentioned above, Broadway authors worked to employ operatic procedures in solo numbers and ensembles in a theatrical manner to appeal to opera fans *and* those skeptical of the genre. In the case of *The Most Happy Fella*, critic Walter F. Kerr acknowledged this infusion of an »operatic« work with energy, but did not care for it. He felt that the abundance of music »tends to choke the movement of the action,« and the show's abundance of energy made him »keep wishing that Mr. Loesser had written six shows in the six years since *Guys and Dolls* instead of packing the energy of all six into one« (Kerr, 1956). Audiences, however, overwhelmingly felt that Loesser had achieved a proper balance, and *The Most Happy Fella* went on to have a long and successful run of 676 performances and earned a Tony Award nomination for Best Musical. When critiquing the »movement of the action,« Kerr was likely not referring to set numbers, for, as has been shown, Loesser packed them with action to please the audience. More likely, the critic was thinking of Loesser's use of recitative. Indeed, as the next section will demonstrate, critics routinely perceived the operatic device as tilting the scales too heavily toward opera.

Recitative

Recitative became the most contested operatic convention on Broadway, coming under attack as early as the reviews for *Porgy and Bess* in 1935. Atkinson famously critiqued recitative as a nontheatrical device of traditional opera:

> Turning *Porgy* into opera has resulted in a deluge of casual remarks that have to be thoughtfully intoned and that amazingly impede the action. [...] What a theatre critic probably wants is a musical show with songs that evoke the emotion of situations and make no further pretensions. Part of the emotion of a drama comes from the pace of the performance. (Atkinson, 1935)

After the initial production of *Porgy and Bess*, which failed to make a profit, Broadway authors used recitative sparingly.

In 1941, producer Cheryl Crawford launched a successful revival of *Porgy and Bess* in Maplewood, New Jersey, before moving the show to Broadway and then embarking on a national tour that ran into 1944. The secret to her success resided in part in the reduction of the amount of recitative. Though some important recitatives remained, such as those that distinguished the African American characters as more musical than the white police officers, many were cut or converted to spoken dialogue. The collaborative team, moreover, touted these revisions in their publicity before the show's opening, establishing the criteria by which critics and audiences judged the work. In a press statement, conductor Alexander Smallens admitted that in its original form »there was too much music and much of the recitative […] slowed up the movement of the drama.« He concluded that »*Porgy and Bess* as it is now […] [is] alive, compact, and dramatic« (Press Release, Cheryl Crawford Papers). Kronenberger's review, for example, absorbed Smallens's talking points: »With the recitative that presumably slowed it down omitted, it is very likely richer and more continuously satisfying now than it was [in 1935].« (Kronenberger, 1942)

Crawford's *Porgy and Bess* inspired Hammerstein to create his own »operatic« work for Broadway. As Annegret Fauser reports,

> Just over two weeks after Hammerstein attended *Porgy and Bess*, a letter (19 February 1942) by producer Richard Berger to Mrs. Cornelius Vanderbilt Whitney (the opera singer Eleanor Searle) reveals that he and Hammerstein were starting to raise money for a new production scheduled for the fall of 1942, an African American show set in North Carolina and based on Bizet's *Carmen*. (Fauser, 2010, p. 134)

After detailing the plans for the production, the letter reads, »We are really hot about this and have great hopes for its success, particularly on the strength of the fine reception of *Porgy and Bess* received on its revival« (Fauser, 2010, p. 134). Although production was delayed until 1943, Hammerstein indeed updated *Carmen*, resetting the opera in a contemporary army parachute factory in North Carolina and titling the work *Carmen Jones*. Emulating the revival of *Porgy and Bess*, moreover, Hammerstein cut many of the recitatives and publicly touted that he did so »in order to maintain the dramatic pace« (Guernsey Jr., 1943). But also like *Porgy and Bess*, Hammerstein left some of the recitatives in place, notably the final scene of the work when Joe (based on *Carmen*'s Don José) murders the titular femme fatale and commits suicide.

In the introduction to the published libretto, Hammerstein portrayed this final scene as unlike traditional opera. The amount of space he devoted to this reveals much about his anxiety over operatic conventions like recitative:

> [Joe] makes the last desperate effort to get [Carmen] to come back to him. For twelve minutes they sing—not *Hit Parade* melodies, verses and choruses, but sincere musical expressions of their emotions. […] Throughout this distinctly »operatic« sequence, the audience is held as at no other time in the evening. They are tense and still in their seats. There is no doubt that they are interested and there is no doubt that this is opera. In one respect it is better-than-usual opera, because the characters look their parts. And they are acting as well as singing. They are not waving their arms and pounding the stage like heavy-footed mastodons. They are not using that phony sob-in-the-throat trick of grand-opera singers in emotional passages. They are portraying two human beings in terrible trouble, two confused souls moving towards their destruction with every word they sing. The au-

dience, knowing what the words mean, are held in a tight grip of interest until the tragedy finds its inevitable end and Carmen sinks to the floor, stabbed by her crazed, heart-torn lover. (Hammerstein, 1945, pp. xvi–xvii)

Hammerstein addressed all the popular concerns about opera. By emphasizing that the acting and singing was realistic, the words intelligible, and the music interesting, Hammerstein presented *Carmen Jones* as a theatrical drama that was »better-than-usual opera«—usual opera, of course, referring to the Metropolitan's productions.

Largely owing to the perception that it slowed dramatic momentum, most Broadway composers used very little recitative. Bernstein's score for *West Side Story*, for example, contains only a few fleeting instances of the operatic device. In their act 2 duet, Anita confronts Maria about her romantic relationship with Tony, who has just killed Maria's brother Bernardo in a gang fight. The duet consists of two seamlessly linked songs. In the first, »A Boy Like That,« Anita urges Maria to leave Tony, a member of a white gang, and to »stick to your own kind,« in this case, Hispanic men. In the next song, »I Have A Love,« Maria tells Anita that she loves Tony and »there's nothing to be done.« Maria is convincing, and Anita joins her at the conclusion of the song, singing »When love comes so strong, there is no right or wrong, your love is your life.« »A Boy Like That« begins in the common AABA form and then includes a brief section of recitative as Maria sings »Oh no, Anita, no! Anita, no!« This recitative is followed by a kind of development of earlier material, making the form of »A Boy Like That« AABA-recitative-BA'B'. At this point, Maria repeats and slightly extends the recitative—»Oh no, Anita, no, you should know better! You were in love or so you said. You should know better [...]«—leading into »I Have A Love,« which unfolds in an AABA' form of new musical material.

While most Broadway composers used recitative sparingly, Menotti utilized the device much more than spoken dialogue. While not nearly as successful as hits like *Oklahoma!*, which featured very little music that could be considered recitative, Menotti's works succeeded because there was what musicologist Kim H. Kowalke describes as »a broad enough target audience for musical theater in New York and a small group of idealistic producers sufficient to sustain« the presentation of such works on Broadway (Kowalke, 2003, p. 293). As critical responses to his works indicate, their success was owed in part to the perception that Menotti's works were more theatrical than traditional opera. While reviewing *The Telephone* and *The Medium*, Otis L. Guernsey Jr., for example, noted that all aspects of Menotti's works are entwined with the action of the story. »Menotti's perfect triple rhyme of the lyrics, the music and the action,« he wrote, »never falter, as his staging makes a perfect fit with accents of his composition.« While there were occasional passages in which the action slowed, Guernsey generally felt it to be more theatrical than opera:

True, they are dramas whose lines of dialogue are sung, and whose action occasionally pauses for lyric passages, but perhaps the term »opera« is too conventional a label to put upon them. Perhaps, at the risk of immediate contradiction, one might decide that they are their own form of musical theater, a sort of halfway mark between the number called »Soliloquy« in *Carousel* and grand opera as it exists today. (Guernsey Jr., 1947)

The Fate of Operatic Conventions on Broadway

In general, it seems that the more operatic procedures a show employed, the shorter was its run on Broadway. Heavily operatic works like the original *Porgy and Bess*, *Regina*, *Street Scene*, and *The Consul* had relatively short runs, while *Oklahoma!*, *Carousel*, and *West Side Story* enjoyed long success on Broadway. But there were also anomalies. Why, for example, did *The Most Happy Fella*, which included an abundance of ensembles, recitatives, and ariosos, enjoy a long run of 676 performances, while *Regina* only played 56 times? Furthermore, why did *The Consul*, which featured much more recitative and no popular music, have a longer run—269 performances—than Marc Blitzstein's work the year before? Obviously, audiences judged the works according to more criteria than simply the amount of operatic music they contained, but these inconsistencies speak of the difficulty that Broadway authors had in striking a balance between operatic and musical-comedy conventions. Partly because of this difficulty, Broadway authors did not pursue opera in the 1960s to the degree that they had in earlier decades. Weill died tragically in 1950, Hammerstein in 1960, and the next generation of authors largely turned to the musical language of rock and the more fragmented narrative strategy of the so-called »concept musical.«

At the same time, the New York City Center, home to the City Center Opera Company, emerged as the institution best suited for the production of American operas. There, works like *Street Scene* and *The Consul*, which featured an abundance of operatic content, became repertoire items, and the popular perception of opera as a nontheatrical genre continued to shape the development of new works. Publicizing the City Center, which frequently produced his operas, composer Douglas Moore critiqued the out-of-date quality of the Metropolitan's American operas, writing, »It was as if the composer, awed by the red plush and the masterpiece repertory of the Metropolitan, was afraid to keep pace with the modern theatre.« The point of the article, he made clear, was to show that »the City Center shows an entirely different point of view« (Moore, 1959). In a separate article, Moore situates his opera, *The Ballad of Baby Doe,* in opposition to the popular perception that opera was action-less theater. He wrote, »I hoped we could have some extended arias without slowing up the action; thanks to [librettist John] Latouche's remarkable theater sense, this was achieved« (Moore, 1961, p. 11). Modern theatrical techniques, pace, and action—the same concerns as those who explored operatic conventions on Broadway—were the concerns of the City Center. Therefore, although Broadway largely turned away from the exploration of operatic conventions in the 1960s, the popular perception of opera, shaped by the Metropolitan and solidified in the 1930s, continued to exert its influence on the development of opera in America.

References

(No date). Press Release. In Cheryl Crawford Papers, Box 20, Folder 6. New York Public Library for the Performing Arts.

(1909). How to Appreciate Opera. *Musical America,* 4 December.

(1916). »Barber of Seville« Reaches Centennial. *Musical America*, 12 February.

(1922). Restore Mozart to Metropolitan with Enchanting »Così fan tutte.« *Musical America*, 1 April.

(1933). $ 350,000 Deficit Again Threatens Opera; New Pay Cuts, Shorter Season Discussed. *New York Times*, 3 February.

(1935). »Porgy« into Opera. *Time*, 30 September, 55.

Atkinson, B. (1935). Dramatic Values of Community Legend Gloriously Transposed in New Form with Fine Regard for its Verities. *New York Times*, 9 October.

Atkinson, B. (1947). Review of »The Telephone / The Medium.« *New York Times*, 2 May.

Bernstein, L. (1959). American Musical Comedy. In L. Bernstein, *The Joy of Music* (pp. 152–179). New York: Simon and Schuster.

Chapman, J. (1956). »The Most Happy Fella« a Superb Musical Romance, Superbly Done. *Daily News*, 4 May.

Downes, O. (1934). Broadway Greets New Kind of Opera. *New York Times*, 21 February.

Downes, O. (1943). Broadway's Gift to the Opera: »Oklahoma« Shows One of the Ways to an Integrated and Indigenous Form of American Lyric Theatre. *New York Times*, 6 June.

Downes, O. (1950). Opera on Broadway. *New York Times*, 2 April.

Engel, L. (1967). *The American Musical Theater: A Consideration*. New York: MacMillan.

Fauser, A. (2010). ›Dixie Carmen:‹ War, Race, and Identity in Oscar Hammerstein's »Carmen Jones.« *Journal of the Society for American Music*, 4 (2), 127–174.

Gershwin, G. (1935). Rhapsody in Catfish Row. *New York Times*, 20 October.

Guernsey Jr., O. L. (1943). The Playbill: Hammerstein, a Broadway Dynasty. *New York Herald Tribune*, 12 December.

Guernsey Jr., O. L. (1947). Review of »The Telephone« and »The Consul.« *New York Herald Tribune*, 2 May.

Hammerstein II, O. (1945). *Carmen Jones*. New York: Alfred A. Knopf.

Hawkins, W. (1949). »Regina« Is Exciting Musical Exposition. *New York World-Telegram*, 1 November.

Kerr, W. F. (1956). Review of »The Most Happy Fella.« *New York Herald Tribune,* 4 May.

Kolodin, I. (1933). What Hope for the Opera? *Theatre Arts*, October.

Kolodin, I. (1934). Opera in a Changing World. *Theatre Arts*, October.

Kowalke, K. H. (2003). Kurt Weill and the Quest for American Opera. In Hermann Danuser & Hermann Gottschewski (Eds.), *Amerikanismus/Americanism/Weill: Die Suche nach Kultureller Identität in der Moderne (1900–1950)* (pp. 283–301). Schliengen: Edition Argus.

Kronenberger, L. (1945). A Famous Team Scores Again. *New York Newspaper PM*, 20 April.

Kronenberger, L. (1942). »Porgy and Bess« Improves with Age. *New York Newspaper PM*, 23 January.

Levine, L. (1988). *Highbrow Lowbrow: The Emergence of Cultural Hierarchy in America.* Cambridge: Harvard University Press.

McClain, J. (1956). This Musical is GREAT. *Journal American*, 4 May.

Millstein, G. (1956). The Greater Loesser. *New York Times*, 20 May.

Moore, D. (1959). Opera as Theatre: American Composers Have Learned Public Demands a Good Libretto. *New York Times,* 12 April.

Moore, D. (1961). Something about Librettos. *Opera News*, 30 September, 8–13.

Mordden, E. (2014). *Anything Goes: A History of the American Musical Theatre.* New York: Oxford University Press.

Stempel, L. (2010). *Showtime: A History of the Broadway Musical.* New York: W. W. Norton.

Stempel, L. (1986). »›Street Scene‹ and the Enigma of Broadway Opera.« In Kim H. Kowalke (Ed.), *A New Orpheus: Essays on Kurt Weill* (pp. 321–341). New Haven, CT: Yale University Press.

Swain, J. P. (2002). *The Broadway Musical: A Critical and Musical Survey.* Lanham, MD: Scarecrow Press.

Taylor, D. (1933). What's Wrong with Opera? *Saturday Evening Post*, 3 June, 6, 7, 66–68.

Wagner, R. (1995). *Opera and Drama.* Translated by William Ashton Ellis. Lincoln: University of Nebraska Press.

Weill, K. (1936). The Alchemy of Music. *Stage*, November, 63–64.

Weill, K. (1947). *Liner notes for the Original Cast Recording of »Street Scene.«* Columbia Masterworks set M-MM-683.

Micah Wittmer

Toward an American Folk Opera
Performing Primitivism and Negro Folk Culture in Hall Johnson's *Run, Little Chillun!* (1933)

»When will we have a real American opera?« asked Olin Downes, theater critic of the *New York Times*, in an article discussing the state of American opera in 1933. To Downes, the fourteen operas and ballads by American composers produced at the Metropolitan Opera in New York did not fit his definition. He explained, »But we have yet to see on that stage an opera which is genuinely American. Such an opera must have substance and style indigenous to this land and people.« He claimed that the African American composer, choral conductor, and playwright of Hall Johnson's musical drama *Run, Little Chillun* was a precursor to a truly native American opera because it was a folk drama with »real life and genuine musical quality.« According to Downes, the final scene of *Run, Little Chillun,* which depicted a black[1] Baptist church revival, was the most impressive nod toward a new genre of American opera because it seamlessly merged music that was distinctly American with the drama. His conclusion is worth quoting at length:

> No doubt the future of American opera as a whole is much broader and more inclusive than that of Negro folk-play. Certainly, the white Americans will take to other subjects and to more elaborate forms for self-expression when at last they create. But it is possible that before that time the race which has not the white's self-consciousness and culture, but retains primitive impulse and emotion, and extraordinary musical sense, and a considerable folklore and folk-music of its own, may be able to produce a species of opera or lyric play which the public will value and to which it will listen. *Run, Little Chillun* is far from finished drama or opera either, but it has real life and genuine musical quality. Such qualities, in fact, as seem hardly to survive in the sterile and artificial music of the day (Downes, 1933, p. X5).

---

1   In this essay, the choice of racial descriptors such as »black,« »African American,« and »Negro« are deliberate. The term »Negro« is employed as it was used by black artists and intellectuals during the time period covered here (e.g., »Negro folk culture« or »New Negro«). »Black« is used when describing a general unifying notion of race that includes African Americans, black Americans of Caribbean descent, and Africans. »African American« is used when emphasizing the hybridity of the culture of Americans from the United States who are descendants of slaves.

According to Downes, *Run, Little Chillun* provided a template for what he considered to be »distinctly American« folk operas and folk plays because it was primitive and lacked the cultural restraints that he felt hindered white artists. This attitude reveals the common notion at the time that African American culture—particularly parts of their culture that was perceived as primitive, folk, and unadulterated by modernism—could provide a necessary, distinctly American character to opera, theatre, and many other cultural forms. The belief is a carry-over from Antonín Dvořák's statement that »an American school of composition would be formed when composers drew from American folk music—specifically Negro folk music and Native American music« (*Real Value of Negro Melodies*, 1893; *Dvořák's American School of Music*, 1893). The Czech composer promoted this ideology during his tenure at the National Conservatory (1892–1895) where he was hired to help young American composers develop an American school of composition (Beckerman, 2003, S. 3–4). During the Great Depression, the American folk in general (not just African Americans), who were idealized and seen as primitive and unspoiled by modernism and capitalism, took on greater significance. Drawing from folk culture became one way artists redefined American culture during this national crisis. Dramas like *Run, Little Chillun* provided American composers and playwrights with innovative models for depicting the culture of African Americans during the 1930s (Allen, 2004). The accounts of influential classical musicians, such as Jascha Heifetz and Arturo Toscanini, many of whom attended multiple performances of *Run, Little Chillun* as well as concerts performed by the Hall Johnson Choir, show just how interested these musicians were in observing what many considered to be authentic performances of black culture (*Robert Rockmore Presents Run, Little Chillun*, 1933; Van Vechten, 1934; Hammond, 1933; Glinsky, 2000, p. 157). Virgil Thomson was so inspired by a performance of *Run, Little Chillun* that he decided that his opera, *Four Saints in Three Acts*, should be performed by an all-black cast, and George Gershwin, who attended multiple performances of *Run, Little Chillun*, likely drew inspiration from it as he was working on his opera, *Porgy and Bess*.

Run, Little Chillun was one of the most popular theatrical works with both book and music created by an African American during the 1930s. After its opening at the Lyric Theater on Broadway on March 1, 1933, *Run, Little Chillun* had immediate box office success. It ran for 126 performances after its premiere at the Lyric Theater, placing fifth for the longest running show on Broadway in May of 1933, just three months after its opening (*Run is 5th Place*, 1933, p. 5). It then enjoyed a brief run at the historic Lafayette Theater in Harlem as well as revivals in Chicago, Los Angeles, and San Francisco during the 1930s—the West Coast revivals were performed under the auspices of the Works Progress Administration (Hatch & Hamalian, 1996, p. 228).

I assert that Johnson's musical play strategically capitalizes on what many white American critics believed to be primitive—and therefore genuine—black culture. I explain that Johnson's portrayal of Africanisms and Negro folk culture played off white people's imagination of black culture because he was greatly influenced by the complex and often paradoxical New Negro ideals of racial uplift—especially those espoused by Locke during the Harlem Renaissance. Part of Locke's strategy for promoting racial uplift was to encourage New Negro artists to emulate European artists, such as Pablo Picasso, who enjoyed great success when they enthusiastically embraced African Art and used it as an inspiration for their works. Although Johnson does not quote Locke directly in his essays on Negro spirituals, like Locke, he goes to great lengths to describe and legitimize racial essentialism and primitivism in spirituals to prove that they are truly the basis of high art. He carefully constructs an image of African American musical culture by highlighting primitivisms—especially the African Americans' innate gift of rhythm and use of drums—by using essentialist language to explain the history of African American music. As seen through the lens of Locke's ideals of racial uplift, I argue that Johnson's complex and nuanced portrayal of African Americans in *Run, Little Chillun* subtly challenged racist stereotypes. I focus on the two elaborate, sensational musical numbers that ended both acts of the drama: an orgiastic song-and-dance ritual of the New Day Pilgrim cult and an emotional revival in the local Hope Baptist Church (Van Vechten, 1933; Hammond, 1933, p. 10). Both scenes depicted contrasting examples of primitivism and Negro folk culture in carefully constructed ways that also appealed to the white audience's imagination of an authentic black culture. They also received considerable attention from critics, some mentioning, like Downes, the similarities to opera and *Run, Little Chillun's* example of the potential of a distinctly American opera.[2]

Portraying Africanisms in Negro Folk Culture

Set in the rural south in 1929, *Run, Little Chillun* centers on Jim, a Baptist minister's son, and his struggle with sin and temptation. In the first act, the audience learns of the tension between the members of the Hope Baptist Church and their rival group, the cult of the New Day Pilgrims. At the center of this tension is Jim who is married to the pious Ella, but who is having an affair with Sulumai, the town's wayward vixen. Although she knows that Jim had been cheating on her for some time with Sulumai, Ella is confident that he will return to her and pleads with Jim not to break

---

2 In addition to the articles cited, I have reviewed over 50 reviews and concert reports on the 1933 Broadway production, many of which attribute the success of the musical drama to the finale of the first and second acts. Some notable ones are Carl Van Vechten's *New York Times* article (1933), and esteemed drama critic Percy Hammond's article (1933).

his father's heart and »follow up these African devils« (Johnson, 1933, p. 242). Sulumai, on the other hand, insists that Jim should accompany her to the New Day Pilgrim meeting, explaining to him that the leader of the Pilgrims, Brother Moses, teaches about sin in a way that causes her to believe that she is supposed to be with Jim. At the end of the first act, Jim and Sulumai attend a New Day Pilgrim meeting held outdoors on a moonlit night.

The finale of act I, often referred to as the »New Day Pilgrim scene,« was described by one reviewer of the *Baltimore Afro-American*, a prominent African American newspaper of the time, as »so weird, so fantastic, so nerve tinkling […] that the savagery of it all seems to draw the audience out of its seats to become a part of this mob of humanity that seems to turn itself loose to riotous abandon« (*Play is Novel Production*, 1933, p. 18). Johnson went to great lengths to establish that the New Day Pilgrims are a purely fictional cult, giving him the freedom to experiment with African-inspired representations of religion and primitivism. In the script, he makes a clear distinction between an authentic vodun cult and the New Day Pilgrims by stating:

> The general impression should be of something approaching voodoo—not too directly African, but with a strong African flavor. Since the cult is not designated by any familiar name, any feature may be introduced which serves to make the whole scene more striking without any chance of controversy or any possibility of offense to any existing religious group. (Johnson, 1933, p. 251)

By incorporating vague and symbolic Africanisms in the New Day Pilgrim ceremony, Johnson created a fictional cult that some white critics found authentic. To put it bluntly, audiences assumed authenticity from black performers in theatrical acts that were deemed primitive, like the New Day Pilgrim ceremony; and Johnson exploited this expectation. His use of Africanisms and primitivisms in the music and dance in this scene was multilayered and contradictory.

Johnson's incorporation of vaguely Africanist exoticism and primitivism reflects the influence of the Harlem Renaissance ideology that Johnson's colleague Locke promoted. In an essay in his edited volume, *The New Negro: An Interpretation* (the seminal text of the Harlem Renaissance), Locke stated:

> […] there would be little hope of an influence of African art upon the western African descendants if there were not at present a growing influence of African art upon European art in general. But led by these tendencies, there is the possibility that the sensitive artistic mind of the American Negro, stimulated by a cultural pride and interest, will receive from African art a profound and galvanizing influence. The legacy is there at least, with prospects of a rich yield. In the first place, there is in the mere knowledge of the skill and unique mastery of the arts of the ancestors the valuable and stimulating realization that

the Negro is not a cultural foundling without his own inheritance. (Locke, 1925, pp. 256–257)

He saw an opportunity for African American artists to capitalize on the allegedly inherent connection to the African ancestors that he believed African Americans possessed. Although he claimed that African Americans were disconnected from the African artist expression due to the Westernization and Christianization that they underwent in America, he believed that their ancestral connection to Africa would give them an advantage over European artists who were inspired by African art (Locke, 1925, p. 256; see also Lemke, 1998, pp. 120–121).

Yet, Locke, and many of the African American artists who shared Locke's belief in the importance of drawing from African sources, created a symbolic and pieced-together African heritage that was not rooted in historical or anthropological research. Historian Michael Feith believes that Locke's encouragement to young Harlem Renaissance artists to »reclaim« primitive characteristics of an imagined African heritage was not a rediscovery, but a deliberate creation of a racial identity (Feith, 2001, p. 61). Carefully crafted Negro culture proved that the New Negro could compete with the intellectual and artistic currents of early twentieth-century modernism through »a questioning of the Western tradition from a (rediscovered) African diasporic standpoint« (Feith, 2001, pp. 66–67).

Locke believed that this idealistic art of the New Negro proved that African Americans were a race of artists who possessed the same level of reason, intelligence, and cultural refinement as the elite Anglo Americans, and therefore was a means of uplifting the race. Importantly, according to Locke, these black artists should not create art that was protest art or propaganda (Locke, 1928). That is, it was not to be art that was confrontational in nature, exposing socio economic and racial injustices, but it was to prove to whites that blacks were a race of sophisticated artists and therefore intelligent and fully human.

The scene begins with four solitary beats of the drums signaling the beginning of the processional. The lone drum beats punctuate each phrase of the music of the processional, prominently featuring one of the most stereotypical theatrical tropes of Africanism. However, other than the use of the drums, the scene's music includes few of the imagined elements of primitive music. In the music of the processional, Johnson creates a sense of gravitas by featuring musical elements that exists in Negro spirituals and Western choral music alike (see Example 1).

Run, Little Chillun: Processional

Hall Johnson

Example 1: Processional (mm 1–9).

After three more solitary beats of the tom-tom, the entire choir (except for the first sopranos) repeats the opening phrase at fortissimo, creating a voluminous response. The technique of alternating between a few voices presenting a phrase and the entire choir repeating it creates a responsorial format. As in plainchant, the texture of the Processional is monophonic and, with the exception of a few measures (which are briefly homophonic), remains so throughout the entire procession, adding to the Western prepolyphonic religious feel that this piece evokes. As the Processional builds to a climax, the piece becomes more homophonic and the alternation of phrases between voices becomes more frequent. In the final eight measures, a phrase punctuated by a dotted eighth-note rhythm followed by a half note rhythmically propels the music toward a dramatic finale, and this phrase is rapidly exchanged by two groups: the first soprano and altos versus the bass, tenor, and 2nd sopranos (see Example 2).

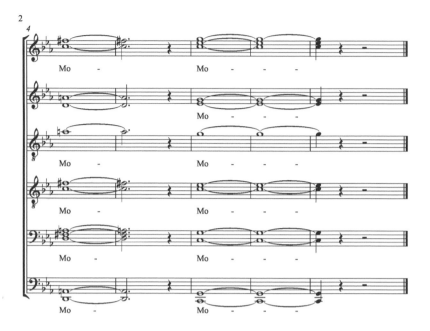

Example 2: Processional (Final Eight Measures).

In this excerpt, the Pilgrims are chanting »Tongola po manekola vedea« in a language that Johnson created, which he named Tongola after the cult's elderly African founder. Johnson allegedly drew from Latin, Greek, and Sanskrit—liturgical languages associated with ancient religious practices. Significantly, he did not use African or Haitian languages. Much like his employment of certain compositional techniques, his choice in the origins of the stage language is a deliberate one that creates a religious, yet exotic, sound (*Hall Johnson Invented Own Language*, 1933, p. 19).[3]

Following the Processional, a speech was delivered by Brother Moses (the Oxford educated spokesman of the cult) that caused a few critics of the mainstream newspapers, such as John Martin, dance critic for the *New York Times*, to dismiss the authenticity of the cult. The style of this speech, which was about the history and theology of the cult, is in stark contrast to the stereotypical dialect spoken by the Hope Baptists throughout the drama—and moreover—constituted a significant departure

---

3   Johnson disliked the comparison of Tongola to Hog-Latin and, according to this article, he took the language very seriously, holding classes in Tongola for the actors and choir members in *Run, Little Chillun.*

from representations of African Americans in other theatrical works of the period. According to Martin, Brother Moses's speech »is not essentially Negroid.« This is because, as Martin explains, Brother Moses spouts »philosophical doctrines in three-syllable words with more than ordinary punctiliousness about subordinate clauses and other grammatical niceties not usually to be found in colloquial speech« (Martin, 1933, p. X7).

To conclude the speech that so disturbed critics like Martin, Brother Moses sings an eerie intonation of a Credo (see Example 3). In this song, we see an antiphonal form similar to the Processional, but with a more developed counterpoint and harmonies derived from the European classical tradition, similar to those used by Johnson in his choral arrangements of Negro spirituals.

Example 3: Credo Intonation.

The solemn, dignified Credo was followed by a dance that critics praised as wild, barbaric, fantastical, and authentic. The dance scene began with a slow solo performed by a female member of the cult, but gradually got faster until the famous Bahamian dancers leapt out of the woods and booming drums began beating wild rhythms (*Run, Little Chillun*, 1933, p. 5). These dancers were not wearing the white robes of the other Pilgrims, but were scantily clothed, wearing loin cloths and feathered headdresses. Some of these dancers were originally assembled by Zora Neale Hurston who taught them the choreography of the Bahamian Fire Dance based on fieldwork she carried out in the Bahamas for a 1932 Broadway revue that she created called *The Great Day*. According to Hurston's research, the Bahamian Fire Dance originated in Africa and was brought to Florida by migrant Bahamian laborers. Under Hurston's direction, the Bahamian dancers sought to amend whites' misguided beliefs about Caribbean dance, attempting to provide researched and accurate choreography that both entertained and dispelled the »jungle dancing« stereotype (Kraut, 2008, p.188).[4] Unfortunately, *The Great Day* was not commercially success-

---

4   There is significant overlap between the Bahamian Fire Dance as performed in Hurston's review, *The Great Day*, which opened two months before *Run, Little Chillun* on January 10, 1932, and the New Day Pilgrim dance. The Bahamian Fire Dance, which was described as originating in Africa and »brought to Florida by immigrant Negro workers from the Bahama Islands,« consists of three parts that celebrate the arrival of spring: the Jumping Dance, Ring

ful, and Hurston could not pay her dancers well. Greatly influenced by the lucrative demand for primitive dancing, the dancers went on to accept many performance opportunities that billed them as African or voodoo jungle dancers, and Johnson's *Run, Little Chillun* was one such occasion (Kraut, 2008 pp. 162–165). This allowed Johnson to include what was perceived, by himself as well as his audience, as African artistic elements in this scene. As an unidentified critic of the prominent African American newspaper *The New York Amsterdam News* claimed, Johnson probably had his white audiences in mind when he created the dance finale, explaining that the scene was »cut and dried from the darkest Africa,« yet the costumes were typical theatrical primitive garb (*Little Ones Not Running*, 1933, p. 7).

Portraying the Black Church of Negro Folk Culture

In the second act, Jim, who was not impressed with the New Day Pilgrims, decides to return to Hope Baptist Church. Afraid she will loose Jim, Sulumai claims that she is pregnant with his child and threatens to parade his baby in front of the congregation. Jim then changes his mind and proposes that they start a new life together, taking the train to a town where nobody knows them. Sulumai refuses and Jim leaves frustrated. In the finale of the second act, Jim attends a revival meeting held at Hope Baptist where he repents of his sins and is reunited with his wife and church. In this scene that Olin Downes believed provided the greatest example of a prototype for an American opera, Johnson reconstructed a southern Baptist church-revival service featuring diagetic choir performances of hymns and spirituals. As in a real church revival, the songs grew spontaneously out of prayers, testimonies, and sermons. Because of this, many reviewers, both black and white, praised the scene for its authenticity. Like the finale of the first act, this finale also exploits the expectations of what was deemed as authentic Negro folk culture. But the mixture of realism with a Negro folk culture crafted by elite whites and blacks to prove the significance of African Americans as cultural contributors to American society makes this scene even more complex and messy than the New Day Pilgrim celebration. Chappy Gardner, an African American theatre critic for *The Chicago Defender,* nostalgically wrote:

> So true to life, and the characters of the revival scene inject so much honest-to-goodness reality into their work that many in the audience about me found themselves completely controlled by the spirit of the play. I found it hard to keep from joining in the singing of

---

Play, and Crow Dance. Not only were some of the dancers the same in both shows, but the choreography in Hurston's review bore striking resemblance to that in *Run, Little Chillun.* Hurston complained that Johnson stole her dancers and even claimed that the New Day Pilgrim dance was the »spitting image« of the Bahamian Fire Dance.

the old spirituals and hymns sung by my mother and hers—and now given more artistic fullness and appreciation by Hall Johnson's masterful direction (Gardner, 1933, p. 5).

He claimed that *Run, Little Chillun* was »an authentic history of a great people in the raw« (Gardner, 1933, p. 5). Echoing Gardner, Morton Eustis, a white theater critic for the *Theater Arts Monthly*, explicitly linked primitivism and authenticity in *Run, Little Chillun*:

> Mr. Johnson and his fellows recreated effectively the life of the primitive Negro at moments of high emotional tension. A revival meeting in a small Negro church in the South was so true and so stirringly expressed that it took the audience completely out of the theatre into the black belt. [...] The revival scene repeated an event which transpires in any primitive Negro community in the South. (Eustis, 1933, p. 338)

Gardner's and Eustis's conflation of the primitive and authentic is an example of how Negro folk culture—in this case, Negro religious practices—were defined not just by white cultural »outsiders,« but by educated African Americans who promoted Negro folk culture as the basis of American culture. The foremost example of this is found in W.E.B. Du Bois's seminal work, *The Souls of Black Folk* (1903). In this collection of essays, Du Bois provided what has since become an oft-quoted DuBois, 1903, p. 191). It is important to note that Du Bois, and later Gardner and Eustis, were not employing these adjectives in a derogatory manner, but rather were explaining what they viewed as the admirable primitive African retentions in African American Christianity.

Du Bois also emphasized the hybridity of African American religious practices, especially that of Negro spirituals, constantly reminding the reader that they were both African and American. Significantly, Du Bois provided an origin story for Negro spirituals that emphasized a vague and somewhat imagined African past and an overly romanticized slave past (Feith, 2001, p. 51). He explains:

> The Music of Negro religion is that plaintive rhythmic melody, with its touching minor cadences, which, despite caricature and defilement, still remains the most original and beautiful expression of human life and longing yet born on American soil. Sprung from the African forests, where its counterpart can still be heard, it was adapted, changed, and intensified by the tragic soul-life of the slave, until, under the stress of law and whip, it became the one true expression of a people's sorrow, despair, and hope. (Du Bois, 1903, p. 191)

Du Bois emphasized the African and American origins of a Negro folk culture that was specifically southern and rooted in slavery, thereby helped to establish the definition of Negro folk culture that would be used by Harlem Renaissance intellectuals in the 1920s and artists and cultural critics in the 1930s (Schenbeck, 2012, p. 74; Anderson, 2001, p. 29; Baker, 1987, pp. 58, 66).

Throughout his work, Du Bois employs a language of romantic nationalism that can be traced back to eighteenth-century Europe when the »discovery of the folk« was inextricably linked with the belief that primitivism—what was untouched by modernism and less civilized, was closer to authenticity. The French philosopher and composer Jean Jacques Rousseau and the German philosopher and theologian Johann Gottfried Herder were early promoters of this theory (Taruskin, 2001). Essential to this romantic, nationalistic ideology was the theory that music »of the soil« from a particular folk defines the music of a nation. However, even more directly, Du Bois's romantic, nationalistic rhetoric reflected that of Dvořák. In *The Souls of Black Folk,* Du Bois used *much of the same rhetoric as* Dvořák, who stated that »the future music of this country must be founded on what are called Negro melodies.« Through his publication, Du Bois helped to define the role of Negro spirituals in shaping both the American and African American culture. For example, Du Bois wrote:

> [...] there are to-day no truer exponents of the pure human spirit of the Declaration of Independence than the American Negroes; there is no true American music but the wild sweet melodies of the Negro slave; the American fairy tales and folklore are Indian and African; and, all in all, we black men seem the sole oasis of simple faith and reverence in a dusty desert of dollars and smartness. (Du Bois, 1903, p. 11)

Likely motivated by *The Souls of Black Folk,* Locke encouraged young black artists to draw inspiration from the folk music of slaves. Locke was in favor of choral arrangements of spirituals because they captured the community essence of the songs as originally sung by slaves. He claimed that the Eva Jessye and the Hall Johnson Choirs were the closest example of a »genuine Negro way of singing these songs« as, in his opinion, they have »about restored the spirituals to their primitive choral basis and their original singing style« (Locke, 1936, p. 24). According to Locke, the Eva Jessye and Hall Johnson Choirs successfully achieved »the actual mechanics of improvised Negro choral singing, with its syllabic quavers, off-tones and tone glides, improvised interpolations, subtle rhythmic variation«—in short, they performed the nontranscribable aspects of the Negro spiritual (Locke, 1936, p. 22).

Like Locke, Johnson also emphasized the importance of preserving the choral aspect of Negro spirituals, lamenting the increasing interest in solo performances of these songs as well as the lack of recordings of the true spiritual (Johnson, 1965, p. 272). Although his 1965 essay, »Notes on the Negro Spiritual,« was published over thirty years after Locke's essay, he used language similar to Locke. In this essay, Johnson claimed that the lack of recordings was a tragedy because published arrangements could not portray their style of performance, which included many nontranscribable elements including bent notes, rhythmic improvisation, and »the unconscious, but amazing and bewildering counterpoint produced by so many voices in individual improvisation« (Johnson, 1965, pp. 271–272). Johnson stated, »The racial tendency to improvise ›between-notes‹ [and] the great variety of characteristic tone-color and rhythmic accent—all of these Negro techniques simply defy notation in any known system. They must be recorded from the living sound« (Johnson, 1965, p. 272). Johnson asserted that the *Green Pastures* and *Run, Little Chillun* were the only modern examples of how the spirituals were supposed to be sung, primarily because of the large a-cappella ensembles (*Green Pastures* and *Run, Little Chillun* had choirs of over 100 singers). Johnson's claims replicate those of Locke's in *The New Negro and His Music* (1936) where Locke stated that »Before they completely vanish in their original form, this congregational folk-singing, with its unique breaks and tricks, should be recorded by phonograph, the only way their full values can be gotten« (Locke, 1936, p. 22).

Johnson also echoes one of the most important ideas that Locke campaigned for throughout the Harlem Renaissance as one of the primary means where black composers could achieve racial uplift—that of using the spirituals as a basis of modern, classical music compositions. As we have already seen, Locke was convinced that the setting of symphonic, choral arrangements of spirituals in modern, classical compositions would equal and surpass that of Russian folk and choral-based compositions (Locke, 1936, p. 21). Likewise, Johnson believed that a program note along with »the plain folk melody unadorned« (a transcription of the melody) should accompany the ideal recording of the spirituals, even in 1965—long after the Harlem Renaissance. Continuing his classical form metaphor where the »plain folk melody unadorned« is the theme, Johnson explains that there should be »a development-section, along racial lines, showing future possibilities for composition. Such a record-library would not only rescue the grandest American art-form from oblivion, [but] would immeasurably heighten the artistic stature of the United States among the other civilized nations« (Johnson, 1965, p. 275).

Johnson's version of the history of the Negro spiritual emphasized the primitive African roots of the spirituals and the process of merging them with European harmony. Tracing the history of the spirituals back to African drums, he stated, »The musical instruments of the primitive African tribes were crude and undeveloped so that the songs were dependent on the voices of the singers. Only the drum, in manufacture and performance, left nothing to be desired« (Johnson, 1965, p. 269).

Just as Du Bois described what he viewed as the primitive characteristics of African retentions in African American culture with admiration and respect, Johnson also purposefully describes the dignity of African culture. For example, in a 1954 lecture, he explained that some of the early African slaves who were brought to America were kings, chieftains, and soldiers in their home country whose previous stature translated to moral courage, curiosity, and imagination that could not be harmed by the harsh conditions of slavery (Johnson, 1954, p. 252). Then, according to Johnson's history, the English introduced harmony and melody to the African slaves who combined it with their instinctive rhythmic talent.

Johnson, like Locke, also promotes the idea that the merging of European and African musical traditions was and is the basis of American music. The result was Afro-American music, which was »a combination of syncopation, the pentatonic scale, unison singing, and a combination of part singing, plus the poetry of the lyrics that grew out of the culture of the nation« (Johnson, 1944, p. 230).

Johnson claimed that the final scene in *Run, Little Chillun* was an attempt to »work out in dramatic form the community background in which Negro spirituals were born« (»Broadway Play is Novel Production,« 1933, p. 18). As in the outline of the final scene shown below (see Example 4), singing and praying were interchangeable: Congregants and church leaders sang songs as their prayers or as part of their prayer. Testimonies begin with songs that are relevant to the congregant's testimony. In addition to this, Johnson indicates in the script that the sermon delivered by Elder Jones and the prayer by Reverend Sister Luella Strong were intoned—a dramatic sing-speech that usually begins with formal, measured phrasing and escalates to the »celebratory gestures of intoned speech« (Johnson, 1933, p. 163–164). There was also an active Amen Corner—a group of congregants that lead others in responses to sermons, prayers, and testimonies by shouting »amen,« »preach it,« etc.

1. A woman kneeling at mourners bench hums »Steal Away«
2. Rev. Ebenezer Allen *lines out* »Amazing Grace« (hymn) as church fills up—as congregants come, they join in the singing and more voices are added.
3. Sister Luella Strong from Mobile Alabama *leads the congregation in prayer, beginning her prayer by singing* »Oh, Jesus, come dis-a-way!«
4. *Testimony time interspersed with songs*—two congregants begin their testimony with songs and then tell their testimony; Brother Abbalom Brown, a veteran Christian, sings »Done written Down-a My Name« and new convert Minnie Williams sings »Is Dere Anybody Here Dat Loves My Jesus.« The final testimony is Ella's (she's the only one that doesn't sing).
5. Jim enters the church and sits beside Ella. *The congregation sings* »Run, Little Chillun little chillun,« then Elder Jones preaches.
6. Jim throws himself at the mourner's bench asking congregation to pray. Congregation sings/prays »O Lord, Have Mercy.«
7. Jim sings »So Glad.«
8. Jim lines out the hymn »Return oh holy dove, return sweet messenger of Rest« (hymn).

Example 4: Outline of songs sung in Finale.

When the scene opens, the congregants are kneeling at the mourner's bench (a bench at the front of church where people go to pray and often repent their sin), some prostrate on the floor. The primary focus is on a woman kneeling at the bench humming the spiritual »Steal Away« as people filter into the church. Singing hymns or spirituals as prayers is a common practice in many black Baptist churches and Johnson demonstrates this in three key moments in this scene (Dargan, 2006, pp. 25, 142). By having characters hum and sing spirituals or hymns as part of a prayer, Johnson shows the highly personal nature of these songs and how they were sung during worship services. In *Run, Little Chillun,* Reverend Sister Luella Strong, an evangelist from Mobile, Alabama, who was visiting the Hope Baptist Church for a camp meeting and who had led the congregation in a prayer, began by singing the spiritual »O Jesus come dis-a-way.« This kind of prayer encourages congregants to participate actively in the prayer—an act of agreement where, in this case, the congregation collectively asks for Jesus's presence to be in the midst of their service. After Reverend Sister Luella Strong finished singing the spiritual, Johnson notes in the script that the congregants continued to hum the spiritual while the Reverend prayed, which is also a common practice in black Baptist churches (Dargan, 2006, p. 142). Finally, at the end of the scene, when Jim throws himself at the mourners' bench, dramatically and publically repenting for his transgressions with Sulumai, he asks the congregation to pray for his soul, and the entire congregation sings »O Lord, Have Mercy on Me." In a sense, the congregation helps Jim to articulate his own prayer of repentance by singing »Oh, Lord have mercy on me, on me, / Oh, Lord have mercy on me, I'm gonna fall down on my knees / And I'm gonna face de risin' sun.« In the script, Johnson indicates that this song is not to be performed as if the choir was singing it for a concert audience, but that it should have »the sound of prayer and supplication—in shrill, high voices of old women, resonant, deep-throated tones from men […]« (Johnson, 1933, p. 277). The congregation continues to sing the spiritual, supporting Jim in his prayers until he is so invigorated by his sense of repentance and redemption that he rises with a shout from the mourners' bench and leads the congregation in the spiritual »So Glad.«

An aspect of black Baptist worship traditions was the tradition of lining out hymns. In *Run, Little Chillun,* the hymns »Amazing Grace« sung at the beginning of the service as congregants filter into the church and »Return oh Holy Dove,« the very last song of the drama, are lined out. Lining out is an oral tradition of hymn singing practiced by black Baptists in the United States in a call-and-response format. A hymn text is chanted by a worship leader in a slow tempo. Syllables are often drawn out and embellished with improvised melismas and, at times, melismatic moans (Dargan, 2006, p. 26). Then, the congregation responds, often repeating some form of the improvisation sung by the worship leader. Although this tradition has its roots in the eighteenth- and nineteenth-century worship practice of the Protestant group English Dissenters, the adaptation of this practice by slaves which has been passed down for generations bears little audible resemblance to its forbearer.[5] The lined-out version is almost unrecognizable in comparison to the hymnal version. »Amazing Grace« is one of the traditional hymns that are lined out in the black Missionary Baptist tradition (Dargan, 2006, p. 27). By including lined-out hymns in this scene along with Negro spirituals as they would be sung in a church service, Johnson provided a replica of a worship service as it would actually have been experienced at a real revival meeting.

Though many aspects of this scene were attempts to show how Negro spirituals were sung in religious worship settings by incorporating well-known spirituals and hymns into the drama, the title spiritual »Run, Little Chillun!« was actually composed by Johnson. This was an opportunity for Johnson to demonstrate his ability to compose in the manner of a Negro spiritual according to the criteria of authenticity he adhered to. The Hall Johnson Choir recorded this song in 1939, making it possible to hear those elements that Johnson claimed could only be captured on recording (bent notes, rhythmic improvisation, and »the unconscious, but amazing and bewildering counterpoint produced by so many voices in individual improvisation« [Johnson, 1965, pp. 271–272]). The song is sung after Ella (Jim's wife) testified to the church about her unwavering faith in God's ability to bring Jim to repentance. Jim then wanders into the church and sits next to her, and the congregation sings the title song. In the 1939 recording, a folk quality is audible as the soloist does not have an operatically trained voice, however, the choir is impeccably unified and in tune and there are no bent notes, slides, or improvisation—markers of musical authenticity that Johnson lamented was lacking in performances of spirituals. The choir and soloists sing exactly what is composed (with the exception of a few bent notes), and the counterpoint and harmony is standard choral music fare. The only identifiable musical elements of a spiritual are a call-and-response form; a minor, pentatonic key; and lyrics that warn the believer against the wiles of the devil.[6] The title song is an example of how a composed spiritual could pass as an authentic Negro spiritual when performed within the context of a dramatic scene that portrayed all of the carefully constructed elements of Negro folk culture.

---

5   For an example of how »Amazing Grace« is traditionally lined out in a north-central Piedmont, South Carolina church, see musicologist William Dargan's transcription in his book *Lining Out the Word: Dr. Watts Hymn Singing In The Music of Black Americans*.

6   Spirituals such as »Doncher Let nobody turn you roun!,« »Run, Little Chillun, Sinner, Run, Little Chillun!,« and »You Better Min!« all have lyrics exhorting believers to avoid the temptations of the devil and stay on the »straight and narrow.«

Conclusion

This essay began with a quote from Downes who suggested that African Americans would be the ones to produce a »species of opera or lyric play« because they possess the primitive emotions, lack of restraint and self consciousness, superior musicality, and a distinctive folklore and folk culture that is American. In his opinion, the rhetoric of which can be traced back to Dvořák's published opinions on drawing from the folk music of Negroes and Native Americans, the final acts of *Run, Little Chillun* provided examples of what an American opera could be because it portrayed contrasting spectacles of primitivism in religious practices of a pseudo-voodoo cult and a black Baptist church revival. But for Johnson, these scenes were more than just depictions of primitivism that would capture the imagination of his white audience—*Run, Little Chillun* was a product of the New Negro ideals of the Harlem Renaissance that used primitivism as a source of pride and as a way to command the attention of white audiences. The belief that art reflecting the modern currents of primitivism popular in European art, and the emphasis on portraying the folk without directly challenging current sociopolitical issues, was commonly held amongst African American artists who were influenced by Locke's ideology. Capitalizing on the perceived primitivism of black American's African heritage, Johnson aspired to create a work that portrayed Negro folk culture in the way that elite African Americans, such as Du Bois, had been defining it: as both African and American. Their carefully constructed definition of Negro folk culture was not always historically accurate, and much of their understanding of African culture was imagined, yet they told the same story of the hybridity of African American culture and its significant role in American culture. That Downes and other important figures in the musical and theatrical world believed *Run, Little Chillun* was a prototype of an American opera *because of* the primitivisms and folk elements proves that Negro folk culture was viewed by some in artistic circles to be legitimate material for creating a distinctly American opera.

Just two years after the premiere of *Run, Little Chillun*, Gershwin's *Porgy and Bess: An American Folk Opera* was premiered. Gershwin deliberately subtitled his opera »an American Folk Opera,« which was considered to be the first great American opera—an extremely significant descriptor for this opera, with an all-black cast that focused on southern blacks and had a score that Gershwin claimed was based on Negro folk music such as spirituals and work songs. The discussion of Negro folk culture and primitivism in *Run, Little Chillun* provides insight into how African Americans were included in the redefinition of American culture that was taking place during the Great Depression. Works like *Run, Little Chillun* also provide a glimpse into the often personal process of black artists creating works that challenged conventionally held views on race, civil rights, and national freedom in ways that were usually not obvious to audiences, but were often complex and messy.

References

(1893). Antonin Dvořák on Negro Melodies. *New York Herald*, 28 May, 31.

(1893). Dvořák's American School of Music. *New York Herald*, 8 May.

(1893). Dvořák on His New Work. *New York Herald*, 15 December.

(1893). Real Value of Negro Melodies. *New York Herald*, 21 May.

(1933). Broadway Play is Novel Production: Hall Johnson Tops Heights in Offering. *Baltimore Afro-American*, 11 March, 18.

(1933). Hall Johnson Invented Own Language for Play: Run Little Chillun. *Baltimore Afro-American*, 25 November, 19.

(1933). Little Ones Not Running: At Least Not Fast Enough to See Hall Johnson's »Run, Little Chillun.« *New York Amsterdam News*, 20 December, 7.

(1933). Play is Novel Production: Hall Johnson Tops Heights in Offering. *Baltimore Afro-American*, 11 March, 18.

(1933). Robert Rockmore Presents Run Little Chillun. *Shubert Theater Billboard*.

(1933). »Run is 5th« in Place for Longest Running Show. *The Chicago Defender*, 27 May, 5.

(1933). »Run, Little Chillun« Has Dancing as Well as Song. *The Chicago Defender*, 20 May, 5.

Allen. R. (2004). An American Folk Opera? Triangulating Folkness, Blackness, and Americaness in Gershwin and Heyward's Porgy and Bess. *The Journal of American Folklore*, 117 (465), 243–261.

Anderson, P. (2001). *Deep River: Music and Memory in Harlem Renaissance Thought*. Durham, NC: Duke University Press.

Baker, H. (1987). *Modernism and the Harlem Renaissance*. Chicago, IL: University of Chicago Press.

Beckerman, M. (2003). *New Worlds of Dvořák: Searching in America for the Composer's Inner Life*. New York: Norton.

Dargan, W. (2006). *Lining out the Word: Dr. Watts Hymn Singing in the Music of Black Americans*. Berkeley, CA: University of California Press.

Downes, O. (1933). Final Scene of Hall Johnson's Negro »Folk-Play« Indicates One Direction for Developing Native Genre. *New York Times*, 2 April, X5.

Du Bois, W. E. B. (1903). *The Souls of Black Folk: Essays and Sketches*. Chicago, IL: A.C. McClurg & Co.

Eustis, M. (1933). The Optimist on Broadway. *Theatre Arts Monthly*, 338.

Feith, M. (2001). The Syncopated African: Constructions of Origins in the Harlem Renaissance (Literature, Music, Visual Arts). In G. Fabre & M. Feith (Eds.), *Temples for Tomorrow: Looking Back at the Harlem Renaissance* (pp. 51–72). Bloomington, IN: Indiana University Press.

Gardner, C. (1933). Hall Johnson Docks Choir Duties; Sails into Dramas: And »Run Little Chillun« Is the Result of Trip. *The Chicago Defender*, 5.

Glinsky A. (2000). *Theremin: Ether Music and Espionage*. Chicago: University of Illinois Press.

Hammond, P. (1933). The Theaters: Negro Folk-Songs and Melodrama. *New York Herald Tribune*, 10.

Hatch, J. & Hamalian, L. (1996). Frances Hall Johnson. In J. Hatch & L. Hamalian (Eds.), *Lost Plays of the Harlem Renaissance, 1920–1940* (pp. 227–229). Detroit, MI: Wayne State University Press.

Johnson, H. (1933). Run Little Chillun. In J. Hatch & L. Hamalian (Eds.), *Lost Plays of the Harlem Renaissance, 1920–1940* (pp. 230–279). Detroit, MI: Wayne State University Press.

Johnson, H. (1965). Notes on the Negro Spiritual. In E. Southern (Ed.), *Readings in Black American Music* (pp. 268–275). New York: W. W. Norton.

Johnson, H. (1954). Lecture-Demonstration on the Origins of the Negro Spiritual. In E. Simpson, *Hall Johnson: His Life, His Spirit, and His Music* (pp. 248–253). Lanham, MD: Scarecrow Press.

Johnson, H. (1944). Some Distinctive Elements in African-American Music. In E. Simpson, *Hall Johnson: His Life, His Spirit, and His Music* (pp. 229–234). Lanham, MD: Scarecrow Press.

Kraut, A. (2008). *Choreographing the Folk: The Dance Stagings of Zora Neale Hurston*. Minneapolis, MN: University of Minnesota Press.

Lemke, S. (1998). *Primitivist Modernism: Black Culture and the Origins of Transatlantic Modernism*. New York: Oxford University Press.

Locke. A. (1925). The Legacy of the Ancestral Arts. In A. Locke (Ed.), *The New Negro: An Interpretation* (pp. 254–267). New York: A. and C. Boni.

Locke. A. (1928). Art or Propaganda? *Harlem*, 1 (1), 12–13.

Locke. A. (1936). *The Negro and His Music*. Washington, DC: The Associates in Negro Folk Education.

Martin, J. (1933). The Dance: A Negro Play: Work of Doris Humphrey in »Run, Little Chillun« Merits Praise. *New York Times*, 12 March, X7.

Schenbeck, L. (2012). *Racial Uplift and American Music, 1878–1943*. Jackson, MI: University Press of Mississippi.

Taruskin, R. (2001). Nationalism. *Grove Music Online. Oxford Music Online*. New York: Oxford University Press. http://www.oxfordmusiconline.com/subscriber/article/grove/music/50846 (accessed 17 September 2014).

Van Vechten, C. (1934). Introduction. *Four Saints in Three Acts: An Opera to Be Sung*. New York: Random House.

Van Vechten, C. (1933). On »Run, Little Chillun!« *New York Times*, 19 March, X2.

Nils Grosch

Oper als Strategie der kompositorischen Selbstinszenierung und Wertbegriff: *Street Scene* (1946) und *West Side Story* (1957)

> »[...] Leonard Bernstein had already released his definitive, final version of the work [*West Side Story*] with a handpicked orchestra and the opera singers of which he always dreamed.«[1] Elisabeth A. Wells (2011)

> »When I arrived in this country [USA], in 1935, another dream began to get hold of me – the dream of an American opera.«[2] Kurt Weill (1947)

1.

Die von Komponisten und Biographen etablierte Denkfigur des Traums von der amerikanischen Oper hat wesentlich mit der Positionierung respektive Selbstpositionierung des Komponisten im so wahrgenommenen – oder auch nur so konstruierten – Spannungsfeld von Kunst und populärer Kultur und somit dem Verhältnis zum Broadway Musical zu tun. Im Falle von Kurt Weills oben zitierten Schallplattentext ist dies augenfällig: Die gattungshistorischen Kontextualisierungen von Elmer Rices, Langston Hughes' und Kurt Weills Bühnenwerk *Street Scene,* das am 09.01.1947 am Broadway im Adelphi Theater eröffnete, werden in obigem Zitat um ein Jahrzehnt zurückverlegt. Weill integriert in sein Narrativ Gershwins *Porgy and Bess* von 1935 und *Lady in the Dark* von ihm selbst, Moss Hart und Ira Gershwin aus dem Jahr 1941, die er als Beispiele für einen Trend zum opernhaften Komponieren am Broadway anführt. Die anderen beiden von Weill hier explizit genannten Werke – *Carmen Jones* von 1943 und *Carousel* von 1945 – stammen nicht zufällig von den damaligen »Marktführern« Richard Rodgers und Oscar Hammerstein II., konnte er doch so suggerieren, Gershwin und er seien schon früher an dieser Tendenz beteiligt gewesen.

---

1   Wells, 2011, S. 16.
2   Weill, 1947; in dt. Übersetzung in Hinton & Schebera, 2000, S. 182–184.

Das Publikum hatte nämlich schon nicht mehr, wie noch in den 1930er Jahren, dominant die klassische Musical Comedy als erfolgreiches Subgenre nachgefragt, sondern eben jene als neuartig empfundene Theaterform des Musical Play, die 1943 mit *Oklahoma!* den Siegeszug angetreten hatte und die in der öffentlichen Wahrnehmung mit dessen Autorenteam Rodgers & Hammerstein assoziiert wurde. Gerade die Tatsache, dass deren Werken – nach *Oklahoma!* folgte mit ähnlichem Zuspruch 1945 *Carousel* – von der Presse Innovationskraft im Sinne einer zunehmenden Integration der theatralischen Elemente zugesprochen wurde, scheint Weill besonders geärgert zu haben, ging er doch davon aus, dies früher und engagierter getan zu haben als Rodgers.[3]

Die explizite Erwähnung von *Porgy* und *Lady* in dem Schallplatten-Begleittext sollte ganz offensichtlich die Arbeiten der mächtigen Konkurrenten historisieren und so der Einzigartigkeits- und Innovationsrhetorik entziehen, mit der sie in der Theaterkritik bisweilen diskutiert wurden. Hier wird auch allzu deutlich, dass die nationale Attribuierung »Amerikanische Oper« zur Aufwertung im Sinne einer traditionellen Kunstwertigkeit mit der Zuschreibung zur Operngattung quasi in eins gedacht ist.

2.

Schaut man sich die Ankündigungen von *Street Scene*, das im Programmheft mit dem Gattungsuntertitel »A Dramatic Musical« bezeichnet worden war, an, so gewinnt man den Eindruck, Weill selbst habe sich noch im Vorfeld der Premiere ganz bewusst gegen die Zuschreibung des Werkes zur Operngattung verwahren wollen. In einer Vorankündigung des Stücks im »Musical Digest« unter dem Titel »Broadway-Opera, Our Composer's Hope for the Future« wurde das Stück als »ernstes Musical mit opernhaften Zügen nach Elmer Rices mit dem Pulitzer-Preis ausgezeichneten Sprechtheater-Stück *Street Scene*, produziert von Dwight Deere Wiman in Zusammenarbeit mit der Playwrights' Company« bezeichnet (Hinton & Schebera, 2000, S. 511). Zweifellos stellen die »opernhaften Züge« Bestandteile einer Argumentation zur Aufwertung als Kunstwerk dar, zu der gleichermaßen der Pulitzer-Preis der Buchvorlage, die Produktion durch die Playwrights Company und die Ernsthaftigkeit des Stoffs gehören. Der Artikel stellt Weills Herkunft aus der »traditionellen europäischen Opernszene« heraus – eine Formulierung, über die man trefflich streiten könnte, hatte doch Weill in den europäischen Operndebatten vor 1933 (Werken und ästhetischen Schriften) nicht selten einen provokativ-antitraditionellen Standpunkt bezogen.

---

3   »So Rodgers ›is defining a new directive for musical comedy.‹ I had always thought I've been doing that – but I must have been mistaken. Rodgers has certainly won the first round in that race between him and me. But I suppose there will be a second and a third round.« Weill, Brief an Lenya, 18.05.1945, zitiert nach Symonette & Kowalke, 1996, S. 460.

Weill selbst hingegen erklärte in dem an gleicher Stelle abgedruckten Interview in einer Formulierung, die zeigen sollte, dass der Gattungsuntertitel wohl überlegt war: »Ich nenne mein Werk nicht Oper. Ich würde es eher als dramatisches Musical bezeichnen.«[4] Er begründet diese Entscheidung mit formalen, dramaturgischen und anderen strukturellen Argumenten, die sich insbesondere aus dem Ziel herleiten, Handlung »realistisch« zu erzählen, was in der Notwendigkeit resultiert sei, »das gesprochene Wort mit dem Song« zu verknüpfen statt die »ganze Geschichte in Musik« zu erzählen (dieser Anspruch war nach Weills Ansicht im Musical eher als in der Oper zu realisieren).

Hier wird erkennbar, dass man eine allzu deutliche Zuordnung zur Operngattung vermeiden wollte, wie sie die Presse im Umfeld der Premiere propagierte. Das in diesem Zusammenhang gern zitierte Bonmot von Oscar Hammerstein, Oper sei ein Weg, sein Geld zu verlieren (Hammerstein II, 1945, S. xiii), zeugt von Berührungsängsten mit dem Operngenre nicht nur der Broadway-Produzenten, sondern auch des Publikums.

3.

Schon in der Frühphase der Konzeption der *West Side Story* sei man sich, so notierte Bernstein nachträglich in sein (teilweise fiktives) *West Side Story*-Log, über ein Gattungskonzept einig gewesen: »idea of making a musical that tells a tragic story in musical comedy terms, using only musical comedy techniques, never falling into the ›operatic‹ trap.«[5] Mit der ›operatic trap‹ hatte man sicher an die jüngsten Opernversuche von Weill, Blitzstein, auch Bernsteins *Trouble in Tahiti* gedacht. Das Umschlagen ins Opernhafte galt den Autoren als eine Falle, die auf keinen Fall zuschnappen sollte. Das Positionbeziehen für die scheinbar paradoxe Option einer »tragic story in musical comedy terms« zeugt von der Nähe solcher generischer Überlegungen zum »Dramatic Musical« bei Weill. Dieser hatte schon nach seiner Einwanderung die Theaterlandschaft in den USA in einer aufschlussreichen Vortragsskizze folgendermaßen bewertet:

> Metropolitan, schlimmstes Beispiel für altmodische Oper (Museum) einerseits, musical comedy, die gleichzeitig intellektuell und anspruchslos zu sein versucht, andererseits. Nichts dazwischen. Enormes Feld für ein musikalisches Theater. Zusammenarbeit von Stückeschreiber und Komponist. – Komponist als Dramatiker (Mozart, Verdi, Wagner).[6]

---

4   Weill, zitiert nach ebd., S. 179. Er wählte damit die gleiche Bezeichnung, die er auch in seinem Programmhefttext benutzte.

5   Bernstein, 1957. Vgl. auch Bernstein, 1983, S. 84.

6   Weill, zitiert nach Hinton & Schebera, 2000, S. 145.

Für das »Dazwischen«, in dem Weill sein Arbeitsfeld sah, verortete er indes die mit Abstand bedeutendste institutionelle Verwirklichungsmöglichkeit am Broadway. Und die Werke, die er bis zu *Street Scene* komponierte, waren in der Tat Broadway Musicals – wenngleich alle mit einem eigenen Gattungskonzept, manche davon (wie *Knickerbocker Holiday* und *One Touch of Venus*) sehr nah an der traditionellen Musical Comedy, andere (wie *Lady in the Dark*) formal experimenteller, aber in jedem Fall stilistisch weit von etwas entfernt, das man im engeren Sinne als Oper hätte bezeichnen können. Zahlreiche Broadwayproduktionen der 1940er und 50er Jahre bezeugen eine tendenzielle Abkehr von der Musical Comedy, und um den Ort des »Dazwischen« wenigstens anzudeuten und dem Publikum eine Orientierungshilfe zu geben, wurden zahlreiche Genre-Subtitel erfunden.[7]

Dass das Musical auf andere Gattungen musikalisch verweist, sich ästhetisch und stilistisch bei ihnen bedient, gehört zu seinen konstruktiven Selbstverständlichkeiten. Warum aber wurden Werke wie *Street Scene* oder *West Side Story* als Ganzes dem Operngenre zugeschrieben? Für die Bewertung dieser Beobachtung leihe ich eine Idee aus dem Kapitel »Wann ist Kunst?« in Nelson Goodmans *Weisen der Welterzeugung* (Goodman, 1990). Goodman meinte hier, die Frage »Was ist Kunst?« sei falsch gestellt, richtiger müsste es heißen: »Wann ist Kunst?« Entsprechend wäre die Frage: »Wann ist Oper?«, oder für unseren Fall: »Wann ist ein Musical Oper?«, nicht im Hinblick auf innere Werkstrukturen, sondern auf das zu diskutieren, was Goodman das »Funktionieren als Symbol« nennt, denn »ebenso wie ein Objekt zu gewissen Zeiten und unter gewissen Umständen ein Symbol sein kann […], so kann es sein, daß ein Objekt zu gewissen Zeiten ein Kunstwerk ist und zu anderen nicht« (Goodman, 1990, S. 87). Und genauso kann es sein, dass einem Musical in einem bestimmten Kontext die Zugehörigkeit zum Operngenre zugesprochen wird, und diese »symbolische« Zuordnung (Goodman, 1990, S. 90–91) wäre zunächst als Faktum *sui generis*, d.h. diskursiv, und nicht aus der Struktur des ihm zugeschriebenen Werkes legitimiert. Allerdings ist ja nicht auszuschließen (wenngleich auch nicht zwangsläufig Ursache), dass ein Werk in sich Elemente enthält, die dem erwähnten Diskurs absichtsvoll zuarbeiten.[8]

Das von Goodman gewählte Beispiel des Steins, der auf der Straße liegt, kommt unserem Beispiel entgegen: »Der Stein ist normalerweise kein Kunstwerk, während er auf der Straße liegt, aber er kann es sein, wenn er in einem Kunstmuseum aufgestellt wird« (Goodman, 1990, S. 87), so heißt es bei Goodman. Denn immerhin scheint es doch etwas mit dem Kunstcharakter eines Musicals zu tun zu haben, wenn man es

---

7   Vgl. zu dieser Problematik Kowalke, 2002.

8   Dennoch plädiere ich – im Sinn von Stuart Halls' Vorschlag – dafür, Encodierung und Decodierung als zwei Prozeduren zu betrachten, die analytisch voneinander zu trennen sind; gibt es doch kein klareres Warnzeichen vor dem intentionalen Fehlschluss.

in einem metaphorischen Museum verorten mag, das durch den Gattungsbegriff ›Oper‹ verkörpert wird.

4.

Doch ging es nicht darum, den ›Stein‹, das populäre »lebendige« Theater, von der ›Straße‹ (dem Broadway) in das von Weill so benannte Museum, die Met, zu verfrachten. Noch 1929 avisierte er, im Falle von *Aufstieg und Fall der Stadt Mahagonny*, das Berliner Publikum der kommerziellen Theater, nicht das Opernpublikum, als das seine, und versuchte für die geplante Aufführung in der Krolloper »das Publikum der *Dreigroschenoper* (das zum grossen Teil noch niemals in einem Opernhaus war) für *Mahagonny*« zu interessieren.[9] Auch vor der *Street-Scene*-Premiere hatte Weill eine öffentliche Gattungsinszenierung versucht, die gezielt die öffentliche Rezeption steuern und das Broadwaypublikum für das neue Werk interessieren sollte. In der redaktionellen Vorbemerkung der *Street-Scene*-Vorankündigung wurde Weill mit dem Appell zitiert: »Nehmt die amerikanische Oper aus dem Opernhaus heraus und bringt sie auf das lebendige Theater!« Mit lebendigem meinte er das kommerzielle Theater des Broadway. Doch auch dies musste noch nicht zwangsläufig bedeuten: »Mein neues Werk ist eine Oper!«

Die Presse war da freigiebiger. »Opera on Broadway« titelte die hier beispielhaft angeführte, überschwängliche Kritik von Olin Downs in der *New York Times*, und mit ihm eine große Anzahl von Kritikern (Kowalke, 2003, S. 287, Fn 16). *Life* brachte am 24.02.1947 eine vierseitige Kolumne unter dem Titel »New version of Street Scene is a major step toward American operas« und schrieb die Oper dem »German composer Kurt Weill« zu – eine Formulierung, die Weill zu einer giftigen Replik veranlasste, denn er, inzwischen US-amerikanischer Staatsbürger, wollte sich durchaus nicht mehr als deutscher Komponist zugeordnet wissen.[10] Dennoch übernahm er in Folge die Gattungszuschreibung für *Street Scene*.

Das bedeutete nun doch eine deutliche Verschiebung, die die ursprüngliche Bezeichnung »Dramatic Musical« noch bewusst gemieden hatte, und die das Werk (und seinen Komponisten) in einem Trend hin zur US-amerikanischen Nationaloper verortete. Seinen Eltern in Israel berichtete Weill stolz, er sei »nun plötzlich zu

---

9   »Wir müssen alles tun, um die Möglichkeiten zu schaffen, dass das Publikum der *Drei-groschenoper* (das zum grossen Teil noch niemals in einem Opernhaus war) für *Mahagonny* interessiert wird.« Weill, zitiert nach Grosch, 2002, S. 165.

10 In *Life Magazine*, 17[!].03.1947, S. 17, Fotoreproduktion und deutsche Übersetzung in Hinton & Schebera, 2000, S. 186–187.

einer Art ›Klassiker‹ befördert worden, und man beginnt allgemein von der ›historischen Bedeutung‹ meiner Werke zu sprechen.«[11]

Die Kategorisierung von *Street Scene* als Oper ist also zuallererst eine diskursive Zuschreibung, strukturelle Argumente hierfür lassen sich kaum objektivieren. Kim Kowalke hat in seiner Analyse von *Street Scene* eine Vielzahl an musikalisch-stilistischen Verweisen herausgearbeitet, die das Werk auszeichnen; diese reichen von folkloristischen Blues-Nummern über Stilelemente verschiedenster Stadien des amerikanischen Musiktheaters (Victor Herbert, George Gershwin, Richard Rodgers) bis hin zu ausgereiften Opernarien, in denen Stilanklänge an Guiseppe Verdi, Richard Wagner und Giacomo Puccini bedeutsam werden (Kowalke, 1998). Der permanente Stilwechsel oder, wenn man so will, Wechsel in der Stilhöhe, ist ein gezielt eingesetztes musikdramaturgisches Mittel: So wie Elmer Rice, der sein Drama *Street Scene* mit Claude Lorrains Gemälde *Landscape with figures* verglich, von welchem es angeblich inspiriert war (Rice, 1963, S. 237), ging es letztlich auch Weill in der musikalischen Dramaturgie um eine unterschiedliche und deutlich unterscheidbare Zeichnung in der Tiefenschärfe der Charaktere. In der Tat sind es vier Figuren, die im Laufe des Stückes als »Hauptfiguren« herausmodelliert werden und im Vordergrund der dramatischen Handlung stehen. Doch wachsen diese aus der Gruppe der Gesamtheit heraus. Und um diese größere Gruppe, die ja paradigmatisch für die US-amerikanische Gesellschaft der Gegenwart einstehen sollte, ging es ja in dem Stück, nicht um das fast austauschbare Einzelschicksal eines Eifersuchtsmordes. Mit der Bildmetapher Rices gesprochen: Opernhaftigkeit kennzeichnet zwar den Vordergrund (die vier Hauptfiguren), die zentrale Thematik von *Street Scene* spielt sich aber nicht im Vordergrund, sondern in der Gesamtkonstellation, im kommunikativen Wechselverhältnis der verschiedenen Ebenen ab. Somit wird »Opernhaftigkeit« ebenso als Marker für eine dramaturgische Ebene des Werkes verwendet wie die populären oder folkloristischen Elemente für eine andere. Die als Realitätsfragment in das Werk eingebrachte Stilebene der »Opernhaftigkeit« ist somit ein durch die Referenz auf die Oper funktionierendes Stilmittel (und eines von vielen), ein Mittel zur Herstellung eines musikdramatischen Gestus, und nicht generischer Rahmen oder musikdramatischer Ausgangspunkt.[12]

Es liegt also der Verdacht nahe, dass es bei der Zuschreibung zum Operngenre weniger um das Modellieren einer Gattungskategorisierung geht, sondern um eine Aufwertungsrhetorik. Diese setzt aber eine bestimmte Rahmung voraus, die das

---

11   Brief Weills an seine Eltern vom 06.09.1949, zitiert nach Symonette & Juchem, 2000, S. 419f.

12   Sieht man einmal von der so genannten Zeitoper der 1920er-Jahre ab, die die ausgeklügelten Pastiche-Mechanismen des Broadway in mancher Hinsicht vorwegnahm und bei der gerade umgekehrt die Adaption populärmusikalischer Stilelemente als prägnant wahrgenommen wurde, wie die Kennzeichnung von Ernst Kreneks *Jonny spielt auf* als Jazzoper verdeutlicht.

amerikanische, leichte, kommerzielle Genre in einem ästhetischen Gefälle zum europäischen, anspruchsvollen, höfischer Tradition und den damit einhergehenden Subventionierungsmodellen entspringenden Operngenre verortet; oder anders gesagt: Wer ein Musical aufwerten will, indem er es als Oper bezeichnet, setzt voraus, dass die Oper etwas prinzipiell besseres ist als ein Musical.

Ein solches Wertungsgefälle kann für Weill definitiv nicht angenommen werden. Für Weill hatte die Beschäftigung mit der Oper immer zwei Seiten. Schon in den Jahren zwischen dem ökonomischen Erfolg seiner *Dreigroschenoper* (1928) und seiner Emigration (1933) hatte er innerhalb des Spektrums zwischen dem kommerziellen Produktionssystem der urbanen Geschäftstheater und demjenigen der subventionierten Staats- und Stadttheater seinen Platz näher bei den Ersteren gesehen (Grosch, 2003). Seine letzten Opernversuche vor der Emigration, *Aufstieg und Fall der Stadt Mahagonny* und *Die Bürgschaft*, lassen sich als Kraftanstrengung lesen, sich im Sektor des staatlich kontrollierten, öffentlichen Theaterbetriebs durch »ernste« Werke zu etablieren – ein Versuch indes, der schon vor 1933 letztlich an den antisemitischen Anfeindungen scheiterte, für die gerade dieses Produktionssystem sich als besonders anfällig erwies (Grosch, 2003). In den Jahren nach seiner Ankunft in New York verstand er das Musical-Theater des Broadway als das lebendige amerikanische Theater, den Opernbetrieb an der Metropolitan Opera hingegen als museal.

Mit der sukzessiv stärker werdenden Zuschreibung von *Street Scene* zur Operngattung durch Weill geht die tendenzielle rhetorische Degradierung der anderen am Werk beteiligten Autoren einher. Denn was war *Street Scene* für Langston Hughes, was für Elmer Rice, wenn es doch primär dem Programm der Traumerfüllung von Weill folgte? Eine solche Änderung der Balance der Autoritäten im Kontext von Autorschaft ist – denken wir an die Gleichwertigkeit der Wahrnehmung solch paradigmatischer Broadway-Produktivteams wie Rodgers/Hammerstein, Lerner/Loewe etc. – für das Musical undenkbar und wird letztlich dadurch legitimiert, dass die Oper, zumal in den Ankündigungsroutinen im europäischen Theaterwesen des 20. Jahrhunderts, primär als musikalische Gattung, und somit als Werk des Komponisten präsentiert wird, und nicht Produkt eines kollaborativen Prozesses.

5.

»[…] one real, moving American opera that any American can understand (and one that is, notwithstanding, a serious musical work)« – einen solchen Kompositionsplan fasste Bernstein Anfang 1948 (Bernstein 1982, S. 131), und erklärte weiterhin in einem Interview: ›I am the logical man to write the Great American Opera‹ (zit. n. Seldes, 2009, S. 43). Aus dem Munde eines »Internationalisten, der glaubt, in unseren Tagen sei ein musikalischer wie ein politischer Nationalismus lebensnotwendig« (Bernstein, 1983, S. 70), erscheint somit die Kontextualisierung des Operngenres mit der nationalen Sache eine Zuschreibung von unmittelbar politischer Bedeutung: Wie Seldes (2009, S. 43f.) verdeutlicht, waren Bernsteins Ambitionen für eine nationale Oper durch sein Engagement für den Präsidentschaftskandidaten Edgar A. Wallace (der Progressiven Partei) motiviert, der indes im November 1948 die Wahl verlor.

Immerhin: *West Side Story* war diese Great American Opera nicht, wie die von Bernstein festgehaltene Äußerung des designierten Buchautoren des Musicals Arthur Laurents aus dem Jahr 1949 deutlich macht: »I want to make one thing clear before we go any further, and that is that I'm not writing any fucking libretto for any goddamned Bernstein opera« (Garebian, 1998, S. 30). Die rhetorische Kopplung des Namens des Komponisten mit dem Gattungsbegriff macht dabei zugleich deutlich, dass zumindest für Laurents die oben geschilderte Wahrnehmung der Autorschaft bei der Operngattung die Entscheidung beeinflusst hat, das Bühnenwerk von den Kriterien der Opernhaftigkeit fernzuhalten.

Es liegt auf der Hand, dass im Kontext des bereits erwähnten, durch Bernstein selbst betriebenen späteren Umwertungsprozesses gerade diese Devise ins Gegenteil umschlagen würde, als der Komponist zu Beginn der 1980er Jahre eine Studio-Gesamtaufnahme der Show konzipierte. Mit dem 1984 veröffentlichten Doppelalbum, das bei einem der renommiertesten Klassik-Labels, der Deutschen Grammophon, herauskam, existierte dann eine neue, als repräsentativ aufgenommene Referenzaufnahme, die das Original-Broadway-Cast-Album von 1957 und das Soundtrack-Album zum Film von 1961 in der Rezeption (und den Rundfunkausstrahlungen) verdrängen sollte. Damit wurden in der öffentlichen Wahrnehmung die Stimmen von Kiri Te Kanawa (die u.a. als Desdemona in Verdis *Otello* Erfolge gehabt hatte) und José Carreras als die Stimmen von Maria und Tony assoziiert.

Noch bevor eine auf breiter Basis sich etablierende wissenschaftliche Diskussion um Bernsteins Oeuvre, und damit auch um sein selbst inszeniertes »Meisterwerk«[13], begann, hatte dieser eine neue, wirkungsstarke (wenngleich weder unumstrittene noch unwidersprochene) Aufnahme vorgelegt, die den verführerischen Charakter der »definitive, final version of the work« des Komponisten hatte, wie Elisabeth Wells pointiert (Wells, 2011, S. 16).

Andreas Jaensch hat 2003 die *West Side Story* als einen Schritt in Bernsteins Musiktheaterschaffen »Auf dem Weg zu einer amerikanischen Oper« interpretiert.[14] Wells setzt einem solchen Werkverständnis eine Lesart der *West Side Story* als »authentic version« entgegen, die »our own communal image« entspricht. Unausgesprochen

---

13 Vgl. zu dieser Debatte das Kapitel »The Unrealized Masterwork« in Seldes, 2009, S. 168–174.
14 Vgl. Jaensch, 2003, S. 71–101. Jaenschs Kapitel zur *West Side Story* ist mit »Musical oder Oper?« übertitelt, und seine Analyse läuft im Wesentlichen auf das Opern-Argument zu.

bleibt dabei, an was für eine abstrakte Gemeinschaft dabei zu denken wäre. Zumindest liegt hier der Verdacht nahe, dass das gleiche »Wir« gemeint ist, das Bernstein als nationales Wir heraufbeschwor, als er (10 Monate vor der *West-Side-Story*-Premiere, in einem Fernsehvortrag zum Musical) meinte, dem Broadway – und damit den USA – möge in Bälde ein amerikanischer Mozart, mit einer amerikanischen »Zauberflöte« im Gepäck, erscheinen (Bernstein, 1976, S. 169). Manche Bernsteinforscher ließen es sich nicht nehmen, die von dem Komponisten suggestiv offen gelassene Lücke mit der Aussage zu schließen, dass sich diese Prophezeiung durch Bernstein und *West Side Story* erfüllen sollte.[15]

Die Denkfigur von der *West Side Story* als Meisterwerk ließ Bernstein und die Deutsche Grammophon das Stück wirkungsmächtig als Oper neu erfinden. Zu der 1984 eingespielten Version wiederum kann kein Korrelat als szenisches Bühnenwerk mehr existieren. Denn im Gegensatz zu *Street Scene*, das in europäischen Mehrspartenhäusern innerhalb der Opernsparte von Opernensembles aufgeführt und als Oper angekündigt wird, sind Opernaufführungen der *West Side Story* im Stil von Bernsteins Studioaufnahme szenisch kaum vorstellbar, so lange für Anita, Riff und andere Figuren nicht erhebliche Kompromisse im Tänzerischen gemacht würden. Gerade die von Bernstein 1984 präsentierte Version, be- und gefangen in der »operatic trap«, markiert eine populäre Lesart im Sinne einer »populären Klassik«, die durch den populären, nationalen Interpreten Leonard Bernstein (im Sinne der Auteur-Theorie) repräsentiert wird und nicht durch einen Autor oder Komponisten. Die »Veroperung« des Musicals erweist sich letztlich als Akt der (Re-)Konstitution, der nachträglichen Umschreibung der *West Side Story* in das Narrativ einer US-amerikanischen Nationaloper hinein. Deren Zweck war nicht zuletzt die Einschreibung ihres Komponisten in dieses Narrativ. Sie ist typisches Beispiel von gezielter Herstellung starker Autorschaft, wie sie in kulturellen Nation-Building-Prozessen oft besonders diskursprägende Bedeutung gewinnt. Die De-Autorisierung populärer Texturen in einem von Massenmedien regulierten kommunikativen Gedächtnis spielt dem Argument Wells' zu, dass sich Musicals »einer populären Bedeutungskonstitution« anbieten.[16]

Kulturelle Nation-Building-Prozesse wirken auf der Suche nach starken Identifikationsfiguren solchen Tendenzen entgegen, Kunst und Wissenschaft tendieren deshalb leicht dazu, im Sinne der Etablierung von Meistererzählungen kollaborative Prozesse in den Hintergrund treten zu lassen oder durch Hierarchisierungen zu ka-

---

15 Beste Beispiele sind Gräwe, 1987, und Stempel, 1988.
16 John Fiske weist darauf hin, dass in der populären Kultur die Künstlerverehrung nicht primär auf Texte und Autoren als vielmehr auf Darsteller resp. Interpreten gerichtet ist, vgl. Fiske, 2010, S. 452.

schieren, und dabei die Zuschreibung zur American Opera unhinterfragt zur Ausgangsbasis zu machen.[17] So vermerkte 1986 Larry Stempel:

> Whatever its merits as a work in its own right, *Street Scene* has come to occupy the keystone in the conceptual arch which connects such American Operas that followed it to Broadway as *Regina* (1949), and *The Saint of Bleeker Street* (1954) with such Broadway »musicals« as *The Most Happy Fella* (1956) and *West Side Story* (1957). (Stempel, 1986, S. 328)

American Opera ist keine strukturell in Werken der Broadwayliteratur festzumachende Kategorie.[18] Es ist eine Zuschreibung, deren Funktion sich aus künstlerischem *Impression Management* der Komponisten, Meistererzählungen der Forschung und Presse zusammensetzt. Beide sind letztlich bezogen auf nationale Diskurse in einer *Imagined Community* und die dazugehörigen historischen Narrative.

Literatur

Bernstein, L. (1957). *Excerpts from Bernstein's West Side Log.* http://www..com/archives_excerpts.php (abgerufen am 10. September 2014).

Bernstein, L. (1976). Das Amerikanische Musical: Fernsehsendung vom 7. Oktober 1956. In ders., *Freude an der Musik* (S. 142–169). Frankfurt am Main: Fischer.

Bernstein, L. (1982). *Findings.* New York: Anchor Doubleday.

Bernstein, L. (1983). *Erkenntnisse.* München: Goldmann.

Fiske, J. (2010). Populäre Texte, Sprache und Alltagskultur. In M. S. Kleiner (Hrsg.), *Grundlagentexte zur sozialwissenschaftlichen Medienkritik* (S. 438–454). Wiesbaden: VS Verlag für Sozialwissenschaften.

Garebian, K. (1998). *The Making of West Side Story.* Oakville: Mosaic Press.

Goodman, N. (1990). *Weisen der Welterzeugung.* Frankfurt am Main: Suhrkamp.

---

17   Ein aktuelles Beispiel hierfür ist Simeone, 2009. Die einseitige Autorenzuschreibung im Titel scheint hier ebenso bezeichnend wie der Titel der Reihe, in der das Buch erschienen ist: »Landmarks in music since 1950«, aber auch der Text selbst tendiert einseitig zu einem traditionellen Meisterdiskurs, vgl. hierzu meine Rezension Grosch, 2013.

18   Aufschlussreich ist, wie Annette Kreuziger-Herr in ihrer klugen, historisch umfassenden Betrachtung der US-amerikanischen Operngeschichte des 20. Jahrhunderts eine Reihe von Broadway Musicals, darunter *Street Scene, West Side Story* sowie Werke von Rodgers/Hammerstein, Frank Loesser bis hin zu *Sweeney Todd* von Stephen Sondheim mit den Begriffen »American Opera on Broadway« oder »Broadway Opera« für »treffend bezeichnet« hält, und zwar weil hier eine »Schnittmenge von Stil, Inhalt und Präsentation angedeutet« sei. Wertsteuernde Zuschreibung als Kriterium thematisiert sie nicht, sie unterläuft ihr aber durchaus, wenn sie unterstellt, dass hier »handwerkliches Können und Solidität über die kommerziellen Aspekte gestellt werden«. Vgl. Kreutziger-Herr, 2000, S. 366f.

Gräwe, K. D. (1987). Ein Mozart für Amerika. »West Side Story« von Leonard Bernstein. In H. Danuser, D. Kämper & P. Terse (Hrsg.), *Amerikanische Musik seit Charles Ives* (S. 163–176). Laaber: Laaber-Verlag.

Grosch, N. (Hrsg.) (2002). *Kurt Weill. Briefwechsel mit der Universal Edition.* Stuttgart: Metzler.

Grosch, N. (2003). Kurt Weill und das kommerzielle Musiktheater 1928–1933. In G. Wagner (Hrsg.), *Jahrbuch des staatlichen Instituts für Musikforschung 2003* (S. 265–295), Stuttgart: Metzler. Leicht überarbeitete englische Fassung dieses Textes: Kurt Weill, Mahagonny and the Commercialization of Berlin Musical Theatre in the Weimar Republic. In J. Hung, G. Weiss-Sussex & G. Wilkes (Hrsg.), *Beyond Glitter and Doom. The Contingency of the Weimar Republic* (S. 192–208). München: Iudicium Verlag.

Grosch, N. (2013). Simeone, N. (2009). Leonard Bernstein: West Side Story. Farnham: Ashgate (Rezension). In *Lied und populäre Kultur/Song and Popular Culture*, 58, 268–271.

Hammerstein II, O. (1945). *Carmen Jones.* New York: Knopf.

Hinton, S. & Schebera, J. (Hrsg.) (2000). *Musik und musikalisches Theater. Gesammelte Schriften. Mit einer Auswahl von Gesprächen und Interviews.* Mainz: Schott.

Jaensch, A. (2003). *Leonard Bernsteins Musiktheater: Auf dem Weg zu einer amerikanischen Oper.* Kassel: Bärenreiter.

Kowalke, K. H. (1998). Kurt Weill, Moderne und populäre Kultur: Öffentlichkeit als Stil. In N. Grosch u.a. (Hrsg.), *Emigrierte Komponisten in der Medienlandschaft des Exils 1933–1945* (S. 171–220). Stuttgart: M & P Verlag für Wissenschaft und Forschung.

Kowalke, K. H. (2002). Das goldene Zeitalter des Musicals. In A. Geraths & C. M. Schmidt (Hrsg.), *Musical. Das unterhaltende Genre* (= *Handbuch der Musik im 20. Jahrhundert, Bd. 6*) (S. 137–178). Laaber: Laaber-Verlag.

Kowalke, K. H. (2003). Kurt Weill and the Quest for American Opera. In H. Danuser & H. Gottschewski (Hrsg.), *Amerikanismus – Americanism – Weill: die Suche nach kultureller Identität in der Moderne* (S. 283–301). Schliengen: Argus.

Kreutziger-Herr, A. (2000). What it takes »to write a real American Opera«: Ein Jahrhundert Operngeschichte in den USA. In U. Bermbach (Hrsg.), *Oper im 20. Jahrhundert: Entwicklungstendenzen und Komponisten* (S. 348–383). Stuttgart: Metzler.

Rice, E. (1963). *Minority Report: An Autobiography.* New York: Simon & Schuster.

Seldes, B. (2009). *Leonard Bernstein: The Political Life of an American Musician.* Berkeley, CA: University of California Press.

Simeone, N. (2009). *Leonard Bernstein: West Side Story.* Farnham: Ashgate.

Stempel, L. (1986). »Street Scene« and the Enigma of Broadway Opera. In K. H. Kowalke (Hrsg.), *A New Orpheus: Essays on Kurt Weill* (S. 321–341). New Haven: Yale University Press.

Stempel, L. (1988). Broadway's Mozartean Moment, or: An Amadeus in Amber. In St. Letbetter (Hrsg.), *Sennets & Tuckets: A Bernstein Celebration* (S. 39–55). Boston: Boston Symphony Orchestra.

Symonette, L. & Juchem, E. (Hrsg.). (2000). *Kurt Weill: Briefe an die Familie: (1914–1950) (= Veröffentlichungen der Kurt-Weill-Gesellschaft Dessau, Bd. 3)* (S. 419–420). Stuttgart: Metzler.

Symonette, L. & Kowalke, K. H. (Hrsg.) (1996). *Speak Low (When You Speak Love): The Letters of Kurt Weill and Lotte Lenya.* Berkeley, CA: University of California Press.

Wells, E. A. (2011). *West Side Story: Cultural Perspectives on an American Musical.* Lanham: Scarecrow Press.

Weill, K. (1947). *Liner Notes for the Original Cast Recording of »Street Scene«.* http://www.kwf.org/liner-notes-for-the-original-cast-recording-of-qstreet-sceneq (abgerufen am 10. September 2014).

Weill, K. (1947). Letters to the Editor. In *Life Magazine*, 17. März, S. 17.

Marie Louise Herzfeld-Schild

The Sound of Music (1959) – »A Great American Opera«?

1.

Im November 2012 konnte man im sozialen Netzwerk *Facebook* einen Online-Wettbewerb verfolgen, bei dem eine Reise nach Salzburg verlost wurde. Es handelte sich dabei um den »Ultimate Sound of Music Fan Contest«, ausgeschrieben von *Tourism Salzburg* und Austrian Airlines und offen für alle US-Bürger über achtzehn Jahren. Hauptpreis war eine einwöchige Flugreise nach Salzburg für zwei Erwachsene und zwei Kinder »to experience the city, including access to Sound of Music attractions.«[1] Interessenten sollten zunächst mindestens fünf von sieben Fragen zu *The Sound of Music* beantworten und dann in 250 Wörtern beschreiben, womit sie eine Woche in Salzburg verbringen würden, wenn ihnen die Familie von Trapp, von der das Musical *The Sound of Music* erzählt, als Fremdenführer zur Verfügung stünde. Unter den zahlreichen Einsendungen gewann ein Eintrag die Online-Abstimmung, der sich am Song »Do-Re-Mi« orientierte, der in der Verfilmung von *The Sound of Music* in einer Vielzahl von Szenenwechseln die Stadt Salzburg beleuchtet, und sehr gute Kenntnisse sowohl des Musicals als auch der Salzburger Attraktionen zeigt:

> Day 1) Do — I would ‚do' the old town area and cross the Mozart footbridge singing and skipping with the von Trapp kids.

> Day 2) Re — I would ‚re-'ally enjoy seeing the Abbey and hearing them sing. Would Maria introduce me to the Mother Superior?

> Day 3) Mi — this trip would be all about ‚me'! Maybe visit a fantastic spa near town? Perhaps the Baroness knows of one?

> Day 4) Fa — I don't think it's that ‚fa-r' to travel to Mondsee to see the church they were married in — I hear it's beautiful. I'd ask Liesl to show me as she was maid of honor.

> Day 5) So — The mountains are ‚so' beautiful! Maybe a long day hike up the Untersberg for some amazing views with Max?

> Day 6) La — ‚La'-ter on at night, a show to see the Salzburg Marionettes would be fantastic with Gretl.

---

1 http://forever-liesl.travellerspoint.com/1/.

Day 7) Ti — I like ‚tea', but a Salzburg coffee house with some yummy pastries sounds even better. Kurt seems like he could recommend a good pastry.

Day 8) Do — What, time to leave? Even though I ‚do-'n't want to, I guess Salzburg will always be there to visit again.[2]

Die Verfasserin dieser Zeilen mobilisierte per *Facebook* alle ihre Freunde, die diese Anfrage wiederum weiterleiteten, und einen Tag vor Wettbewerbsende forderte sogar der Bürgermeister ihres Wohnortes in Massachussets zur Abstimmung auf.

Die vierköpfige Gewinnerfamilie besuchte Salzburg im Juni des darauffolgenden Jahres.[3] Neben dem üblichen ‚Sightseeing' besuchten sie die Original-Drehplätze des Filmmusicals von 1965 und nahmen an der Sound of Salzburg Dinner Show teil, die in einem traditionellen Ratskeller österreichische Küche mit der musikalischen Tradition Salzburgs kombiniert, d.h. eine Live-Performance von Songs aus Richard Rodgers und Oscar Hammersteins Musical sowie Opernmelodien insbesondere von Wolfgang Amadeus Mozart.[4] Dieselben Salzburger Attraktionen zu *The Sound of Music* werden alljährlich von etwa 300.000 überwiegend amerikanischen Touristen besucht.[5]

Diesen Wettbewerb nimmt der vorliegende Beitrag zum Ausgangspunkt, um darüber nachzudenken, worin die Ausmaße der *The Sound of Music*-Begeisterung in der US-amerikanischen Bevölkerung begründet liegen. Betrachtungen der politischen und kulturhistorischen Aufführungsumstände und Reflexionen über die Unterschiede zwischen der Bühnen- und der Filmversion des Musicals werden im Folgenden die außergewöhnliche Rezeptionsintensität näher beleuchten und damit hoffentlich die Suche nach einer »Great American Opera« um ein weiteres, dem populären Musiktheater entspringenden Phänomen bereichern.

2.

Im November 1959 feierte das Musical *The Sound of Music* am New Yorker Broadway seine Premiere. Als Textgrundlage griff es lose auf die Lebenserinnerungen Maria von Trapps zurück, die zehn Jahre zuvor unter dem Titel *The Story of the Trapp Family Singer* in Philadelphia erschienen waren und zu einem Besteller wurden (Maslon, 2007, S. 59). Sie erzählen die Geschichte der Salzburger Sängerfamilie von Trapp, die aus politischer Überzeugung nach dem Anschluss Österreichs an Nazi-

---

2 Ebd.
3 Zu dieser Reise siehe den Blog der Gewinnerin auf ebd.
4 Vgl. http://www.soundofsalzburg.info/history-of-a-dinner-concert.htm.
5 Vgl. http://www.austria.info/uk/art-culture/the-sound-of-music-as-tracht-ambassador-1523 543.html; zum Salzburg-Tourismus siehe den Sammelband Kammerhofer-Aggermann & Keul, 2000.

deutschland ihr Land verließ, in die USA emigrierte und dort eine äußerst erfolgreiche Musikkarriere erlebte.

Die mit diesen Lebenserinnerungen ausgesprochen frei umgehende Musicalshow war die letzte gemeinsame Arbeit des Erfolgsduos Richard Rodgers und Oscar Hammerstein und lebte nicht nur von deren Songs, sondern auch von der berühmten Hauptdarstellerin Mary Martin. Allein die erste Produktion erreichte in vier Jahren Laufzeit 1.443 Aufführungen und war damit ein außergewöhnlicher Publikumserfolg – wenn auch durchaus kein Kritikererfolg, denn vor allem in den intellektuellen Zeitungen der Ostküste wurde *The Sound of Music* als zu »sweet« oder »saccherine« (Hirsch, 1993, S. 8) teilweise harsch angegriffen. Dennoch gewann die Show im Jahre 1960 acht Tony Awards, unter anderem für das beste Musical, die beste Hauptdarstellerin und den besten Komponisten.

Es war jedoch die Verfilmung von Robert Wise aus dem Jahre 1965, die dem Erfolg des Musicals noch die Krone aufsetzte und *The Sound of Music* in den USA zu einem Kultstatus verhelfen sollte. Auch diese Version des Musicals wurde mit Preisen überhäuft, so unter anderem 1966 mit Academy Awards in den Kategorien Bester Film, Beste Regie, Bester Schnitt, Beste Filmmusik und Bester Ton sowie Golden Globes in den Kategorien: Bester Film (Komödie oder Musical) und Beste Hauptdarstellerin (Komödie oder Musical) für Julie Andrews in der Rolle der Maria. Julie Andrews war im Jahr zuvor für ihren ersten Kinofilm *Mary Poppins* ebenfalls (durch einen Golden Globe sowie einen Oscar) ausgezeichnet worden; insbesondere mit ihrer Darstellung der Maria gilt sie als besondere Identifikationsfigur für zahlreiche Generationen von Zuschauern.

Der große Erfolg des Films überraschte nicht nur die Produzenten und Mitwirkenden, die sich allesamt der Gefahr der zu großen »Sweetness« bewusst gewesen waren, sondern auch Kritiker und Fans. Der Film überquerte nationale Grenzen sowie Generationsgrenzen.[6] Bis heute gibt es vermutlich kein Kind in den USA, das die Songs aus *The Sound of Music* nicht kennengelernt hat, sei es zu Hause, im Kindergarten oder in der Schule. Der Film wird außerdem jedes Jahr zu Weihnachten im Fernsehen gezeigt und seit 2005 veranstaltet die Hollywood Bowl in Los Angeles ein alljährliches *Sing-Along*, das stets ausverkauft ist.

Da in der Rezeptionsgeschichte das Bühnenmusical nahezu untrennbar mit dem Film verbunden ist, kann auch in der Betrachtung der Rezeptionsbedeutung von *The Sound of Music* nur schwer ein Unterschied zwischen der Bühnen- und der Leinwandversion gemacht werden. Zwar liegen zwischen den beiden Uraufführungen sechs Jahre, in denen allein die Musicalshow die Grundlage für den Erfolg legte, doch rückte der Film relativ schnell nach und beeinflusste die Rezeption und damit

---

6   Einzig in Österreich und Deutschland war der Film ein großer Misserfolg, vgl. Starkman, 2000, sowie Junin, 2013.

auch zahlreiche folgende Bühnendarstellungen nicht nur in der Festlegung des örtlichen Geschehens auf Salzburg (im Musical-Libretto heißt es nur »The story is laid in Austria early in 1938«), in Bühnenbild, Kostümwahl und Choreographie, sondern auch insofern, als für den Film neu hinzugefügte Songs immer öfter auch Einzug in das Musical hielten. Für die Frage nach einer »Great American Opera« werden hier somit beide Versionen, auch gerade im Hinblick auf ihre Unterschiede, hinzugezogen.

3.

Es mag verwunderlich erscheinen, dass ein Musical, das auf den ersten Blick inhaltlich faktisch rein gar nichts mit den Vereinigten Staaten von Amerika zu tun hat, zu einem so bedeutenden Identifikationsobjekt für die dortige Nachkriegsgeneration werden konnte, wie es die Rezeptionsgeschichte nahelegt – und ebenso für die folgenden Generationen, wobei es sich hierbei zusätzlich um eine Art Rezeptions*tradition* handelt, die ihre eigenen Topoi mit sich führt.[7] Die rege Anteilnahme des breiten Publikums an Show und Film zeigt, dass auch oder gerade die auf den ersten Blick amerikafernen Inhalte einen Nerv der damaligen Nation getroffen haben müssen. Dabei bedingen sich Angebot und Nachfrage gegenseitig: Einerseits konnten offenbar zahlreiche Amerikaner in diesem Musical ihre eigenen Wünsche, Fragen und Lebensthemen wiederfinden, so dass das Musical gewissermaßen einen Spiegel der gesellschaftlichen und kulturellen Gegebenheiten Nordamerikas darstellte; andererseits machte dieses Musical ganz offensichtlich Identifikationsangebote, für die die amerikanische Öffentlichkeit der 1950er und 1960er Jahren besonders empfänglich war. Es konnte damit öffentlichkeitsbildend wirken und erhält so einen zutiefst amerikanischen Inhalt, der zwischen den Ziegelsteinen der österreichischen Fassade hindurchschimmert.

Doch was waren die Umstände und die Inhalte, die die Rezeptionsgeschichte von *The Sound of Music* in den USA so nachhaltig beeinflussen sollte? Und inwieweit lassen sich dabei Unterschiede zwischen Broadwayshow und Film festmachen?

3.1

Fragt man nach den Ursachen für den ungebrochen anhaltenden Erfolg von *The Sound of Music*, so finden sich in erster Linie folgende Gründe: Die Novizin Maria, die aus dem Kloster als Kindermädchen zu den sieben mutterlosen Trapp-Kindern und ihrem strengen Vater Baron von Trapp geschickt wird, die deren Trostlosigkeit

---

7   Aus diesem Grunde beschränken sich die folgenden Ausführungen auf die Generation der direkten Rezeption.

in Fröhlichkeit verwandelt, durch ihre Eheschließung mit dem Vater die ganze Familie zu allumfassendem Glück führt und dadurch nebenbei auch noch den Titel einer Baroness erhält – diese Maria von Trapp verkörpert als moderne Cinderella den sogenannten amerikanischen Traum »vom Tellerwäscher zum Millionär«; so bezeichnet Raymond Knapp Maria als »idealized American« (Knapp, 2004, S. 139).

Ein weiterer, immer wieder aufgegriffener Topos ist der der Familie, die in *The Sound of Music* allgegenwärtig ist. Die siebenköpfige Kinderschar entzückt nicht nur im Film, sondern ist auch in Bühnenproduktionen stets ein besonderes Highlight (vgl. Abb. 1).

Abbildung 1: Programmheft der Original Broadway-Produktion 1959.

Darüber hinaus ist es nicht allein die Liebe zum Baron von Trapp, die Maria ihren ursprünglichen Plan, Nonne zu werden, verwerfen lässt: Es ist insbesondere die Tatsache, dass durch ihre Hochzeit mit dem Vater die Kinder wieder eine Mutter bekommen und sie wieder zu einer heilen Familie werden. Auch ist es das liebevolle Umgehen Marias mit den Kindern, durch das der Baron Gefühle für sie entwickelt. In diesem Zusammenhang sei betont, dass die »echte« Maria von Trapp wenige Jahre vor der Uraufführung des Musicals als »catholic mother of the year« ausgezeichnet wurde.[8]

Dieser Rezeptionsstrang lässt sich historisch untermauern: Die Uraufführung der Musicalshow 1959 fiel in die Eisenhower-Ära. Den Schock des Koreakrieges hatten die USA seit 1953 hinter sich gelassen und bürgerliche Werte wie die behütete Welt der Kleinfamilie waren das propagierte Ideal. Das *Life Magazine* beispielsweise widmet sich in seiner Ausgabe vom 23. November 1959 (S. 137–146) der Uraufführung des Musicals und stellt in Text und zahlreichen Bildern den Eröffnungssong à la Gregorianik im Kloster, Marias christlichen Glauben, ihre Sorge um die Kinder, ihr Hochzeitskleid oder das Spielen in der Familie in den Mittelpunkt (vgl. Abb. 2).

Abbildung 2: Frontcover Life Magazine, 23. November 1959.

Den Kindern auf und hinter der Bühne werden zwei Extraseiten eingeräumt, gefolgt von Reklameseiten, die themengerecht für Eiscreme, für ein Auto »for more frequent family visits« (ebd., S. 14) sowie für besonders weiche Babytücher werben.

Stacy Wolf beschreibt die Geschlechterrollenzuschreibungen in den 1950er Jahre als »sharply delineated and among the most conservative of any period in U.S. history« und als geprägt von einem Frauenbild, in dem »women were supposed to be homemakers and mothers and to find complete satisfaction in those roles« (Wolf,

---

8   http://www.thecatholicuniverse.com/rosemarie-von-trapp-last-sound-music-children-dies.

2011, S. 27); »›Mother‹ [...] was the key identifying role for women in the 1950s«
(ebd.). In diesem Sinne ist das Liebesduett zwischen dem Baron und Maria mit dem
Titel »An Ordinary Couple« ein Spiegel des damaligen Frauenbildes:

Maria	Baron
An ordinary couple, is all we'll ever be	An ordinary couple, that's all we'll ever be
For all I want of living is to keep you close to me	For all I want of living is to keep you close to me
To laugh and weep together while time goes on its flight	To laugh and weep together while time goes on its flight
To kiss you ev'ry morning and to kiss you ev'ry night	To kiss you ev'ry morning and to kiss you ev'ry night
We'll meet our daily problems and rest when day is done	**Maria**
Our arms around each other in the fading sun	We'll meet our daily problems and rest when day is done
An ordinary couple across the years we'll ride	Our arms around each other in the fading sun
Our arms around each other and our children by our side...	**Beide**
Our arms around each other	An ordinary couple, across the years we'll ride
	Our arms around each other and our children by our side....
	Our arms around each other!

Tabelle 1: http://www.theatre-musical.com/soundofmusic/blyrics.html.

Dieses unaufgeregt sanfte Lied ist in Melodie und Text einfach und repetitiv gehalten. Die Aussage entspricht auf den ersten Blick gänzlich dem Frauenbild der
1950er Jahre und malt ein Leben in familiärer Harmonie. Die unruhige Begleitung
der Streicher jedoch, die sich wie ankündigendes Unheil in der Tiefe windet, gibt
dem Lied eine unbehagliche Färbung, die mit der Zukunft dieses Paares resoniert:
Denn eben dieses hier gemalte Leben, das war dem Publikum durchaus bekannt,
wird der Familie von Trapp durch die Nationalsozialisten verwehrt.

Für den Film wurde dieses Liebeslied mit »Something Good« ersetzt, das ebenfalls
als Duett zwischen Baron von Trapp und Maria angelegt, doch musikalisch ab-
wechslungsreicher, selbstbewusster und textlich von Maria wenn schon nicht eman-
zipiert, so doch immerhin Ich-bezogener gestaltet ist:

Maria

Perhaps I had a wicked childhood
Perhaps I had a miserable youth
But somewhere in my wicked, miserable past
There must have been a moment of truth

For here you are, standing there, loving me
Whether or not you should

So somewhere in my youth or childhood
I must have done something good

Nothing comes from nothing
Nothing ever could

So somewhere in my youth or childhood
I must have done something good

Baron

For here you are, standing there,
loving me
Whether or not you should

Maria

So somewhere in my youth or
childhood
I must have done something good

Beide

Nothing comes from nothing
Nothing ever could

Maria

So somewhere in my youth

Baron

Or childhood

Maria

I must have done something …

Beide

Something good

Tabelle 2: http://theatre-musical.com/soundofmusic/lyrics.html.

Der Film ging mit der Ersetzung von »An Ordinary Couple« durch »Something Good« insofern mit der Zeit, als das Frauenbild der 1950er Jahre im Verlauf der 1960er Jahre nach und nach von der zweiten Welle der Frauenbewegung abgelöst wurde (McLeer, 2002), die ihren Ursprung in den Vereinigten Staaten nahm und thematisch unter anderem an die Einführung der neuartigen Schwangerschaftsverhütung gebunden war. Marias im Film erwachendes Selbstvertrauen findet sich dabei nicht nur in »Something Good«, sondern fast noch deutlicher im ebenfalls für den Film neu komponierten »I Have Confidence«, das bezeichnenderweise mit dem Ausruf »I have confidence in me!« endet. Es sei nur nebenbei angemerkt, dass sich dieser Umschwung in der Frauenrolle schon auf dem Frontcover des *Life Magazins* vom 23. November 1959 ankündigt, das neben dem Foto von Mary Martin als frisch verheiratete Maria von Trapp als weiteres Thema die »controversial world question« der Geburtenkontrolle durch die neuen Möglichkeiten der Antibabypille, die

1960 in den USA zugelassen wurde, ankündigt (vgl. Abb. 2). Auf diesem Cover vereint sich damit in gewisser Weise die Gegenwart von *The Sound of Music* in Form der Bühnenshow mit seiner Zukunft in Form des Films.

Wie Stacy Wolf betont, weist in US-amerikanischen Musicals die Liebesbeziehung zwischen Mann und Frau traditionell über sich selbst hinaus. Männlichkeit versus Weiblichkeit sind zwei Pole, die symbolisch für im weitesten Sinne als »weich« versus »hart« verstandene Gegensätze stehen können: Vernunft versus Gefühl, Frieden versus Krieg oder, wie Wolf es für Baron von Trapp und Maria in *The Sound of Music* aufzeigt, »culture« versus »nature« (Wolf, 2011, S. 8). Diese beiden können jedoch noch für zahlreiche weitere Gegensatzpaare stehen, wie zum Beispiel für starr versus lebendig, Musik verleugnend versus Musik machend oder, wie Knapp es formuliert, »sophisticated, worldly Austria and the military order« versus »rural Austria and the religious order« (Knapp, 2004, S. 135). Durch ihre rollentypischen Zuschreibungen repräsentieren sie »larger struggles in U.S. society that are symbolically resolved in marriage« (Wolf, 2011, S. 9).

Knapp betont, dass sich der Film *The Sound of Music* den traditionellen »marriage trope« (Knapp, 2004, S. 134) des amerikanischen Musiktheaters jedoch zusätzlich für einen besonderen dramaturgischen »Schock« zu Nutze macht: »As the wedding [between Maria and the Baron] concludes, an eerie application of associational montage merges the celebratory wedding bells directly into the deeper bells celebrating the Anschluss, the ›peaceful‹ annexation of Austria by Germany« (ebd., S. 133). Unter diesen Vorzeichen zeigt ein Blick auf die politische Situation der USA im Zeitraum zwischen der Uraufführung der Musicalshow 1959 und der Premiere des Films 1965 eine mögliche Erklärung für die Ersetzung von »An Ordinary Couple« durch »Something Good« auf. Denn in diesen Jahren geschah einiges, was die USA in Aufruhr versetzte: Bürgerrechtsbewegungen verunsicherten das Land, 1962 war das Jahr der Kubakrise, 1963 das der Ermordung John F. Kennedys und 1964 das des Eintritts in den Vietnamkrieg, der mit immer stärker werdenden Protesten einherging. Die propagierte familiäre Eintracht und Sicherheit der 1950er Jahre war gestört; insbesondere durch den Vietnamkrieg war es für die USA, deren Rolle in und nach dem Zweiten Weltkrieg die des »Weltretters« gewesen war, wichtiger denn je, diese positive Rolle nicht nur nach außen, sondern auch und vor allem nach innen zu bestätigen.

Vor dem Hintergrund dieser politischen Situation werden die Schwerpunktverschiebungen von Bühnenshow zu Film deutlich: Was 1965 gebraucht wurde, war erstens ein Vorbild von Einstehen für und Liebe zu einem Vaterland, das von äußeren und inneren Kräften angegriffen wurde, und zweitens eine Stärkung der amerikanischen Moral durch Rückgriff auf einen der nationalen »Gründungsmythen« (Knapp, 2004): Amerika als »Kind« Europas. Österreich übernimmt dabei die Rolle des bedrohten Vaterlands und steht gleichzeitig stellvertretend für dasjenige Europa, auf dessen Erbe man sich mit gutem Gewissen berufen konnte – der sogenannten »Opferthese«, dem Mythos, Österreich sei Hitlers erstes Opfer gewesen, wird damit Tür und Tor geöffnet. Das visuell-musikalische Österreichbild, das Musical und Film vermitteln – Berge, Zwiebeltürmchen und Trachten, Walzer, Ländler und Jodler –, war nun nicht mehr bloßes Nationalkolorit, sondern diente zur besseren Charakterisierung eines Vaterlands und bot damit eine deutlicher umrissene Identifikationsfläche. Die sieben Trapp-Kinder waren nun nicht mehr bloß süß und niedlich, sondern schlüpften in die Rolle Amerikas selbst: Denn ihre Kindheit lag in Europa, doch ihre Zukunft – das wusste jeder Zuschauer – lag in Amerika. Marias strikte Ablehnung der militärischen Trillerpfeife, mit der Baron von Trapp seine Kinder zu rufen pflegte, erhält in diesem Zusammenhang eine besonders aktuelle, pazifistische Note.

Auch der Song »Something Good« ist in diesem Lichte betrachtet nicht nur Ausdruck einer demütigen Haltung Marias ihrem großen Glück gegenüber, sondern lässt sich in doppelter Weise für den »Gründungsmythos« Amerikas fruchtbar machen: Fasst man Maria mit Knapp als Verkörperung des ländlichen Österreichs auf, so wird dieses – als »guter«, weil »ursprünglicher« Teil Europas –, mit den Worten »somewhere in my wicked childhood, I must have done something good« von allen Verflechtungen mit dem Nationalsozialismus freigesprochen. Mit diesem Österreich kann sich Amerika selbst, dessen positive, europäische »Kindheit« durch die »Schlechtigkeit« der jüngsten Vergangenheit in ein schlechtes Licht gerückt war, ein letztes Plätzchen »guter« Vergangenheit sichern.[9] Dies, und nicht nur die Familienidylle aus »An Ordinary Couple«, ist es, von der die Frischverliebten im Jahre 1965 singen.

3.2

Neben dem Topos des Familienidylls wird als Grund für den großen Erfolg von *The Sound of Music* auch auf den Topos der Alpenländer oder allgemeiner auf den Topos der Natur bzw. der Naturgewalten hingewiesen, der in der amerikanischen Kultur eine lange Tradition habe (siehe etwa Ralph Waldo Emersons Essay »Nature«, 1836). Während die Bühnenshow diesen Topos durch ihre im Vergleich geringeren Möglichkeiten nur bedingt umsetzen konnte, so huldigt ihm der Film durch großartige Kameraaufnahmen insbesondere in der berühmten Eröffnungssequenz ausgiebig (vgl. Abb. 3).

---

9   Vgl. auch Knapp, 2004, S. 138, der Salzburg in diesem Zusammenhang als »the essentially good heart of Europe« bezeichnet.

*Abbildung 3: Screenshot aus der Eröffnungssequenz des Films
»The Sound of Music« (DVD 5006506, Twentieth Century Fox 2015).*

Der in dieser Anfangssequenz des Films zu beobachtende Übergang von Erhabenheit hin zur individuellen Bestimmtheit – sowohl auf der Ebene des Klangs, wenn
die Naturgeräusche des Windes und der Vögel zunächst in verstreute Instrumental-
klänge und schließlich in geordnete Musik übergehen, als auch auf der Ebene des
Bildes, wenn die Gestalt der Maria als zunächst kleiner Punkt inmitten der gewaltigen Berglandschaft allmählich in den Mittelpunkt gerückt wird – vermittelt ein Ver-
ständnis der Position des Menschen innerhalb des großen Ganzen, das uns alle
umgibt: unendlich klein und doch unendlich wichtig. Dieser Aspekt des Einzelnen
im größeren Verbund ist bisher seltener in den Blickwinkel gerückt, wenn Gründe
für den großen Erfolg von *The Sound of Music* gesucht werden: nämlich die Rolle
des Einzelnen im großen Ganzen, das sich Nation nennt. Auch hier wird wiederum
die symbolische Bühne des Politischen betreten, was sich auf der Ebene des Natur-
topos am Song »Edelweiss« aufzeigen lässt (vgl. Notenbeispiel 1).

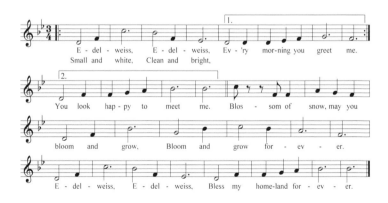

Notenbeispiel 1: Richard Rodgers & Oscar Hammerstein II: »Edelweiss«.

Dieser Song wird oft und gerne als »echtes« österreichisches Volkslied aufgefasst, obwohl er in seiner aus 32 Takten bestehenden AABA-Form einem typischen Tin-Pan-Alley-Song entspricht und auch seine Intervallstruktur weniger für ein volkstümliches als vielmehr für ein »Kunst«-Lied spricht. Seine Inszenierung in *The Sound of Music* jedoch wird dieser Fehlrezeption durchaus gerecht. In der Musicalshow erklingt das Lied auf der Bühne des »Kaltzberg Festivals« nach dem Anschluss Österreichs an Nazideutschland als Abschiedslied des Barons von Trapp. Im Film erhält es zusätzlich einen Platz im familiären Rahmen, als der Vater es mit seiner ältesten Tochter Liesl gemeinsam singt. Hier übernimmt »Edelweiss« tatsächlich die diegetische Funktion eines bekannten Volksliedes. Später, auf der Festivalbühne, inszeniert der Film das Lied jedoch mit politischen Dimensionen eines solchen Ausmaßes, dass bis heute zahlreiche Amerikaner, den ehemaligen Präsidenten Ronald Reagan eingeschlossen (Bernstein, 2005), davon ausgehen, »Edelweiss« sei nicht nur irgendein Volkslied, sondern sogar die österreichische Nationalhymne: Vor den wachsamen Augen zahlreicher Braunhemden und dem Gauleiter in der ersten Reihe lässt Baron von Trapp sein Österreichbild zutiefst emotional und mit brechender Stimme ein letztes Mal vor seiner Emigration musikalisch erstehen, als Reminiszenz und Aufforderung an seine »fellow Austrians«, nicht zu vergessen, was und wo ihre Heimat sei. Schließlich fällt fast das gesamte Publikum aus voller Kehle in seinen Gesang ein.

Dramaturgisch steht »Edelweiss« für Österreich und Vaterlandsliebe, für Widerstand gegen die Bedrohung der Nation von außen (und letztlich auch von innen) und ebenso für Natur und Ursprünglichkeit. Durch die zusätzliche Szene im Film schließt dieser Bedeutungsrahmen noch die familiäre Eintracht mit ein. Die Wortwahl gibt darüber hinaus Konnotationen des Puren, Unschuldigen und Unberührten (Knapp, 2004, S. 140).

Eine eindeutige Funktion im Imagekampf Amerikas der 1960er Jahren erhält »Edelweiss«, wenn man mit Nils Grosch im Musical-Ort »Österreich« nicht einen »regional gemeinten (topischen)«, sondern einen »idealen (utopischen) Raum (nämlich [ein] idealisierte[s], abstrakte[s] Amerika)« (Grosch, 2014, S. 1f.) versteht, vor dessen Folie sich eine Bewegung abspielt, die Grosch als ein »Woher« bezeichnet, im Gegensatz zu einem »Wohin«, wie es in Rodgers and Hammersteins erstem Musical *Oklahoma!* (1943) verhandelt werde (ebd., S. 7). Während mit diesem »Wohin« ein Prozess des Sesshaftwerdens von zuvor umherziehenden Siedlern beschrieben werde, stelle jenes »Woher« in *The Sound of Music* das Aufbrechen von zuvor fest Verwurzelten dar. In den beiden Musicals *Oklahoma!* und *The Sound of Music* finde daher »eine ganz unterschiedliche, ja gegensätzliche Dynamik in der Dramatisierung [der] Räume« (ebd.) statt, die dem Publikum in den USA beide auf ihre Art vertraut waren.

Auch für Raymond Knapp steht in *The Sound of Music* nicht die österreichische, sondern die amerikanische Geschichte auf dem Spiel, und zwar insbesondere die amerikanische »nationhood« (Knapp, 2004, S. 136) mit all ihren Mythen und Symbolen, die jedoch gänzlich »without specific reference to America« verhandelt werde, »although we may note that the von Trapps were at the time of the show already well known in America« (ebd.).

Vor diesem Hintergrund wird auch verständlich, warum in der Rezeption von *The Sound of Music* fast vollständig unter den Tisch fällt, dass sich dieses Musical mit dem Anschluss Österreichs an Nazideutschland befasst. Im Falle des Bühnenmusicals kann diese Rezeptionslücke durchaus der Tatsache geschuldet sein, dass bis in die späten 1950er Jahre hinein die Auseinandersetzung mit dem Nationalsozialismus und dessen Verbrechen in der amerikanischen Öffentlichkeit noch in den Kinderschuhen steckte (Hillman, 2012, S. 11ff.).[10] Im Fall des Films scheint die Übertragung auf ein »idealisiertes, abstraktes Amerika« in den Zuschauern unbewusst eine Übermacht entwickelt zu haben, so dass die Nazizusammenhänge in ihrer tatsächlichen historischen Bedeutung hier seltsam irrelevant erscheinen.

Greifbar wird dies am, aus Sicht des Barons von Trapp, zutiefst ironischen Song »No Way to Stop it«, in dem dessen offene Ablehnung des Nationalsozialismus musikalische Ausgestaltung erhält, während seine Wiener Freunde, Elsa und Max, ihn davon überzeugen wollen, sich den Nazis doch einfach stillschweigend anzuschließen, da man sie sowieso nicht aufhalten könne.

Elsa

You dear attractive dewy-eyed idealist

Today you have to learn to be a realist

Max

You may be bent on doing deeds of derring-d

But up against a shark, what can a herring do?

Elsa

Be wise, compromise!

Baron

Compromise and be wise!

Max (Fortsetzung)

You're a fool if you worry, you're a fool if you worry

Over anything but little Number One!

Baron

That's you!

Elsa

That's I

Max

And I

---

10   Da es sich in diesem Beitrag um die unmittelbare Rezeption von *The Sound of Music* handelt, werden an dieser Stelle bewusst Inszenierungen jüngeren Ursprungs ausgeklammert, die sich dem Nationalsozialismus und dem Holocaust in Bühnenbild, Kostüm und Dramaturgie verstärkt zuwenden.

Elsa

Let them think you're on their side, be non-commitical

Baron

I will not bow my head to the men I despise

Max

You won't have to bow your head, just stoop a little

Elsa

Why not learn to put your faith and your reliance
On an obvious and simple fact of science?
A crazy planet full of crazy people
Is somersaulting all around the sky
And ev'rytime it turns another somersault
Another day goes by!
And there's no way to stop it,
no there's no way to stop it
No, you can't stop it even if you try
So I'm not going to worry, no I'm not going to worry
Ev'ry time I see another day go by

Max

While somersaulting at a cock-eyed angle
We make a cock-eyed circle 'round the sun
And when we circle back to where we started from
Another year has run
And there's no way to stop it,
no there's no way to stop it
if the earth wants to roll around the sun!

Baron

And me! That all absorbing character!

Elsa

That fascinating creature!

Max

That superspecial feature...

Alle

Me!

Baron

So ev'ry star and ev'ry whirling planet, and ev'ry constellation in the sky
Revolve around the centre of the universe, a lovely thing called I!

Max und Elsa

And there's no way to stop it,
no there's no way to stop it
And I know though I cannot tell you why

Baron (gesprochen)

That's charming

Max und Elsa

That as long as I'm living

Alle

Just as long as I'm living there'll be nothing else as wonderful as I!

Elsa

Nothing else as wonderful as I!

Tabelle 3: http://www.theatre-musical.com/soundofmusic/blyrics.html.

Knapp betont »a sense of inevitability by evoking obsessive circular motion« (Knapp, 2005, S. 244) in diesem Song, ausgelöst sowohl durch den auf die kreisenden und Purzelbaum schlagenden Himmelskörper im Text als auch die harmonische und rhythmische Anlage der Musik, die nicht von der Stelle zu kommen scheint.

Für den Film wurde dieser Song gestrichen. Denn mehr noch als das Musical selbst ist der Film, wie Knapp ausführt,

> not really a story of the Nazis, nor even, really, of the Anschluss. While the full weight of what the Nazis would do hangs over the film, we see no direct depiction of their ruthless racial persecution and war-making (much alluded to in *The Story of the Trapp Family Singers*). It's not just that we don't see the Holocaust; we don't see even one Jew who is unmistakably a Jew, and no discussion whatever of this aspect of Nazism (Knapp, 2004, S. 134).

Führt man sich vor Augen, dass in den 1960er Jahren die inneramerikanischen Probleme selbst auf dem Spiel standen, so wird der Verzicht auf »No Way to Stop It« umso einsichtiger.

4.

Doch inwiefern kann *The Sound of Music* abschließend unter das fallen, was dieser Sammelband unter dem Schlagwort »In Search of the ›Great American Opera‹« aus verschiedenen Blickwinkeln betrachtet? Dafür sei der Titel dieses Sammelbandes wörtlich genommen und von hinten nach vorne aufgerollt:

The Sound of Music stellt sowohl in der Bühnenversion als auch im Film eine Form von »opera«, d.h. von Musiktheater dar, wenn auch als Musical bewusst populär angelegt. Es kann als solches sicherlich als »great« im Sinne von »großartig«, »super« und sogar »bedeutend« eingestuft werden – nicht nur aufgrund seines Erfolgs oder seiner Stellung in der amerikanischen Popularkultur, sondern auch aufgrund seiner zwischen den Zeilen vermittelten »großen« Inhalte wie Vaterlandsliebe, Nationalgefühl, Gründungsmythen etc.

Dass *The Sound of Music* außerdem auch »American« ist, und zwar nicht nur im Sinne der Bezeichnung eines geographisch begrenzten Bereichs, eines Staatsgebiets und dessen Staatsbürgern, sondern auch als Bezeichnung einer irgendwie gearteten und sich von anderen unterscheidenden Kultur, einer *National*kultur also, die sowohl die Gegenwart als auch die Zukunft und die Vergangenheit der Nation sowie die ihr eigenen Topoi umfasst und die sich unter anderem politisch oder künstlerisch manifestieren kann, konnte hoffentlich durch die hier angedeutete Einbettung in die amerikanische Geschichte und Kultur der 1950er und 1960er Jahre plausibel gemacht werden.

Darüber hinaus waren die entscheidenden Personen (wie Komponist, Librettist, Regisseur, Drehbuchautor, Produzent etc.) im Entstehungsprozess der Broadwayshow sowie in deren Überarbeitung für den Film immer wieder selbst auf der Suche nach (»in search of«) der Relevanz von *The Sound of Music* für die amerikanische Bevölkerung und trafen ihre Entscheidungen dementsprechend. Die in diesem Beitrag herausgearbeiteten Zusammenhänge mit politischen und kulturellen Zusammenhängen der 1950er bzw. 1960er Jahre in den USA zeigen, dass sich sowohl die Bühnenshow als auch der Film durch die am Musical vorgenommenen Änderungen an zeitpolitischen Themen orientierten und damit den »Geist der Zeit« getroffen haben.

Die Gattung des Broadwaymusicals allgemein ist, mit Knapp (2005, S. 1f.) gesprochen, neben dem amerikanischen Film und dem Jazz eine der drei genuin amerikanischen Kunstformen. Diese seien seit ihrer Entstehung immer wieder als ästhetisch minderwertig kritisiert worden, was es diesen Kunstformen ermöglicht habe »to emerge as specifically American, answering to specifically American demands and shaping American experiences more directly than arts imported from Europe could ever have managed to do« (Knapp, 2005, S. 2). Im Phänomen *The Sound of Music* vereinen sich diese drei amerikanischen Kunstformen: Zunächst war es ein reines Musical, komponiert für den New Yorker Broadway. Dann wurde es zu einem Film, produziert von *20th Century Fox*, einem der wichtigsten Filmstudios Amerikas. Der Spagat zum Jazz schließlich wurde mit dem Song »My Favorite Things« geschlagen, der durch John Coltranes vierzehn Minuten umfassende Interpretation schon ein Jahr nach der Uraufführung des Musicals zu einem Jazzstandard avancierte. In diesem Sinne ist *The Sound of Music* sicherlich einer von unterschiedlichsten Fahndungserfolgen »In Search of the Great American Opera«.

Literatur

(2014). Maria von Trapp, last of the »Sound of Music« children, dies. *The Catholic Universe*, 23. Februar. http://www.thecatholicuniverse.com/rosemarie-von-trapp-last-sound-music-children-dies (abgerufen am 24. September 2014).

Bernstein, R. (2005). The Hills Are Alive With the Sound of Remembrance. *The New York Times*, 24. März. http://www.nytimes.com/2005/03/24/world/europe/vienna-journal-the-hills-are-alive-with-the-sound-of-remembrance.html (abgerufen am 20. Juli 2015).

Grosch, N. (2014). *»The Sounds of (the Earth Are Like) Music«: Notiz zur Verortung der Rodgers & Hammerstein-Musicals.* Unpublished manuscript.

Hillman, J. (2012). *Echoes of the Holocaust on the American Musical Stage.* Jefferson, NC: McFarland & Company.

Hirsch, J. (1993). *The Sound of Music. The Making of Amerika's Favorite Movie.* Chicago: Contemporary Books.

Jubin, O. (2013). The hills are alive with… My Songs, My Dreams? »The Sound of Music« in Germany and Austria. *Studies in Musical Theatre,* 7 (2), 135–156.

Kammerhofer-Aggermann, U. & Keul, A. (Hrsg.). (2000). *»The Sound of Music« zwischen Mythos und Marketing* (= Salzburger Beiträge zur Volkskunde, Bd. 11). Salzburg: ohne Verlagsangabe.

Knapp, R. (2005). *The American Musical and the Formation of National Identity.* Princeton, NJ: Princeton University Press.

Knapp, R. (2004). History, ›The Sound of Music‹, and Us. *American Music,* 22 (1), 133–144.

Maslon, L. (2007). *The Sound of Music Companion.* New York: Simon and Schuster.

McLeer, A. (2002). Practical Perfection? The Nanny Negotiates Gender, Class, and Family Contradictions in 1960s Popular Culture. *NWSA Journal,* 14 (2), 80–101.

Schild, L. (2013). *A Few of Our Favorite Things. Winning a trip to Salzburg.* http://forever-liesl.travellerspoint.com (abgerufen am 24. September 2014).

Starkman, R. A. (2000). American Imperialism or Local Protectionism? *The Sound of Music* (1965) fails in Germany and Austria. *Historical Journal of Film, Radio, and Television,* 20 (1), 63–78.

Wolf, S. (2011). *Changed for Good. A Feminist History of the Broadway Musical.* Oxford: Oxford University Press.

History of a Dinner Concert. http://www.soundofsalzburg.info/history-of-a-dinner-concert.htm (abgerufen am 24. September 2014).

The Sound of Music as Tracht Ambassador. http://www.austria.info/uk/art-culture/the-sound-of-music-as-tracht-ambassador-1523543.html (abgerufen am 24. September 2014).

Mauro Fosco Bertola

Glass *avec* Fukuyama oder Philip Glass' *The Voyage* (1992) und das Ende der Geschichte

> »Tous les événements sont enchaînés dans le meilleur des mondes possibles.« Voltaire, *Candide*

Es ist vielleicht nicht unangebracht, das Nachdenken über die Suche nach »the great American opera« während der 1990er Jahre mit einem Beispiel aus einem Hollywood-Blockbuster einzuleiten; einem Blockbuster, der jene Dekade zum Ende brachte und zugleich das hinter den schillernden Erfolgen der *Clinton-years* lauernde Unbehagen auszudrücken vermag, aus dem die berüchtigten geopolitischen Entscheidungen der Bush-Administration zu Beginn des neuen Millenniums hervorgingen. Gemeint ist *The Matrix*, der mittlerweile zum Kult-Status herangewachsene Film von Lana und Andrew Wachowski aus dem Jahr 1999. Als der Hacker Neo (alias Keanu Reeves) aus dem Koma erwacht, in das jene von einem gewissen Morpheus angebotene Tablette ihn versetzt hat – eine Tablette, welche ihm das Erfahren der realen Zustände der Welt ermöglichen soll – begrüßt ihn Morpheus mit dem Satz »Welcome to the desert of the real«: Die Welt, in der Neo zu leben dachte, ist in Wahrheit eine computergestützte Simulation. Die Maschinen beherrschen die Erde und halten die Menschen bewusstlos, in einer virtuellen Welt gefangen, um aus ihren Körpern Energie zu gewinnen.

Um von *The Matrix* zum Thema des Beitrags zu gelangen, muss man nur eines machen, nämlich Morpheus' bitteren Gruß in sein Gegenteil verkehren. Nicht die Realität, sondern die Illusion, die imaginäre Leinwand aus Wünschen, Neigungen und Hoffnungen, mit denen wir unser Realitätsprinzip, unsere Auffassung von dem, was real ist, konstruieren und aufrechterhalten, ist die Wüste, die wir (zu Recht) in unserem Alltagsleben nicht anzuschauen wagen. Gerade dort scheint Philip Glass' Oper *The Voyage* ansetzen zu wollen.

Für die Metropolitan Opera zum Anlass des 500. *Columbus Day* komponiert, ist Philip Glass' *The Voyage* eine regelrechte *grand opéra* mit Balletteinlagen, ausgedehnten Chören, einem sich von segelnden Karavellen bis hin zu Raumschiffen erstreckenden Dekor und komplexen, zum Teil parallel verlaufenden Szenen. Wie Tim Page zu Beginn des Jahres 2000 bemerkt hat, ist *The Voyage* zumindest vor den späteren Versuchen mit *Galileo Galilei* (2002) oder *Kepler* (2009) und *The Perfect American* (2013), »the densest, most contrapuntal and perhaps the most complicated score that Glass has yet written« (Page, 2000). Aus einer solchen Oper, die zu diesem runden Jubiläum die Figur Columbus und – wie Glass explizit anmerkt – »the spirit of discovery« nicht ohne jenen *de rigeur* gewordenen multikulturalistischen Wermutstropfen für die dadurch unterdrückten Zivilisationen zelebriert, die den Theatersaal mit einem alle sozialen Schichten vertretenden, vom Kritiker der *New York Times* als »a piquant mixture of uptown and downtown, [...] of traditional first-night operagoers and hip explorers from other musical worlds« beschriebenen Publikum zu füllen weiß, und die von einem der international bekanntesten amerikanischen Komponisten jener Zeit geschrieben wurde, aus einer solchen Oper also, sollte in einer vor kaum drei Jahren unter der Vormacht der USA endgültig unipolar gewordenen Welt nicht weniger als ein Triumph werden.[1]

Was sich de facto ereignete, ist stattdessen etwas, das viele Parallelen mit der Rezeption eines Buches aufweist, das im selben Jahr wie Glass' Oper erschien; eines Buches, das nicht nur den globalen Triumph jener spezifisch nordamerikanischen Verbindung von freier Marktwirtschaft und liberaler Demokratie wissenschaftlich belegen zu wollen schien, sondern auch dabei ein durchaus hegelsches Ende der Geschichte bereits im Titel deklarierte. Ich meine natürlich den mittlerweile sprichwörtlich gewordenen Essay von Francis Fukuyama *The End of History and the Last Man*. Dass die kühne These des Titels vom politisch linken Spektrum kritisch aufgenommen wurde, ist sicherlich nicht verwunderlich.[2] Interessant ist es jedoch zu bemerken, dass Kritik auch aus jenem konservativen Spektrum kam, zu dem Fukuyama selbst gehört: Bereits ein Jahr später veröffentlichte Samuel P. Huntington einen Aufsatz in *Foreign Affair*, der 1996 unter dem ebenfalls sprichwörtlich gewordenen Titel *The Clash of Civilizations and the Remaking of World Order* zu einem erfolgreichen Buch wurde. Darin verkehrt Huntington die Thesen Fukuyamas in ihr Gegenteil: Die Geschichte sei längst nicht im Zeichen einer progressiven, globalen Durchsetzung des US-amerikanischen Binoms von Markt und Demokratie zum Ende gekommen, sondern es sei vielmehr ein Kampf auf Leben und Tod zwischen unterschiedlichen, nicht kommunizierenden »Zivilisationen« angesagt.[3]

---

1   Vgl. Rothstein, 1992. Siehe außerdem Davis, 1997, und Gann, 1997.
2   Siehe Derrida, 1994. Derrida schrieb *Spectres de Marx* als kritische Antwort auf den internationalen Erfolg von Fukuyamas Monografie und die darin enthaltenen Thesen. Dabei hob er eine ganze Reihe von Missständen selbst in den damaligen westlichen Demokratien hervor und entwarf das normative Ideal einer »democracy to come« als Antidot gegen die ideologischen Irrwege von Fukuyama, vgl. diesbezüglich auch Schrijver, 2010, S. 326–329.
3   Der entscheidendste Unterschied zwischen beiden Autoren besteht bereits auf der Ebene des jeweiligen Ansatzes; Huntington kehrt expressis verbis Fukuyamas hegelsche These eines Primats des Idealen über das Reale um und bemerkt: »The West won the world not by the superiority of its ideas or values or religion, but rather by its superiority in applying organized violence. Westerners often forget this fact, non-Westerners never do«, vgl. Huntington, 2003, S. 51.

Was sowohl im Fall von Fukuyamas Rezeption als auch in der eher kühlen Aufnahme von Glass' Oper daher auffällt, ist gerade die Tatsache, dass Kritik von jener Seite kam, aus der eine spontane Zustimmung zu erwarten war: 1992, ein halbes Jahrtausend nach der Entdeckung Amerikas, sah die geopolitische Weltkarte so aus, als hätten die USA jenes Projekt eines »amerikanischen Jahrhunderts« wahrlich erfüllt, das mit der Verwerfung der Monroe-Doktrin im Spanisch-Amerikanischen Krieg von 1898 begonnen wurde.[4] Warum hätten gerade die Konservativen dies verleugnen müssen und warum sollte *The Voyage* nicht zumindest zeitweilig zur »great American opera« werden?

The End of History oder von der (bitteren) Wahrheit des Übertreibens

In Zeiten von düsteren Prognosen über das Fortbestehen der Europäischen Union ist es vielleicht nicht verkehrt, an Alexander Kojève zu denken, jenen Hegel-Exegeten, der im Paris der 1930er Jahre die berühmten und für die Interpretation des Stuttgarter Philosophen im 20. Jahrhundert maßgeblich gewordenen Vorlesungen hielt, die 1947 unter dem Titel *Introduction à la Lecture de Hegel* veröffentlicht wurden. Im festen Glauben an die Richtigkeit von Hegels These eines Endes der Geschichte, das mit Napoleons Sieg von 1806 in Jena ideell bereits erreicht wurde und sich nach der Niederlage des Faschismus zumindest auf europäisch-westlichem Boden auch faktisch verwirklicht habe, entschied sich Kojève nach dem Zweiten Weltkrieg, die philosophische Muße weitgehend beiseite zu legen und einen hohen Posten im französischen Außenministerium anzunehmen.[5] Von dort konnte er bis zu seinem Tode bei der Errichtung jener universellen und homogenen Zivilgesellschaft mitwirken, welche die Menschen am Ende der Geschichte erwarten sollten und die er in der Entstehung der Europäischen Union politisch verwirklicht sah. So zumindest möchte uns Francis Fukuyama die eigenwillige Figur Kojève vorstellen und sich selber in den schützenden Schatten des großen Mannes stellen (Fukuyama, 1992, S. 65–67).

Fukuyamas Thesen basieren auf etwas, das sich als eine kühne Verbindung von kontinentaler, deutsch-idealistischer Anthropologie und analytischer angelsächsi-

---

4   In diesem Kontext soll auch auf das sogenannte *Project for the New American Century* erinnert werden, ein 1997 gegründetes und bis 2006 bestehender »Thinktank«, dessen ausdrückliches Ziel es war, »to promote American global leadership«. Viele der Mitglieder kamen unter der Administration Bush zu wichtigen Positionen, wie zum Beispiel im Fall von Dick Cheney und Donald Rumsfeld. Zur Organisation gehörte auch Francis Fukuyama, der das Statement of Principles unterschrieb, vgl. die Homepage des Projektes unter: https://web.archive.org/web/20050205041635/http://www.newamericancentury.org/statementofprinciples.htm (abgerufen am 7. August 2014).

5   Über Kojève und seine Philosophie siehe Butler, 2012, S. 63–78.

scher Empirie beschreiben lässt. Fukuyama konstatiert in der Tat eine progressive Durchsetzung der modernen Naturwissenschaften im Besonderen und ihres heuristischen Modells im Allgemeinen in aller Herren Länder und sieht darin jenen Faktor, welcher der Menschheitsgeschichte ihre »directionality and coherence« verleiht (Fukuyama, 1992, S. xiv). Wir können also sehr wohl von Fortschritt reden und dabei anhand des Aufnahmegrades der Naturwissenschaften bzw. des empirisch-rationalen Argumentationsmodells in verschiedenen Kulturen unterschiedliche Entwicklungsstadien feststellen. Die Verbreitung dieser wissenschaftlichen Denkstruktur stellt für Fukuyama einen nach dem Ende der Ideologien unaufhaltbaren Prozess dar. Die Folge ist dabei eine kulturelle Homogenisierung, die vor allem im Zeichen einer progressiven Durchsetzung der liberalen Marktwirtschaft als der bis ins Alltagsleben eindringenden Verkörperung von Rationalität, Empirie und utilitaristischem Effizienzdenken steht.[6] Dies stellt aber nur die erste Hälfte von Fukuyamas Argumentation dar. Denn warum, fragt sich Fukuyama, hat sich nicht auf der politischen Ebene etwas wie ein bismarcksches, autoritär-zentralistisches Modell etabliert, unter dem wissenschaftlicher Fortschritt und Marktwirtschaft eigentlich am besten gedeihen? Warum also entscheiden sich die durch technischen und wirtschaftlichen Fortschritt aufgeklärten Menschen für die (weniger effiziente) Demokratie?

Hier kommt die deutsch-idealistische Anthropologie zum Einsatz. Auf Kojèves Interpretation der hegelschen Dialektik von Herr und Knecht basierend, postuliert Fukuyama ein menschliches Bedürfnis nach Anerkennung (»thymos«): Der Mensch sei nicht ein allein nach Profitmaximierung strebendes Tier, sondern sei vor allem auf die soziale Anerkennung seines Wertes als Individuum bedacht. Diese Anerkennung kann nur eine Demokratie mit ihrem allgemeingültigen und auf der Egalität aller Bürger untereinander basierenden Recht geben. Hier, im hegelschen Kampf um Anerkennung, findet damit Fukuyama den »missing link«, welcher repräsentative Demokratie und liberale Marktwirtschaft zwangsläufig, zumindest in der Dimension der *longue durée*, zusammenführt.[7]

---

6   »The unfolding of modern natural science has had a uniform effect on all societies that have experienced it [...]. All countries undergoing economic modernisation must increasingly resemble one another: they must unify nationally on the basis of a centralised state, urbanise, replace traditional forms of social organisation like tribe, sect, and family with economically rational ones based on function and efficiency, and provide for the universal education of their citizens. Such societies have become increasingly linked with one another through global markets and the spread of a universal consumer culture. Moreover, the logic of modern natural science would seem to dictate a universal evolution in the direction of capitalism.« Fukuyama, 1992, S. xv.

7   Fukuyama, 1992, S. xvi: »Man differs fundamentally from the animals, however, because in addition he desires the desire of other men, that is, he wants to be ›recognised.‹ In particular, he wants to be recognised as a human being, that is, as a being with a certain worth or digni-

Die Geschichte ist für Fukuyama nicht auf der faktischen Ebene, wo es sehr wohl Konflikte und Krisen geben könnte, aber auf der ideellen bzw. ideologischen Ebene bereits 1806, als die demokratischen Ideale der Französischen Revolution über Preußen siegten, spätestens aber mit dem Kollaps der Sowjetunion 1989 zu Ende. Genau wie für Kojève ist auch für Fukuyama das Politische als eigenständige Kategorie, als Ort der Debatte über grundsätzliche Entscheidungen, in sich wertlos geworden: In der Welt der »post-history« hat die Stunde der Techniker, der Fachmänner, der Verwalter geschlagen. Das Nachdenken über alternative Regierungs-, Produktions- und Verteilungsmöglichkeiten ist nicht mehr gefragt. Alle sollen nur darauf bedacht sein, den sich zwangsläufig durchsetzenden Prozess so gewalt- und problemlos wie möglich entfalten zu lassen. Es ist die Epoche des »letzten Menschen«, wie Fukuyama in expliziter Anlehnung an Nietzsche und mit Wehmut am Ende des Buches konstatiert, eines Menschen, der, von der Effizienz eines uneingeschränkten Konsums versorgt, allein dem Lustprinzip folgt und nur von dem immer präziseren rationalen Kalkül des eigenen Interesses getrieben wird.[8]

Beim Lesen von Fukuyamas Argumentationen ist man vermutlich gut beraten, an Adorno zu denken. Nicht jedoch an den Adorno der »verwalteten Welt« und des Triumphs der »Kulturindustrie« am Ende der *Dialektik der Aufklärung*, sondern an den der intimeren und flüchtigen Töne der *Minima Moralia*. Gerade dort vermerkt Adorno an einer Stelle, wie dem Denken »ein Element der Übertreibung« wesentlich sei.[9] Darin liege die Wahrheit jedes Gedankens, in diesem Moment der Gebrochenheit, bei dem er das Objekt, auf das er verweist, verfehlt. Lässt sich nicht bei

---

ty.« Siehe auch folgende Passage eine Seite weiter: »The inherently unequal recognition of masters and slaves is replaced by universal and reciprocal recognition, where every citizen recognises the dignity and humanity of every other citizen, and where that dignity is recognised in turn by the state through the granting of rights.« Fukuyama, 1992, S. xvii–xviii.

8   »Liberal democracy produced ‚men without chests,‘ composed of desire and reason but lacking thymos, clever at finding new ways to satisfy a host of petty wants through the calculation of long-term self-interest. The last man had no desire to be recognised as greater than others, and without such desire no excellence or achievement was possible. Content with his happiness and unable to feel any sense of shame for being unable to rise above those wants, the last man ceased to be human.« Fukuyama, 1992, S. xxii.

9   Vgl. den Aphorismus Nr. 82 »Drei Schritt vom Leibe« aus dem zweiten Teil, Adorno, 1969, S. 164–165. Siehe auch folgende Anmerkung Adornos in seiner Einleitung zum »Positivismusstreit in der deutschen Soziologie«: »Ohne ein Gebrochenes, Uneigentliches gibt es keine Erkenntnis, die mehr wäre als einordnende Wiederholung. Daß sie dabei gleichwohl die Idee der Wahrheit nicht opfert, wie es dem Positivismus in seinen folgerechtesten Repräsentanten weit näher liegt, umschreibt einen wesentlichen Widerspruch: Erkenntnis ist, und keineswegs per accidens, Übertreibung. Denn so wenig irgendein Einzelnes ‚wahr‘ ist, sondern vermöge seiner Vermitteltheit immer auch sein eigenes Anderes, so wenig wahr ist wiederum das Ganze. Daß es mit dem Einzelnen unversöhnt bleibt, ist Ausdruck seiner eigenen Negativität. Wahrheit ist die Artikulation dieses Verhältnisses.« Adorno, 2003, S. 318–319.

Fukuyama *mutatis mutandis* dasselbe sagen? Wird nicht gerade in der Naivität und unheimlichen Selbstherrlichkeit seiner These die westliche Utopie der 1990er Jahre stillschweigend bloßgelegt? Gerade in seiner Übertreibung lässt sich am deutlichsten jenes sonst implizite Konglomerat ablesen, welches den Glauben an eine naturwüchsige Selbstregulierung der Märkte, die Vorstellung eines Globalisierungsprozesses, der nicht anzuhalten sei und von dem schließlich doch alle Beteiligten (früher oder später) profitieren werden, und die Zuversicht auf eine baldige globale Verwirklichung eines »dritten Wegs« zwischen kapitalistischer Effizienz und sozialistischem Wohlfahrtsstaat zusammenführte; jenes Konglomerat also, welches das kulturpolitische Agieren des Westens in jener Dekade prägte.

Und liefert nicht Fukuyamas Buch zugleich auch seine eigene Dekonstruktion? Was Fukuyama beim Offenlegen dieses konfusen Konglomerats unfreiwillig machte, war, dessen Inkonsistenz vor allen Augen sichtbar vorzuführen. Was daraus resultierte, war die klare Abbildung, dass die Wirklichkeit der realen Welt am Ende des 20. Jahrhunderts viel komplexer und offener war (und ist) als die damaligen Utopien sie haben wollten.

Analogien: Fukuyama at the Opera

Wer 1643 vor dem Erklingen der ersten Noten das Libretto von Monteverdis *L'incoronazione di Poppea* noch schnell aufschlug, konnte ganz am Anfang, bei dem *Argomento*, der Zusammenfassung der Handlung, eine entscheidende Anmerkung des Librettisten Giovanni Francesco Busenello lesen: Sehr wohl habe Tacitus erzählt, dass der in Poppea hoffnungslos verliebte Nero ihren Gemahl Otto mit Vorwänden in die ferne *Lusitania* verschickt hatte, dennoch »qui [alias in dieser Oper] si rappresenta il fatto diverso« (»hier werden die Fakten anders erzählt«).[10] In der ersten auf einem historischen Sujet basierenden Oper der Musikgeschichte zeigt sich ihr Librettist der Realitätsferne durchaus bewusst, welche der Oper als Gattung immanent ist. Es ist nur durch einen – um es mit Busonis Worten zu formulieren – Zauber- bzw. Lachspiegel, welcher unsere Auffassung des Realen auf den Kopf stellt, nur also durch die Unwahrheit des Fiktiven, des faktisch Unmöglichen möglich, dass die Gattung Oper das Wahre unserer Lebenserfahrung wiedergibt.[11] Es soll damit nicht verwundern, wenn knapp 350 Jahre später Philip Glass, der das Libretto zu *The Voyage* zusammen mit David Henry Hwang verfasst hat, Folgendes über

---

10   Der Text des *argomento* ist in Rosand, 2007, S. 394 wiedergegeben.

11   »Es sollte die Oper des Übernatürlichen oder des Unnatürlichen, als der allein ihr natürlich zufallenden Region der Erscheinungen und der Empfindungen, sich bemächtigen und dergestalt eine Scheinwelt schaffen, die das Leben entweder in einen Zauberspiegel oder einen Lachspiegel reflektiert; die bewußt das geben will, was in dem wirklichen Leben nicht zu finden ist.« Busoni, 1916, S. 18–19.

seine eigene mit der historischen Figur von Christoph Columbus weitgehend, wenn auch nicht ausschließlich, sich befassende Oper schreibt: »I've never felt that ‚reality' was well served in an opera house. […] The opera house is the arena of poetry par excellence, […] where, in the world of artistic imagination, a different kind of truth can be discovered« (Glass, 2006, S. 3). Sollten wir nicht die Hypothese wagen, dass das »different kind of truth«, welches *The Voyage* zum Ausruck bringen möchte, nichts anderes ist, als das Imaginäre, die Utopie, welche jener ersten Dekade nach dem zelebrierten Ende der Ideologien 1989 ihre faktische Wirklichkeit stillschweigend verlieh?

Zwei Handlungsstränge verflechten sich ineinander in *The Voyage* und erzeugen dadurch auf der Ebene der Erzählung eine Schachtelstruktur. Der eine Strang setzt sich, wie gesagt, dem Anlass gemäß mit der Figur von Christoph Columbus auseinander: Im zweiten Akt wird von Columbus' Erinnerungen an den Tag der Abreise sowie von seinen Zweifeln und Erwartungen unmittelbar vor der Landsichtung berichtet und im Epilog der Oper zieht der sterbende Columbus in einem imaginären inneren Zwiegespräch mit der Königin Isabella von Kastilien ein bitteres, wenn auch nicht hoffnungsloses Lebensfazit. Der andere Handlungsstrang gehört zum Genre der *Science-Fiction*: Im ersten Akt spielt sich ein Raumschiffunfall ab; die Besatzung ist zur Notlandung auf einem Planeten gezwungen, der nichts anderes ist als die Erde gegen Ende des Eiszeitalters. Der dritte Akt findet im Jahr 2092 n. Chr. statt: Auf einer zwischen einer Raumstation im Weltall und einem archäologischen Forschungsteam auf der Erde geteilten Bühne sind wir Zeuge der Entdeckung jenes Meldegeräts, welches die notgelandete Besatzung im ersten Akt hinterlassen hatte und das auf den Herkunftsplaneten der Crew verweist. Die Menschheit ist nun 2092 ihrem Ursprung auf die Spur gekommen und eine Mission zu diesem fernen Himmelskörper wird organisiert. Der feierliche Abschuss des neuen Raumschiffes schließt den Akt ab.

Die nichtlineare Struktur der Erzählung dient nicht allein der Hervorhebung der Botschaft von Glass' Oper, d. h. der Ewigkeit jenes Entdeckungsgeistes, der alles politisch Korrekten zum Trotz als der Menschheit inhärent und ihren Wert ausmachend gepriesen wird. Sie verweist auch und vor allem auf eine besondere Dimension der (historischen) Zeitlichkeit, welche Glass hier nicht nur dramaturgisch, sondern auch musikalisch zu suggerieren scheint. Als im dritten Akt das Raumschiff die Erde verlässt, stehen wir einen Schritt vor dem Ende der Geschichte: Wenn sie glückt, soll diese Mission sicherlich nicht das Ende der Raumfahrt bedeuten, sie wird jedoch auf *die* Antwort stoßen, welche alle Fragen und alles Fragen ein für alle Male stillt – auf die Antwort über den Ursprung des Lebens auf der Erde. Mit ihrem Erfolg sind der Entdeckungsgeist und der aus ihm hervorgehende und ihm dienende technische Fortschritt zu Ende. Das Ringen der Menschheit um die letzte Wahrheit über sich selbst wird endlich zu Ende sein. Kraft der nichtlinearen Erzählstruktur der Oper sind wir Zuschauer jedoch bereits am Anfang, im ersten Akt der Oper,

Zeugen des Endes der Geschichte bzw. des Lebens in einem, um es mit den Worten Fukuyamas zu formulieren, »post-historischen« Zeitalter.

Der erste, sich 50.000 Jahre vor Christus abspielende Akt wird von einem Quartett eröffnet, bei dem jedes der Besatzungsmitglieder auf unterschiedliche Weise seine Langeweile und Unzufriedenheit bei dem langen und ereignislosen Reisen durch das Weltall zum Ausdruck bringt. Den Ton gibt hier die Kommandantin an, sie singt folgende Worte: »No more choices / Don't rely on options / The concept of free will / Is dead.« Der kurz danach eintretende Schiffbruch verändert dieses glatte Dahinschweben durch das Weltall, was jedoch dabei vor allem auffällt, ist die grundsätzliche Gefahrlosigkeit seines Verlaufs: Nicht nur ereignet sich die Notlandung auf der Erde ohne jegliche (musikalische und szenische) Dramatik, die Crew scheint dabei auch keiner reellen Gefahr ausgesetzt zu sein. Nachdem jedes der drei Besatzungsmitglieder das jeweilige auf den Herkunftsplaneten des Raumschiffes verweisende Meldegerät aktiviert hat, hält jedes der Mitglieder für einen kurzen Moment inne und stellt sich einen Ort und eine Epoche auf dem neuen Planeten (alias Erde) vor, an dem und in der er gerne leben möchte. In einer Art Zeit und Raum überwindenden Teletransport verschwinden sie alle bis auf die Kommandantin von der Bühne.

Sind wir hier nicht in einem post-historischen, von versorgender Rationalität beherrschten Zeitalter, und haben wir es hier nicht mit Fukuyamas »letzten Männern«, mit jenen – wie er schreibt – »›men without chests‹, composed of desire and reason but lacking *thymos*, clever at finding new ways to satisfy a host of petty wants through the calculation of long-term self-interest« zu tun? (Fukuyama, 1992, S. 5). Der technische Fortschritt hat eine individuell maßgeschneiderte Verschränkung von Realität und Imaginärem ermöglicht, welche Tod und Leiden weitgehend ausgemerzt zu haben scheint: Die letzten Männer leben nicht in einer virtuellen, die realen Zustände verschleiernden Welt à la *Matrix*, verändert hat sich dank des Fortschritts die *reale* Welt selbst bzw. das gesamte Universum. Am Ende der Geschichte leben die Männer in einem Kosmos von faktisch real uneingeschränkten Möglichkeiten, welcher jeden individuellen Traum zu verwirklichen verspricht. Ist das nicht die Abbildung jener (fast) perfekten Welt, die Fukuyama 1992 sich vor unseren Augen verwirklichen sah? Und ist auch nicht die einzige Sorge, mit der die Crew ernsthaft zu kämpfen hat, genau dieselbe, die auch Fukuyama für die letzten Männer diagnostiziert hat? Wie der *first mate* im anfänglichen Quartett sagt: »Any fate is better than another supper in the Ship's mess hall.« Dies ist genau der einzige (wenn auch für ihn entscheidende) Kieselstein des Anstoßes, welchen Fukuyama für die Welt der Post-History diagnostizieren konnte. Wie er schreibt: »Is there not a side of the human personality that deliberately seeks out struggle, danger, risk, and daring, and will this side not remain unfulfilled by the ›peace and prosperity‹ of contemporary liberal democracy? Does not the satisfaction of certain human beings depend on recognition that is inherently unequal?«[12]

Aber es ist die Musik selber, welche die gesamte Oper hindurch die ewige Gegenwart eines post-historischen Zeitalters klanglich zu suggerieren scheint. Es ist eine Musik, welche auch auf die durchaus *historische* Zeit von Columbus' Seefahrt einen post-historischen Blick wirft, welcher Spannungen und Konflikte weitgehend ignoriert und in seinem unberührten Dahinfließen leicht melancholisch wirkt.[13] Das be-

---

12 Fukuyama, 1992, S. xxiii. Siehe auch folgende Stelle aus Fukuyamas Artikel von 1989 in *The National Interest*, aus dem die drei Jahre später erschienene Monografie entstanden ist: »The end of history will be a very sad time. The struggle for recognition, the willingness to risk one's life for a purely abstract goal, the worldwide ideological struggle that called forth daring, courage, imagination, and idealism, will be replaced by economic calculation, the endless solving of technical problems, environmental concerns, and the satisfaction of sophisticated consumer demands. In the post-historical period there will be neither art nor philosophy, just the perpetual caretaking of the museum of human history. [...] Perhaps this very prospect of centuries of boredom at the end of history will serve to get history started once again.« Fukuyama, 1989, S. 18.

13 Das Problem einer analytischen und ästhetischen Auseinandersetzung mit Glass' Musik, insbesondere mit den nach *Einstein on the Beach* von 1976 entstandenen musiktheatralischen Werken bleibt bis heute de facto offen und allein negativen Stereotypisierungen bzw. einseitigen Verteidigungen überlassen. Tatsache ist, dass im Fall solcher Werke »traditionelle« Ansätze in der Auseinandersetzung mit dem Phänomen der Minimal Music dem zu untersuchenden Objekt nicht gerecht werden: Es ist kein Zufall, dass Paul Griffiths in seiner erfolgreichen Monografie über die Musik des 20. Jahrhunderts selbst in ihrer dritten, erweiterten Auflage aus dem Jahr 2010 kein Wort den Werken Glass' ab den 1980er Jahren widmet und sich auf die frühe Phase seines Schaffens beschränkt, vgl. Griffiths, 2010, S. 235–236. John Richardsons 1999 erschienene Monografie über Glass' Oper *Akhnaten* von 1984 stellt vielleicht den einzigen großangelegten Versuch dar, sich mit dieser stilistischen Wende (aber längst keine Zäsur) in Glass' Œuvre auseinanderzusetzen, gibt leider zusammen mit vielen interessanten Anmerkungen und Beobachtungen kein schlüssiges Gesamtbild wieder, vgl. Richardson, 1999, insbesondere S. 53–89. Dieser Mangel wurde auch von Robert Adlington in seiner Rezension von Richardsons Buch mit folgenden Worten deutlich hervorgehoben: »I feel that Richardson's extraordinary resourcefulness – the sheer quantity of reference and connection drawn into his discussion – sometimes also provides to be his downfall. [...] To have such a range of philosophies and critical practices at one's fingertips potentially opens up exhilarating hermeneutic possibilities; that Richardson's account falls short of this potential is in part due to the rather casual way in which these tools are introduced.« Vgl. Adlington, 2001, S. 488. Für einen rezenten, anregenden ersten Überblick über die Möglichkeiten einer analytischen Auseinandersetzung mit dem gesamten Phänomen der Minimal Music siehe Evans, 2013. Meinerseits habe ich in einem weiteren Artikel versucht, mich Glass' späteren musiktheatralischen Werken unter einer musikästhetischen Perspektive anzunähern; einer Perspektive, die im Rahmen des vorliegenden Textes zugunsten einer kulturgeschichtlichen Kontextualisierung Glass' im Panorama der 1990er Jahre mit Absicht weitgehend unberücksichtigt bleibt, siehe Bertola, 2014.

rühmt-berüchtigte Wiederholen melodisch-harmonischer Floskeln, welches die Musik von Glass der auffälligen stilistischen Veränderungen im Laufe seiner Karriere zum Trotz bis heute prägt (und ihm das problematische Etikett des »Minimalisten« eingebracht hat), scheint bereits auf der Ebene des musikalischen Satzes die Wahrnehmung eines Zeitalters vermitteln zu wollen, das keine substanzielle, sondern allein rein akzidentelle Veränderungen kennt; eines Zeitalters also, welches das Tragische einer radikalen Offenheit vor den zu treffenden Entscheidungen und der Unberechenbarkeit von deren Konsequenzen überwunden hat. Das überall waltende minimalistische Wiederholungsprinzip stellt jedoch eine für Glass' Schreibweise allgemeingültige Charakteristik dar und kann daher nur bedingt als gezielte, der klanglichen Ausgestaltung einer post-historischen Perspektive dienende Entscheidung seitens des Komponisten gedeutet werden. Deshalb soll hier nicht allein das Konstruktionsverfahren, sondern auch das klanglich-stilistische Material, mit dem Glass operiert, in Betracht gezogen werden. Denn vor allem dadurch schafft es Glass, *The Voyage* in einem post-historischem Zeitalter à la Fukuyama musikalisch zu verorten. Gerade in dieser Oper und mehr als in anderen musiktheatralischen Werken des Komponisten ist die Musik von einer unersättlichen Gier durchzogen, sich alles an Stilen und musikalischen Idiomen einzuverleiben: Ein sammelnder Eifer spielt sich vor unseren Ohren ab, welcher unter dem Deckmantel des Wiederholens das gewundene Fortschreiten in Quartparallelen des mittelalterlichen Organums (Epilog), das Unbeholfen-Feierliche einer Blaskapelle (Akt III, 2), die barocken Musiktopoi des Meeresturmes (Prolog und Akt II, 1), die gewaltigen Chöre der *grand opéra* (Prolog) sowie das Primitiv-Fauvistische eines strawinskyschen Frühlingsrituals zusammenzieht bzw. aufreiht. Wir sind auch klanglich bei jener Epoche am Ende der Geschichte angelangt, die, wie Fukuyama es formuliert, nur den »perpetual caretaking of the museum of human history« kennt.[14] Nicht das klanglich und satztechnisch Neue, sondern das Virtuose eines *omnium gatherum*, eines kunterbunten Anhäufens, das keine Grenze zwischen »high« und »low« mehr kennt, ist hier musikalisch entscheidend.

Bis hier haben wir Analogien, dramaturgische und musikalische Korrespondenzen zwischen Glass' Oper und Fukuyamas Thesen hervorgehoben, d. h. wir sind zu dem Schluss gekommen, dass beide Werke aus einem imaginären Punkt am Ende der Geschichte (bzw. der Musikgeschichte) argumentieren. Was wir uns jedoch nun fragen sollten ist, ob Fukuyama und Glass ihr jeweiliges Werk *aus demselben Punkt* entwerfen, d. h. ob beide *genau dasselbe Ende* der Geschichte meinen. Die Frage soll nicht politisch verstanden werden, es soll also nicht gefragt werden, ob Glass trotz seiner Nähe zur kontrakulturellen Szene des *Green Village* und dem spirituellen Brick à Brack des New Age doch faktisch ein hartgesottener Konservativer ist oder umgekehrt, ob doch wohl nicht Fukuyama trotz seiner konservativen Gebärde de

---

14   Fukuyama, 1989, S. 18.

facto das Tor zu einem neosozialistischen Paradies vom allgemeinen Wohlstand plus kultureller Vielfalt eröffnet. Die Frage ist vielmehr, ob beide ungeachtet ihres jeweiligen politischen Credos dieses Ende der Geschichte ideell bzw. strukturell auf dieselbe Art und Weise konzipieren.

Glass *avec* de Maistre: Reisen bis ans Ende der Geschichte

Die allerseits bekannte altgriechische Anekdote jener spartanischen Mutter, welche beim plötzlichen Wiedersehen ihres längst für tot erklärten Sohnes auf der Stelle stirbt, steht sicherlich nicht für die eher banale Weisheit, jeglichem Exzess, und sei es auch ein freudiger, wohne ein zerstörerisches Potenzial inne. Was uns hier erzählt wird, ist stattdessen, dass das Auftreten des Undenkbaren, die plötzliche Konfrontation mit einer radikal unvorstellbaren Alterität, *das* ist, welches das Fortsetzen des Lebens in seinen gewohnten Bahnen unmöglich macht. Es ist dieses unvorstellbare Andere, dieses überbordende Neue, welches uns das radikale Neudenken der Kategorien aufzwingt, auf denen unser Leben und unsere Auffassung der Realität basiert. Und das ist es gerade, was die letzten Männer am Ende der Geschichte nicht mehr kennen. In Fukuyamas Welt der »post-history« werden Ereignisse weiterhin Ereignissen folgen und es wird ebenfalls Probleme geben. Die Kategorien, mit denen diese letzten Männer sie aufzufassen und zu bewältigen haben, werden jedoch immer dieselben bleiben: liberale Demokratie, freie Marktwirtschaft und technischer Fortschritt. Denn nur diese Kategorien ermöglichen auf lange Sicht für Fukuyama das Zufriedenstellen jenes Dranges nach der sozialen Anerkennung des eigenen Wertes als Individuum und des eigenen Tuns, jenes hegelschen Kampfes um Anerkennung, welcher kulturunabhängig den Menschen als Spezies auszeichnet. Es ist die Ausmerzung des radikal Neuen auf der konzeptuellen Ebene, des traumatischen Kerns, der jeglicher wahrer Alterität innewohnt, d. h. jenes unheimliche Andere, wofür man zunächst keine Konzeptualisierungsmöglichkeit parat hat, in der die *summa summarum* von Francis Fukuyamas Vision eines Endes der Geschichte liegt. Und am Ende des ersten Aktes spricht Glass das Thema des radikalen Anderen am deutlichsten an.

Nachdem die anderen Besatzungsmitglieder des notgelandeten Raumschiffes an den gewünschten Ort und in die gewünschte Epoche auf der Erde *tele-* bzw. *chrono-*transportiert wurden, entscheidet sich die auf der Bühne alleine gebliebene Kommandantin, den Nativen direkt zu begegnen, d. h. jenen Neandertalern, die sich in der Zwischenzeit vor dem Raumschiff versammelt haben. Auf indirekte Weise also nähert sich Glass der problematischen Thematik der Begegnung zwischen Columbus und den Indigenen an, wie er in seiner kurzen Einführung zur Oper explizit anmerkt.[15] Und vor allem hier trifft der letzte Mensch schließlich auf das radikale Andere, das unberechenbare, unvorhersehbare, traumatische Neue in Gestalt der Neandertaler. Vor dem Hinausgehen fantasiert nun die Kommandantin über die Nativen und ihre Reaktionen bei der Begegnung, sie füllt also das unheimlich Unbekannte mit ihren kulturspezifischen Fantasien über das Andere. Noch bevor die Ausgangstür geöffnet wird, singt jedoch der Chor der Nativen praktisch *dieselben Worte* der Kommandantin. Lassen wir uns nicht von dem unbeholfen anmutenden Anachronismus eines Chors der Neandertaler verwirren, der sich über die »photos in color« sorgt, welche die außerirdische Kreatur vermutlich machen wird: Dieser Anachronismus geschieht hier nicht zufällig, genau wie die Tatsache, dass sowohl die Kommandantin als auch die Nativen dieselbe Musik singen. Nachdem die Kommandantin aus dem Raumschiff ausgestiegen ist, folgt ein weiterhin auf demselben musikalischen Material basierendes klangliches und emotionales *crescendo*, bei dem sie mit den Nativen gemeinsam singt. Das Nirwana der Überwindung aller Differenzen liegt hier nicht, wie in *Tristan und Isolde*, im Nicht-Sein des Todes, sondern in einem diesseitigen dionysisch-orgiastischen Gruppenritual à la Strawinsky: Wie es in den Regieanweisungen an diesem Punkt zu lesen ist: »The Commander is *absorbed* by the Natives, performing the Rites of Spring.«[16]

Der Punkt ist aber, dass dieses dionysische »Einswerden« eine Täuschung ist: Zwar findet nicht jene willige Aufopferung des Einzelnen im Namen des Kollektiven wie im strawinskyschen Originalballett statt, welche bekanntermaßen Adornos Strahlen auf sich zog. Was die ganze Szene dennoch vermittelt, ist die Abwesenheit jeglicher substanzieller Differenz zwischen unterschiedlichen Kulturen. Während die Matrosen im zweiten Akt historisch gerecht auf Spanisch singen, sind hier die Nativen im Englischen durchaus flüssig, die Kommandantin und die Neandertaler füllen das jeweilig radikal Neue eines unbekannten Anderen mit denselben Fantasien und singen schließlich noch vor ihrer Begegnung dieselbe Musik. Hier zelebriert Glass nicht die Gleichberechtigung und die mutuelle Anerkennung der jeweiligen Alterität zwischen unterschiedlichen Kulturen, wie er beabsichtigte. Gegen seinen Willen liefert Glass also hier nicht die Abbildung der »richtigen« Landung Columbus' an der Küste Amerikas, der Landung wie sie sich in der besten aller Welten hätte ereignen müssen: anstatt des gegenseitigen Schlachtens – ein gemeinsames, fröhliches Erlernen der jeweiligen Kulturen. Dieses Finale des ersten Aktes wird stattdessen zur *mise en scène* eines eskapistischen *One World – One Nation*, bei dem das Andere so lange auf der Bühne erscheinen kann wie es keine wahre, alias radikale und

---

15   »That particular cultural confrontation [zwischen Columbus und den dort ansässigen Zivilisationen, d. V.] takes place in a different time and place and serves as the finale to Act One, and is every bit as traumatic and dramatic as the ›real‹ historical ›Columbus‹ event must have been.« Vgl. Glass, 2006, S. 3. Aber nicht nur das tatsächliche Libretto, sondern auch die Musik scheint den hier von Glass formulierten Vorsatz zu dementieren.

16   Vgl. das Libretto der Oper in der CD Orange Mountain, omm0017 2006, S. 9.

traumatische Alterität darstellt. An der Küste Amerikas angelangt, trifft Columbus nichts anderes als sich selber, nur mit einem folkloristischen Kostüm bekleidet.

Und gerade hier, an dem Punkt also, wo die beabsichtigte Botschaft von einem »gesunden«, die mutuelle Begegnung unterschiedlicher Kulturen ermöglichenden Entdeckungsgeist dramaturgisch unfreiwillig untergraben wird, erweist sich Glass als jemand, der mit Noten besser als mit Worten umgehen kann. Die Musik zu dieser Szene scheint in der Tat das ganze Geschehen auf der Bühne als eine Täuschung demaskieren zu wollen: Hier liefert der erfahrene Opernkomponist Glass nicht nur das spektakuläre Finale des Aktes, das sein Publikum erwartet. Er spielt vor allem eindeutig mit musikalischen Stereotypen und schreibt eine Musik, die geschickt einen fauvistischen, forciert primitivierenden Gestus (man denke zum Beispiel an die lange Passage von Ziffer 70 bis einschließlich Ziffer 76 des Klavierauszuges, wo die Schlagzeuge dominieren) mit dem Topos des Feuertanzes à la De Falla des *El Amor Brujo* oder à la Pizzetti der *Sinfonia del fuoco* und deren exotisierendem, »orientalischem« Flair vermischt. (Hier sind nicht nur die rekurrierenden Melismen der Singstimme zu erwähnen: Über weite Strecken steht die Szene in einem phrygischen Modus, der an einigen Stellen kurz in ein phrygisches Dur übergeht, siehe zum Beispiel Ziffer 26 bis 29 des Klavierauszuges; man höre auch die insistierenden Einschübe der Pikkoloflöte ganz zu Beginn der Szene, wo das Instrument eine hypophrygische Skala mehrmals wiederholt, Ziffer 15ff.). Alle diese, zuerst separat eingeführten Elemente werden entlang eines unaufhaltsamen, 16-minutigen *crescendo* progressiv aufgeschichtet, bis sie zu einem abschließenden, effektvollen orgiastischen Bacchanal zusammengeführt werden, welches die durchaus kinematografische, hollywoodsche Qualität dieser Szene musikalisch endgültig bestätigt.[17] Die Musik scheint uns hier daran erinnern zu wollen, dass sich diese kulturelle Begegnung im Bereich des Imaginären abspielt, dass die Kommandantin hier nicht dem Realen, sondern, genau wie die anderen Besatzungsmitglieder davor, einem imaginären Anderen begegnet, d. h. dem Spiegel ihres Selbst.

Als 1794 Xavier de Maistre, der jüngere und weniger bekannte Bruder des piemontesischen Philosophen und erbitterten Feindes der Französischen Revolution Joseph de Maistre wegen eines unerlaubten Duells unter Hausarrest gestellt wurde, schrieb er während seiner Inhaftierung jenes Werk, mit dem er seinen kleinen, aber dennoch beständigen Platz in der Literaturgeschichte errang: *Voyage autour de ma chambre* (»Reise um mein Zimmer«). Das schmale Büchlein stellt eine reüssierte Parodie des damals weit verbreiteten Genres des Reiseromans dar: Anstatt die großen Abenteuer und die atemberaubenden (wahren oder erfundenen) Gefahren einer Reise in die weite Welt, beschrieb de Maistre mit demselben rhetorischen Pathos seine »Reisen« vom Bett zum Schreibtisch, vom Lehnstuhl zum Fenster etc. Ist nicht

---

17   Es ist natürlich kein Zufall, dass Pizzettis *Sinfonia del fuoco* für eines der ersten Epen der Kinogeschichte geschrieben wurde: *Cabiria* von 1914, siehe diesbezüglich Sala, 2004.

The Voyage ebenfalls die *ungewollte* Parodie des westlichen Diskurses um das Reisen; jenes Diskurses, der große Entfernungen mit großen Erkenntnissen gleichsetzt? Zeitlich und räumlich deckt Glass' Oper enorme Abstände ab, bei dem großen Reisen treffen wir jedoch auf nichts anderes als auf uns selbst. Und auch hier, wie bei Fukuyama, liefert die Oper ihre eigene Dekonstruktion: Sie legt offen, wie hinter dem politisch korrekten Zelebrieren der kulturellen Vielfalt in einer harmonischen, von den angeblich kulturell neutralen Kräften der Demokratie und des freien Marktes zufriedengestellten Welt am Ende der Geschichte de facto das Aufzwingen der eigenen Werte steckt. Die Kommandantin begegnet nicht den Nativen, sondern ihrer eigenen Fantasie über das Andere.

Kundrys Schmach, Columbus' Tod: Reisen als Kreisen

Und dennoch ... am Ende meines Artikels sei mir noch eine letzte, kurze Anmerkung erlaubt. Das bis jetzt Gesagte gilt nur, wenn die Oper ohne den abschließenden Epilog geschrieben worden wäre. Denn gerade am Ende, in Columbus' Sterbeszene, lehnt Glass das anthropologische Modell explizit ab, auf dem Fukuyamas Thesen aufgebaut sind. Hier erklärt Glass die hegelsche These eines dem Menschen immanenten Kampfes um Anerkennung als nichtig und verneint damit implizit die Möglichkeit eines Endes der Geschichte, d. h. ein Zufriedenstellen dieses Kampfes und dadurch die Beseitigung jeglicher radikalen Alterität.

Als Isabella ein letztes Mal erscheint, wirft ihr der sterbende Columbus vor, ihre Versprechen nicht gehalten zu haben: Aus seiner Entdeckung ist für ihn kein Reichtum, keine Macht und selbst keine richtige Tat im Sinne Gottes gefolgt. Isabella, die im zweiten Akt bei all diesen Versprechen die Gebärde einer halb heiligen Gottesgesandten angenommen hatte, verwandelt sich nun wie Edward Munchs berühmte *Madonna* in ihr Gegenteil und macht ihm ein unverblümtes sexuelles Angebot. Und nun erst, indem Columbus wie Parsifal die allerletzte Versuchung dieser Isabella-Kundry ablehnt, entdeckt er *in actu mortis* das Wahre über seine Reise: Nicht für den Reichtum oder die Macht oder die Veredelung seiner Seele hat er sich den Gefahren des Ungewissen ausgesetzt. In seiner Kurzeinführung zur Oper bemerkt Glass: »It is the driving force in Columbus that draws us to him« (Glass, 2006, S. 3). Man sollte hier den Ausdruck »driving force« wortwörtlich nehmen: Was Columbus bei der Ablehnung aller rationellen Gründe und Anlockungen für seine Reise entdeckt, ist der in ihm blind pulsierende Trieb nach Wissen, nach Entdeckung ohne Rücksicht auf die Konsequenzen. Glass' Oper entpuppt sich also als Eulogie, nicht eines »spirit of discovery«, sondern eines »drive of discovery«, nicht eines Entdeckungsgeistes, sondern eines Entdeckungstriebes. Dies, und nicht wie bei Fukuyama der Wunsch nach sozialer Anerkennung, ist das, was den Menschen als Spezies ausmacht.

Und hier also, erst im Epilog, wird die bis jetzt erklungene Musik neu semantisiert: Das gierige Ansammeln von Stilen und musikalischen Topoi, ihre Zusammensetzung in einem vom Wiederholungsprinzip strukturierten Satz steht hier nicht mehr für ein das radikal Neue ausschließende Dahinfließen am Ende der (Musik-)Geschichte. In einem retroaktiven Gestus wird das bis jetzt Gehörte als Zeichen einer unersättlichen, unbeherrschbaren Kraft umgedeutet, die hinter Rationalität, Kultur und dem Wunsch nach sozialer Anerkennung im Menschen unaufhaltsam pulsiert und alle diese Komponenten perpetuell infrage stellt. Das Motorisch-Hypnotische, welches im Herzen von Glass' Musik liegt, ihr fortwährendes Kreisen zwischen Wiederholung und Neuem, zwischen dem Spiel mit Stereotypen und Spektakulärem soll als musikalische *chiffre* dieses Triebes, dieses perpetuellen Kreisens um Wissen gelesen werden; eines Triebes, der nie gestillt werden kann und immer bereit ist, das Bekannte, das Rationelle und das kulturell Tradierte über Bord zu werfen, um sein wissensvermehrendes Kreisen um sich selber fortsetzen zu können. Hier also kommt die Geschichte in *The Voyage* doch nicht und nie zum Ende.

Literatur

Adlington, R. (2001). Singing Archaeology: Philip Glass's Akhnaten by John Richardson. *Music & Letters*, 82 (3), 487–491.

Adorno, T. W. (1969). *Minima Moralia. Reflexionen aus dem beschädigten Leben*. Frankfurt am Main: Suhrkamp.

Adorno, T. W. (2003). Einleitung zum »Positivismusstreit in der deutschen Soziologie«. In R. Tiedemann (Hrsg.), *Theodor W. Adorno. Gesammelte Schriften* (Bd. 8, S. 280–353). Frankfurt am Main: Suhrkamp.

Bertola, M. F. (2014). Oper und Film als Anamorphose: »Orphée« zwischen Jean Cocteau und Philip Glass. *Kieler Beiträge zur Filmmusikforschung*, 11, 10–36.

Busoni, F. (1916). *Entwurf einer neuen Ästhetik der Tonkunst*. Leipzig: Insel Verlag.

Butler, J. (2012). *Subjects of Desire. Hegelian Reflections in Twentieth-Century France*. New York: Columbia University Press.

Davis, P. G. (1997). Star Drek (1992). In R. Kostelanetz (Hrsg.), *Writings on Glass: Essays, Original Writings, Interviews, Criticism* (S. 271–273). New York: Schirmer.

Derrida, J. (1994). *Specters of Marx. The State of the Debt, the Work of Mourning and the New International*. New York, London: Routledge.

Evans, T. (2013). Analysing Minimalist and Postminimalist Music: An Overview of Methodologies. In K. Potter, K. Gann & P. Siôn (Hrsg.), *The Ashgate Research Companion to Minimalist and Postminimalist Music* (S. 241–257). Farnham: Ashgate.

Fukuyama, F. (1989). The End of History? *The National Interest*, Summer, 3–18.

Fukuyama, F. (1992). *The End of History and the Last Man*. New York: The Free Press.

Gann, K. (1997). Midtown Avantgardist (1992). In R. Kostelanetz (Hrsg.), *Writings on Glass: Essays, Original Writings, Interviews, Criticism* (S. 265–270). New York: Schirmer.

Glass, P. (2006). Preface. In *Philip Glass: The Voyage, Solisten und Chor des Landestheaters Linz, Bruckner Orchester, Dennis Russell Davies* [CD]. Orange Mountain, omm0017.

Griffiths, P. (2010). *Modern Music and After. Directions since 1945*. Oxford: Oxford University Press.

Huntington, S. P. (2003). *The Clash of Civilizations and the Remaking of World Order*. New York, NY: Simon & Schuster.

Page, T. (2000). *The Voyage*. Grove Music Online. http://www.oxfordmusiconline.com.ub proxy.ub.uni-heidelberg.de/subscriber/article/grove/music/O002769 (abgerufen am 13. August 2014).

Richardson, J. (1999). *Singing Archaeology. Philip Glass's Akhnaten*. Hanover, NH: University Press of New England.

Rosand, E. (2007). *Monteverdi's Last Operas. A Venetian Trilogy*. Berkeley, CA: University of California Press.

Rothstein, E. (1992). Philip Glass Offers More than Memorial Just to Columbus. *The New York Times*, 14. Oktober 1992. http://www.nytimes.com/1992/10/14/arts/review-opera-p hilip-glass-offers-more-than-memorial-just-to-columbus.html?pagewanted=all&src=pm (abgerufen am 14. August 2014).

Sala, M. (2004). Dal muto al sonoro: Le musiche di Pizzetti per Cabiria e Scipione l'Africano. In R. Illiano (Hrsg.), *Italian Music during the Fascist Period* (S. 157–189). Turnhout: Brepols Turnhout.

Schrijver, G. (2010). *The Political Ethics of Jean-François Lyotard and Jacques Derrida*. Leuven: Peeters Ephemerides theologicae Lovanienses.

Frédéric Döhl

About the Task of Adapting a Movie Classic for the Opera Stage: On André Previn's *A Streetcar Named Desire* (1998) and *Brief Encounter* (2009)

A Three-Step-Adaptation-Formula

On May 1, 2009, André Previn's second opera, *Brief Encounter*, was premiered at the Houston Grand Opera.[1] This was the second time that Previn took a piece of theatre that has already been adapted as a classic movie as his starting point for an opera: On September 19, 1998, his first opera, *A Streetcar Named Desire*, based on Tennessee Williams's play and Elia Kazan's film of the same name (with a screenplay written by Williams himself) was premiered at the San Francisco Opera.[2]

This adaptation formula in three steps—a classic play or novel made into a popular movie made into an opera—is a lively trend in contemporary American opera (Kirk,

---

1   The author attended the performances on May 1 and 3, 2009, in person. Both operas are published by G. Schirmer, New York. On the publisher's website, the full scores have now been made accessible for reading via http://www.musicsalesclassical.com/composer/works/1249/12 (accessed 22 September 2015). A vocal score and an edition of the libretto of *A Streetcar Named Desire* were also published. Both works have also been released in live recordings from the premiere productions in San Francisco and Houston, respectively: *A Streetcar Named Desire* (1998, Deutsche Grammophon 459 3662 8); *Brief Encounter* (2011, Deutsche Grammophon 477 9351 9). Furthermore, the original production of *A Streetcar Named Desire* has also been released on DVD (1999, Image Entertainment UPC 0143815 78829 [US] and Arthaus 100 138 [Europe], respectively), accompanied by a documentation *André Previn—A Portrait. The Kindness of Strangers* (1998, Arthaus [Europe] 100 150; 2001, Image Entertainment UPC 14381926729 [US]; director: Tony Palmer) that is focused on the process of creating the opera and the first production in San Francisco.

2   This article is based on extensive research on André Previn by the author that was funded for four years (2007–2010) by the German Research Foundation (DFG) through the Collaborative Research Centre 626 *Aesthetic Experience and the Dissolution of Artistic Limits* at the Freie Universität in Berlin, the city where the cosmopolitan Previn was born on April 6, 1929. It presents for the first time in English—while pushing them further—results from this research that have been previously published partly in German, especially in the monograph Döhl, 2012a and several journal articles, e.g. Döhl, 2012b, Döhl, 2013a and Döhl, 2013b. With regard to Previn's most prominent characteristic as a musician, his versatility, which can be just touched in passing here, see Döhl, 2013c, and the full catalog raisonné, filmography, and discography in Döhl, 2012a, as well as in Döhl, 2013d.

2005, p. 207; Kramer, 2007a, p. 67; Döhl, 2016). Most works go even further in the 'Americanization' of this formula, using a classic play or novel by an American author made into a popular movie by an American film company and director for an opera in American English by an American composer. This trend that the *New York Times* called the »operafication of American literature«[3] is so significant that critic Alex Ross rightfully called it, in the *New Yorker*, a genre of its own:

> [...] American opera composers have been playing it safe these days, glomming on to one classic book or play after another, preferably one that Hollywood turned into an equally classic movie [...]. (Ross, 2007)

Of course, it is not an easy task to define what is American and what is not (Döhl, 2015). And, naturally, there are contemporary operas that fit the very same adaptation formula, too—as do a few older works (Halliwell, 2008)—without touching the question of ›American opera‹ at all that seems to be at stake here. One example would be Poul Ruders' opera *The Handmaid's Tale*: Canadian novelist, German filmmaker/director with Japanese film composer, and, finally, Danish opera composer.

With regard to questions of national identity or agenda and opera (Calico, 2002; Kelly, 2008; Goehr, 2011; Ther, 2011; Aspden, 2012), this may be an issue (Döhl, 2015), but with regard to the three-step-adaptation-formula of a classic play or novel made into a popular movie made into an opera that I am dealing with here, this difference is of minor significance. The key problems and challenges of the genre I am interested in lie elsewhere. So at least for the purpose of this paper, it is enough to recognize that this adaptation formula has become a genre of its own with significant, constant production since the 1990s—but only in the United States and with a special American twist in the discourse accompanying this genre (Döhl, 2015; Döhl, 2016).

With the term genre I borrowed here from Ross, I mean a cluster of orientations, expectations, and conventions within a distinctive cultural web of production, circulation, and signification. This cluster integrates, amongst other things, musical, social, economic, historical, and ideological factors to create a relatively stable »genre world« where the emphasis is on structuring discourse, producing meaning, and the continual production of familiarity. As it is shown here, this broader understanding of the term addresses the specific configuration that this three-step-adaptation-formula presents.[4]

---

3   *A Nathanael West Novel Gets Its Turn on the Opera Stage*, 2006.

4   This definition with which I work here is a combination of observations and conclusions by Neale, 1980, pp. 19–22; Fabbri, 1982, pp. 52, 55; Frith, 1998, pp. 87, 94; Negus, 1999, p. 25; Glendhill, 2000, p. 223; Samson, 2001; Frow, 2006, p. 10; Holt, 2007, p. 2; Lena & Peterson, 2008, p. 698. Genre theory is a complex field. And it is obvious that the idea of genre I use

Naturally, not every work that should be considered as a contribution to this new genre of American opera realizes the aforementioned definition as clearly as Previn's *A Streetcar Named Desire*: a famous play, first turned into a classic movie and now a much performed opera. For example, in some cases, the movie adaptations are not as well known, they are produced outside of Hollywood, or several notable film versions exist. Some movies own a widely acknowledged film score, others do not. Some operas by American composers have an English instead of an American original as their starting point, such are e.g. Heggie's *The End of the Affair*, Schwartz's *Séance on a Wet Afternoon*, and Previn's *Brief Encounter*.[5] In some cases, the movie adaptation has become the main reference point in place of the original play or novel. Some novels or plays or movies have become a bit out of fashion after being popular for a while. Nonetheless, the specific challenges that this three-step-adaptation-formula presents remain intact while the trend is significant and still running strong after two decades in American opera.

Thereby, the following operas should be considered as further examples for recent works within this genre:

- William Bolcom's *McTeague* (premiered in Chicago on November 3, 1992 [Lyric Opera production]), based on the novel by Frank Norris (1899) with a classic silent movie directed by Erich von Stroheim (*Greed*, 1924);
- Mark Adamo's *Little Women* (premiered in Houston on March 13, 1998 [Houston Grand Opera production]), based on the novel by Louisa May Alcott (in two volumes in 1868 and 1869) with a movie directed by Mervyn LeRoy (1949) starring Elizabeth Taylor and

---

here contradicts other models, the most prominent of which are all concepts whose emphasis is on the immanent dynamic and hybridism of genres; see, e.g., Derrida, 1980; Jameson, 1982; Adorno, 2004, pp. 262–268. Or theories that contradict the idea of genre at all; for a discussion, see Carroll, 2009, pp. 95ff. In the genre, aspects of stabilization and dynamic are in constant battle. Furthermore, there are several other areas of debate. This includes, first and foremost, the question of how genres form and what preconditions (e.g., sociocultural, socioeconomical, and medial preconditions) exist for the formation of genres; see Peterson & Anand, 2004; Bourdieu, 1993, p. 29. A detailed discussion of genre theory cannot be made in the context of this article. The definition I follow here fits the current trend in American opera with which I deal.

5   Jake Heggie's *The End of the Affair* (premiered in Houston on March 4, 2004 [Houston Grand Opera production]), based on the novel by Graham Greene (1951) with a movie directed by Neil Jordan (1999) starring Julianne Moore and Ralph Fiennes (Soundtrack: Michael Nyman). Stephen Schwartz's *Séance on a Wet Afternoon* (premiered in Santa Barbara on September 26, 2008), based on the novel by Mark McShane (1961) with a movie directed by Bryan Forbes (1964) starring Kim Stanley and Richard Attenborough.

Janet Leigh—like Previn's *A Streetcar Named Desire*, this opera is widely played, especially in the University circuit;[6]

- William Bolcom's *A View from the Bridge* (premiered in Chicago on October 9, 1999 [Lyric Opera production]), based on the play by Arthur Miller (1955—Miller also wrote the libretto) that was the main influence on the classic French-Italian movie *Rocco and His Brothers* (1960) directed by Luchino Visconti starring Alain Delon (Soundtrack: Nino Rota);[7]

- John Harbison's *The Great Gatsby* (premiered in New York on December 20, 1999 [Metropolitan Opera production]), based on the novel by F. Scott Fitzgerald (1925) with a movie directed by Francis Ford Coppola (1974) starring Mia Farrow and Robert Redford;[8]

- Carlisle Floyd's *Cold Sassy Tree* (premiered in Houston on April 14, 2000 [Houston Grand Opera production]), based on the novel by Olive Ann Burns (1984) with a movie directed by Joan Tewkeybury (1989) starring Faye Dunaway and Richard Witmark;

- Jake Heggie's *Dead Man Walking* (premiered in San Francisco on October 7, 2000 [San Francisco Opera production]), based on the nonfiction book by Helen Prejean (1993) with a movie directed by Tim Robbins (1995) starring Susan Sarandon and Sean Penn—this opera is also widely played;

- Scott Eyerly's *The House of the Seven Gables* (premiered in New York on December 6, 2000), based on the novel by Nathaniel Hawthorne (1851) with a movie directed by Joe May (1940) starring George Sanders;

- Paula Kimper's *The Bridge of San Louis Rey* (premiered in New York on March 16, 2003), based on the novel by Thornton Wilder (1927) with a movie directed by Rowland V. Lee (1944) starring Lynn Bari (Soundtrack: Dimitri Tiomkin, Academy Award Nomination for »Best Score«);[9]

- Richard Danielpour's *Margaret Garner* (premiered in Detroit on May 7, 2005), based on the novel *Beloved* by Toni Morrison (1987) – who also wrote the libretto for the opera – with a movie by Jonathan Demme (1998), starring Oprah Winfrey and Dani Glover;

- Tobias Picker's *An American Tragedy* (premiered in New York on December 2, 2005 [Metropolitan Opera production]), based on the novel by Theodore Dreiser (1925) that was the main influence on the movie *A Place in the Sun* (1951) directed by George Stevens starring Elizabeth Taylor and Montgomery Clift (Soundtrack: Franz Waxman, Academy Award Winner for »Best Score«);

---

6   This is the classic and best-known film adaptation. There have been several others. A second successful movie adaptation was produced in 1994, directed by Gillian Armstrong and starring Susan Sarandon and Winona Ryder.

7   Visconti was directing a stage version of the play at the same time in Italy; see Marino, 2013, pp. 195f. In 1962, the play was also adapted directly to a French-Italian movie called *Vu du pont* which was directed by Sidney Lumet.

8   This is the classic and best-known film adaptation, but there have been several others. A second successful movie adaptation was produced recently in 2013, directed by Baz Luhrmann and starring Leonardo DiCaprio and Tobey Maguire.

9   It is debatable to include this work in this list. The story takes place in South America.

- Ned Rorem's *Our Town* (premiered in Bloomington/IN on February 2, 2006), based on the play by Thornton Wilder (1938) with a movie directed by Sam Wood (1940) starring William Holden and Martha Scott (Soundtrack: Aaron Copland, Academy Award Nomination for »Best Score«);
- Lowell Liebermann's *Miss Lonelyhearts* (premiered in New York on April 26, 2006), based on the novel by Nathanael West (1933) with a movie directed by Vincent J. Donehue (1958) starring Montgomery Clift;
- Ricky Ian Gordon's *The Grapes of Wrath* (premiered in Saint Paul, Minnesota, on February 10, 2007), based on the novel by John Steinbeck (1939) with a movie directed by John Ford (1940) starring Henry Fonda—this opera is also widely played;
- Robert Aldrige's *Elmer Gantry* (premiered in Nashville, Tennessee, on November 16, 2007), based on the novel by Sinclair Lewis (1926) with a movie directed by Richard Brooks (1960) starring Burt Lancaster and Jean Simmons (Soundtrack: André Previn, Academy Award Nomination for »Best Score«);
- Lori Laitman's *The Scarlet Letter* (premiered in Conway/AR on November 6, 2008), based on the novel by Nathaniel Hawthorne (1850) with a movie directed by Roland Joffé (1995) starring Demi Moore, Gary Oldman, and Robert Duvall;[10]
- Phillip Martin's *Tom Sawyer* (premiered in Hartford/CT on April 16, 2010), based on the novel by Mark Twain (1876) with a movie directed by Norman Taurog (1938);
- Jake Heggie's *Moby-Dick* (premiered in Dallas on April 30, 2010), based on the novel by Herman Melville (1851) with a movie directed by John Huston (1956) starring Gregory Peck;
- Margaret Garwood's *The Scarlet Letter* (premiered in Philadelphia on November 19, 2010), based on the novel by Nathaniel Hawthorne (1850) with a movie directed by Roland Joffé (1995) starring Demi Moore, Gary Oldman, and Robert Duvall;
- Charles Wuorinen's *Brokeback Mountain* (premiered in Madrid on January 28, 2014), based on the short story by Annie Proulx (1997—Proulx also wrote the libretto) with a movie directed by Ang Lee (2005) starring Heath Ledger and Jake Gyllenhaal (Soundtrack: Gustavo Santaolalla, Academy Award Winner for »Best Score«);
- Jennifer Higdon's *Cold Mountain* (premiered in Santa Fe/NM on August 1, 2015), based on the novel by Charles Frazier (1997) with a movie directed by Anthony Minghella (2003) starring Nicole Kidman, Renée Zellweger and Jude Law (Soundtrack: Gabriel Yared, Academy Award Nomination for »Best Score«);
- Paul Moravec's *The Shining* (premiered in Minneapolis/MI on May 7, 2016), based on the novel by Stephen King (1977) with a movie directed by Stanley Kubrik (1980) starring Jack Nicholson.

This genre came into being when, in the late 1980s/early 1990s, even major American opera houses and companies like the Metropolitan Opera New York, the San Francisco Opera, and the Houston Grand Opera started again to commission oper-

---

10 There is also an interesting movie adaptation directed by Wim Wenders starring Senta Berger (1973).

as (Kirk, 2001, pp. 359ff., 389; Taruskin, 2010, p. 515). It is part of a renewed interest in the search for a »Great American Opera.« Since 1990 about 700 new operas (in the widest sense of the term, Koch, 1999) have been written in the US and, to some extent, in Canada (Opera America, 2016). The number of institutions and companies performing opera in the US has doubled since 1980 (Midgette, 2007, p. 81). Rightfully, Philip Glass summed up: »We're in a boom« (Glass, quoted in Midgette, 2006). This recent boom is even more impressive in size and longevity taking into account that not much public money is invested here compared, for example, to opera's biggest market, Germany.[11] While at the same time most of the new operas that are performed do not survive its premiere production (Abbate & Parker, 2013, p. 641; Garrett, 2013, p. 225; Hutcheon & Hutcheon, 2014, p. 179). But there are works that have received constant attention and productions. And many like Adamo's *Little Women* or Previn's *A Streetcar Named Desire* belong to the new genre I deal with here that is a smaller but significant trend within the general renaissance of the search for a »Great American Opera.«

The central counter-arguments against this new genre are of course one of playing it safe and one of a missing necessity to add the old, comparatively slow-moving form of opera to stories that are recognized to have already found ideal realizations in novels/plays and movies. But this critical debate is not the topic here. The question is not one of value. And, of course, this genre is just one narrative amongst many in the long history of the search for an »American opera« (Kirk, 2001; Kirk, 2005; Goehr, 2011; Griffel, 2013) and just one storyline in the rich current field of commissions and productions of newly written contemporary operas (Döhl, 2015; Döhl 2016).[12] Nonetheless, we shall see that this three-step-adaptation-formula is not just a very lively and robust trend. It is an artistically significant one.

Adaptations are complex phenomenons, especially when artistically successful. An intermedia network of relations and differences arises, a plural stereophony of »quotations, references, echoes,« as Roland Barthes (1989, pp. 59–60) called it. And there are many examples that it works both ways. It is not easy to deal with *A Streetcar Named Desire*, the play, and forget about Marlon Brando whose performances as Stanley in the theatre are lost to us now but whose iconic performance in the movie is alive and present as ever. With the three-step-adaptation-formula, this two-way street becomes a triangle of relations and differences. It is how this three-dimensional stereophony is shaped in case of the works listed above that I am interested in (Döhl, 2016): To approach the question if and how this new genre is distin-

---

11   With regard to economics, see Pierce, 2000; Mulcahy, 2003; Höhe, Schmidt & Wittmann, 2005; Payne, 2005; Abfalter, 2008; Agid & Tarondeau, 2010; Kim & Jensen, 2011; Towse, 2011; Payne, 2012; Fraser & Fraser, 2014; Fryer, 2014; Belina-Johnson & Scott, 2015.

12   For an overview, see also Griffel, 2013 (especially the introduction), and the statistics on http://www.operaamerica.org/ (accessed 22 September 2015).

guished from ›normal‹ opera that most of the times is also based on a preexisting novel, play or movie (Schmidgall, 1977; Speedie, 1991; Rosmarin, 1999; Halliwell, 2005, pp. 28f.; Huwiler, 2010, p. 137; Hutcheon & O'Flynn, 2013, pp. 5, 48).

In the following, I want to showcase one aspect to illustrate that there is more to this new genre than just a question of value and a critique of playing it safe. This new genre possesses a unique twist regarding the challenges it presents to the authors of new operas: It is that the audience comes to the opera house with existing knowledge of a specific earlier audiovisual adaptation of the same original (Kramer, 2007a, pp. 68, 74). It is not that they only already know the storyline that is a standard situation in opera, a genre in which many works are based on preexisting and well-known literary or theatrical models, the audience also tends to attend the opera with a previous visual and audible imprint of how the story is told. This imprint can be so strong that it uplifts the earlier movie adaptation to the status of a quasi-original with regard to the opera that follows: The earlier movie adaptation is not just another adaptation, but as much of a point of reference for the opera as the original play or novel—and sometimes it is even the main point of reference.

If there was a well-known play upon which the opera is based, there may also be a previous visual and audible imprint of how the story is told (and even if the opera is based on a well-known novel, this may also be true because quite often people tend to audiovisualize while reading and/or audiovisual descriptions are central to the writing). For example, Williams's original version of *A Streetcar Named Desire* for the theatre is still performed regularly today and is as well-known as Kazan's movie. It is likely that many people in the audience of the opera will have previously seen the play at one point or another. So even if there was no canonical movie adaptation based on the play, the authors of the opera would have to assume that their audience will attend the opera with previous visual and audible imprints of how the story is told or needs to be told. Nonetheless, there is a crucial difference in the situation if there is a popular movie adaptation involved in between the play/novel and the opera: The point of reference and arguably the main previous visual and audible imprint is—at least for most of the audience—the same and, at the same time, is known to the authors of the opera.

Furthermore, this imprint can be of iconic proportions. Just remember what Previn faced when dealing with his two adaptation projects: Marlon Brando's half-naked Stanley Kowalski at the bottom of the staircase desperately shouting »Hey Stella!« over Alex North's jazzy soundtrack in *A Streetcar Named Desire* (Henderson, 2003, pp. 113ff.; Davison, 2009, pp. 125ff.). Or Celia Johnson's haunting facial expressions of longing while sitting in the train, her cockney accent coming in from offscreen, summing up the story and melting into one with excerpts from Sergei Rachmaninov's epic *Second Piano Concerto in c-Minor op. 18* in *Brief Encounter*.[13] The connection made between story, picture, and sound is so strong in these two cases that statements about these two adaptations by Kazan and David Lean, respectively, regularly refer to it—like, for example, Lawrence Kramer (»The music is no mere accessory to the story: it is that story.« 2007b, p. 101) and Richard Dyer (»*Brief Encounter* without Rachmaninov is unimaginable.« 1993, p. 49) did when talking about *Brief Encounter*. At least it is safe to say that very specific comparisons are unavoidable when working within this genre and its three-step-adaptation-formula. Almost all critics of Previn's two operas compare movie and opera in this way, and they even seem to feel that they have to make judgments in this regard when they acknowledge that, at least from their point of view, strong connections are missing. Or as one critic of *Brief Encounter* exemplarily noted: »He mercifully avoids referring to Rachmaninov« (Ashley, 2011)—as if Previn's metrical instable, harmonically much more dissonant, rhythmically challenging, and jazz informed art music would tend to sound like the music of Rachmaninov in the first place at any point of his career as a composer.[14] It is just Lean's film that suggests asking if there is any musi-

---

13   At least as far as I can see, there have not been any detailed analyses published of the soundtrack of *Brief Encounter*, just passing remarks here and there although the film is a constant topic for scholarly comments, especially with regard to close-up, gender, Englishness, and in general studies dealing with the British Film or the work of Coward and Lean, respectively. At first, this seems to be astonishing if, at the same time, there seems to be a general consensus of how effective this soundtrack works. The likely reason is that Lean's movie has no »original soundtrack,« that is, no originally composed soundtrack for the movie in question.

14   At least there is no evident reference to Rachmaninov in Previn's art music despite maybe in some passing moments on the more or less superficial level that occasionally does »enjoy making an orchestra ›sound,‹ making it project and play with the wish to sound beautiful,« André Previn, in *TIME* (September 4, 1972), http://content.time.com/time/magazine/article/0,9171,910404,00.html (accessed 22 September 2015). But these moments, although they occur in most of Previn's art music works, are passing ones. See, for detailed comments on this side of Previn's aesthetic as a composer with references to specific moments in several works, Döhl, 2012a, pp. 92–98. However, the situation is different with Previn, the classical conductor and pianist, who has a strong record in performing and recording Rachmaninov. See (P = pianist; CD = conductor; G = Grammy Award winner; Sop = Soprano; Ten = Tenor; Bari = Baritone; LSO = London Symphony Orchestra; RPO = Royal Philharmonic Orchestra): *Sergei Rachmaninov: Piano Concerto No. 1 F sharp-minor op. 1, Piano Concerto No. 4 G-minor op. 40*, Leonard Pennario[P], RPO (1965, RCA Victor LSC 2788)[CD]; *Sergei Rachmaninov: Symphony No. 2 E-minor op. 27*, LSO (1966, RCA LM2899/60791.2RV)[CD]; *Sergei Rachmaninov: Symphony No. 3 A-minor op. 44, The Rock op. 7*, LSO (1968, RCA LM2 990/6801-2-RG/60791.2RV)[CD]; *Sergei Rachmaninov: Piano Concertos No. 1–4, Rhapsody on a Theme of Paganini op. 43*, Vladimir Ashkenazy[P], LSO (1972, London Records CS 6773/CS 6774/CS 6775/417 702-2/425 576-2/Decca SXL 6554/6555/6556/Decca 444 839-2)[CD]; *Sergei Rachmaninov: Symphony No. 2 E-minor op. 27, Vocalise op. 34/14, Aleko: Intermezzo, Aleko: Women's Dance*, LSO (1973, HMV ASD 2889/EMI 2 67969-2)[CD]; *Sergei Rachmaninov: Music*

cal relation between the famous Russian piano concerto und Previn's score. As in the case of *Brief Encounter*, Previn widely ignores the score for the movie in his version of *A Streetcar Named Desire*. Within this three-step-adaptation-formula at least, Previn is dealing with the plays and their earlier adaptations as movies, not with the music of the plays and the movies. Interestingly, this observations hold true for most works written within this genre (Döhl, 2016).

So, on the one hand, working within this three-step-adaptation-formula means to set out on an endeavor that is accompanied by strong, very precise expectations about the story and how it is told in audiovisual terms. On the other hand, this general framework does not need to be only a burden: To know expectations that precisely in advance also allows for working with them creatively. This is the road that Previn and his collaborators[15] followed. With regard to both operas and in special consideration of their music, one aspect in each of the two works is highlighted in the following to illustrate how Previn tried to meet head on with the specific challenge that the three-step-adaptation-formula presents and how he accomplished this differently in the two pieces: Firstly, in *A Streetcar Named Desire*, Previn developed the role of Blanche in a different way in his opera version compared to Kazan's movie. And secondly, in *Brief Encounter*, he adopted the role of visual close-up that is central to Lean's filmic storytelling, while transforming that idea of visual close-up into a musical role in his opera score.

In doing so, we find ourselves addressing, at the same time, a second type of expectation with which an opera composer is regularly confronted when he or she is working within this three-step-adaptation-formula. This type of expectation is no less powerful and just as constantly expressed in comments about operas, like Previn's works, as the first type of expectation described previously with which the second type is interrelated: the idea that there is a strong tendency to »compose film music« for the opera stage within this three-step-adaptation-formula. Some exam-

---

for Two Pianos. Suite No. 1 op. 5, Suite No. 2 op. 17, Symphonic Dances op. 45, Vladimir Ashkenazy[P] (1974, London Records CS 6893/Decca 444 845-2)[P]; *Sergei Rachmaninov: Symphony No. 1 D-minor op. 13*, LSO (1975, HMV ASD 3137/EMI CMS 7 64530-2)[CD]; *Sergei Rachmaninov: Piano Concerto No. 3 D-minor op. 30*, Alicia de Larrocha[P], LSO (1976, Decca SXL 6746)[CD]; *Sergei Rachmaninov: The Bells*, Sheila Armstrong[Sop], Robert Tear[Ten], John Shirley-Quirk[Bari], LSO Chorus, LSO (1976, EMI ASD 3284/3 81513-2)[CD, G]; *Sergei Rachmaninov: Symphonic Dances op. 45, The Isle of the Dead op. 29*, LSO (1976, HMV ASD 3259/Angel CDM-69025/EMI 2 37616-2)[CD]; *Sergei Rachmaninov: Symphony No. 3 A-minor op. 44, Aleko: Intermezzo, Aleko: Women's Dance*, LSO (1977, HMV ASD 3369/Angel CDM 7-69564-2/EMI CMS 7 64530-2)[CD]; *Sergei Rachmaninov: Symphony No. 2 E-minor op. 27*, RPO (1985, Telarc CD-80113)[CD].

15   For *A Streetcar Named Desire*, the libretto was written by Philip Littell and the premiere directed by Colin Graham. For *Brief Encounter*, the libretto was written and the premiere directed by Caird.

ples[16] from reviews about Previn's *A Streetcar Named Desire* shall illustrate this diagnosis:

> *Streetcar* offers a warm bath of nostalgia. Its recurrent splashes of symphonic jazz recall, perhaps deliberately, every soundtrack ever composed for a movie about steamy, jazz-drenched New Orleans. (Kramer, 2007, pp. 72f.) Mr. Previn is not ashamed to incorporate Hollywood code words, especially the wailing thrusts of saxophone, trumpet and clarinet to introduce dissolution and lurid sex. (Holland, 1998, p. E2) If anything, I should have liked Previn to take this aspect of the score a little further, to have set up a more dangerous apposition to the plushy, Gothic, 1940s film noir complexion of his musical mis-en-scène. (Gramophone, April 1999, p. 107) With its mixture of sax-heavy blues and gnawing nostalgia, Previn's score is not unlike Alex North's music for Elia Kazan's 1951 film. True originality is infrequent in this opera. (One of the most striking sections is in Act III, Scene One, during which Previn depicts the intervals of passing time with music that sounds as if it has been electronically accelerated.) However, although one cannot praise Previn for breaking new ground, one can admire the strength and sincerity of his workmanship.

---

16 For more details, see Döhl, 2012a, pp. 239–241. It has to be said that, interestingly, some commentators lament the lack of film music in Previn's opera. See, e.g.: »Previn is an outspoken admirer of Benjamin Britten's music, and he includes an interlude that is pure homage to Britten in its glassy sound and long, arched phrasing. Much of the strength of the score comes from what Previn does not do. There is no New Orleans jazz and no real reference to it. There are no Southern references, no local color. Occasionally, the raw edge of a saxophone tears the emotional fabric, and a vibraphone, sparingly employed, suggests the wavering stability of the heroine.« (Webster, 1998) »More drastically, where is the common aroma of the lower classes? Alas, it isn't here. Aside from a few blues licks, a sliding around in the brass, a clarinet wailing between phrases, the composer writes music dead serious in modern opera style. For ambience of lowdown New Orleans one ought to depend on the music; moreover, in the play Williams asks for offstage blues piano and raucous polkas. In the opera this power of vulgarity is missing. ›Jazz would be too easy,‹ Previn has said. Pity; for that's just what is needed and he's very good at jazz. Instead, one hears an orchestra mired in figurative details that work at odds with the simplicity of the words on stage, an amalgam of musical styles from a myriad of musical sources. The eclectic Previn has acknowledged the influence of Britten, Barber and Strauss; one also hears a touch of Honegger, Milhaud, Berg, and in the orchestration, even Korngold. These musical giants form the now-conservative musical language of 20th century orchestral styles; where is Previn's own language?« (Tartak, 1998) Because Previn's score does relate to the music of classical composers he explicitly admires, like Richard Strauss, Benjamin Britten, or Samuel Barber who have not worked much for the film, it is not only possible but also plausible to hear Previn's score without connecting it to the genre of movies at all, instead referring it to a specific tradition of modern art music. So the reception phenomenon of film music analogies that this paper deals with clearly is not a one-way road, but just the one most often traveled in reviews and other forms of critical comments. But it is hoped that the following arguments will illustrate convincingly that it is at least a road worth traveling, even beyond the musical surface of sounding like symphonic film music here and there.

(Tuttle, 1999) The mix of jazz, blues and classical themes in Previn's score makes for some occasionally uneasy listening, particularly as Williams' words are merely placed on top, rather than within, the music. And while that music doesn't quite match the drama, the director and performers do. (Boland, 2007) For all of Previn's craftsmanship—sensible, sensitive vocal lines; deftly colored, wonderfully assured orchestration—the music often [comes] across as a film score with sung dialogue. Still, Previn's mix of lush, occasionally Broadway-style lyricism with sultry and insinuating inflections strikes many of the right notes for such a tale. He applies jazzy touches, such as a wailing sax and slurring trombone, with admirable subtlety; he turns a simple little jazz riff for a very satisfied Stella at the end of Act 1 into a most revealing glimpse into her character. (Smith, 2004a) For all of Previn's craftsmanship—sensible, sensitive vocal lines, brilliant orchestration—the music suggested a film score with sung dialogue. It still sounds that way now and then in the Washington staging, but the opera somehow comes across as a stronger force. The mix of the lushly romantic with the sultry and insinuating adds up to a more consistently effective musical package. (Smith, 2004b) The chief problem with Previn's Streetcar Named Desire is that it doesn't have enough music in it. It's theatrically effective (but then of course, so is the Tennessee Williams play) and operatically paltry, its deficiencies all the more glaring when the opera is heard but not seen. The instruments are kept busy in the background, and the trumpet riffs, saxophone plaints, and clarinet noodling add splashes of color, but much the same way they might if Previn had simply written a film score. (Lucano, 1999, p. 194) The brassy wah-wahs that open the opera, signifying »Big, Bad City« (and sounding suspiciously like the chords that close each act of Berg's *Lulu)*, plonk us straight into the land of cliché, as does the subsequent garnish of garden variety discordances and trumpet rips. The transitional music that brings characters on and off the scene is the most humdrum sort of hurry-scurry stuff, and the recitatives are punctuated with unimaginative instrumental writing that sounds like discards from an Alex North or David Raksin soundtrack—and not one of their better ones. (McKee, 2000, p. 719) The composer's first opera is crafted with fluency and skill. Previn draws on his jazz background with its bluesy strains—as with Stella's wordless vocalise after an impassioned session with Stanley—and the music is artfully scored and flows easily, a treatment to Previn's Hollywood years. (Johnson, 2013) The initial criticism of the operatic »Streetcar« was that Mr. Previn's hybrid—with hazy Impressionist harmonies, evocations of sultry New Orleans jazz, bursts of agitated angst that recall his work in film, soaring Straussian lyricism, even hints of Berg to convey Blanche's inner demons—simply did not contribute enough to the drama. That remains its shortcoming, though it was interesting to hear the work performed with the orchestra onstage, where the fine points, richness and variety in Mr. Previn's instrumental writing came through. (Tommasini, 2013) Listening to the way Previn's score fits the stage action and libretto it is indeed very cinematic and works in the same way a skilled screen composer (which Previn is) underscores action, giving the visuals a musically dramatic undercurrent equal to the emotional content of the scene. (Magnusson, 2009)

The response to *Brief Encounter* is quite similar, as the following excerpt exemplarily documents: »He may underscore what the characters say or feel, but he doesn't spell out time and place. His real genius here is to, like a film composer, set a mood and, like a jazz musician, let the music take him where it will« (Swed, 2009).

Connecting Previn and film music is not a difficult task and almost suggests itself: He worked between the mid-1940s and the late 1960s in Hollywood, amongst other things winning the remarkable amount of four Academy Awards out of thirteen nominations in his most distinguished area of expertise: the adaptation of Broadway musicals for the silver screen.[17] But to ask Previn to write an opera was not as self-explanatory. Although he had also started to gain attention as a composer of art music since the 1970s (Döhl, 2012a, pp. 219–221, 223ff.), he had at least widely avoided the field of opera as a conductor until Lotfi Mansouri called.[18] Asked why, he had clearly distanced himself from the genre:

> I confess that I am out of sympathy with whole chuncks of the operatic repertoire.[19] I have aspirations to do opera, yes, certainly, but not to the degree that some of my colleagues do. Some of them, certainly Zubin Metha, basically like opera better than anything else and I basically don't. I love the symphony literature and its endless variety too much, and I find it depressing to think of all the music that I will never in the world get to conduct. [...], but if I thought I was going to spend the major part of my every musical day listening to opera singing, I would not be happy. [...] Yes, I am terribly interested in musical drama, but then I think there is such enormous musical drama also in non-singing music. (Previn & Hopkins, 1971, pp. 101–103)

Mansouri, the long-term director of the San Francisco Opera, argued indeed from a different angle when he approached Previn in 1994 with the idea of commissioning an adaptation of *A Streetcar Named Desire* for his opera house: »I love his sound-

---

17 Academy Awards for *Gigi* (1958), *Porgy and Bess* (1959), *Irma la Douce* (1963), and *My Fair Lady* (1964). *Gigi* was an original score for Hollywood by Frederick Loewe and Alan Jay Lerner. See, for a detailed discussion of Previn's work in the film musical business, Döhl, 2012a, pp. 147–150. Previn did the same in jazz where he started, with Shelly Manne and Leroy Vinnegar, a massive trend in the late 1950s/early 1960s of recording jazz albums based exclusively on material from single Broadway shows. See in Döhl, 2013b.

18 As a composer for the stage, his output had also been very limited until this point. It included two musicals for Broadway and West End, respectively, *Coco* (1969; Lyrics: Alan Jay Lerner, starring Katharine Hepburn) and *The Good Companions* (1974; Lyrics: Johnny Mercer, starring Judi Dench). Both shows had solid runs. Original cast albums exist: *Coco* (1969; Paramount PMS 1002) and *The Good Companions* (1974; EMI EMC 3042). Besides this, Previn had written one experimental piece with Tom Stoppard, *Every Good Boy Deserves Favour* (1977), which was also recorded (1978; RCA RL-12855). Furthermore, for Stoppard's play *Rough Crossings* (1984), Previn had written three songs.

19 Previn, quoted in *The Times* (30 May 1972), part of »Clippings André Previn,« New York Public Library.

tracks because they have an incredible sense of drama and personality. Listen to ›Elmer Gantry,‹ ›Bad Day at Black Rock.‹ I told André, ›You're a born opera composer‹« (Mansouri, quoted in Hamlin, 1998, p. 2). So the second type of expectation for film music is not just a phenomenon in the reception of Previn's operas. That he started to work in this genre at all was already caused by the very same expectation, now on the side of his future commissioner.

In the long-term view, Mansouri's statement is not without irony, at least from Previn's perspective, because Previn started already, in advance of the premiere and has continued ever since, to argue against any comparison between his opera scores and the genre of film music: »I am sure, someone, important or unimportant, will accuse me of having composed film music. The work might seem like nothing more than a soundtrack with sung dialogues. But I will contest that view« (Previn, quoted in McKay, 2007). This mindset is not just caused by the bad experiences that Previn had during the 1960s when he tried to establish a career as a conductor of classical music after spending years in Hollywood (Döhl, 2012a, pp. 178–191), an experience whose lasting impression on him was described several times in harsh terms by Previn: »Some critics [...] will forgive you being an axe murderer, but never for scoring a film.«[20] »But somehow, having worked in Hollywood is like being a well-known whore.«[21] More than that, Previn gave reasons for his opposition which are obviously based on his inside knowledge of the film music business: »Writing an opera has nothing to do with writing a film score. A film score is an accompaniment to an already existing series of images. An opera is a musical extension of the word« (Previn, quoted as in Singer, 2009). This argument deals with the differences in the working process and the diverse hierarchies between the artists and arts involved in the kind of collaborative efforts that operas and movies both are. Hereby, Previn's position is in line at least with the mainstream of film music studies.[22]

It is noticeable that, in the reviews etc. I quoted here, it remains widely unclear what film music constitutes and how it differs from opera music in terms of a necessary and sufficient condition. Of course, every kind of music can be part of an opera or film score and in this spirit become opera and film music, respectively (Rosar, 2002, p. 14). More than that, there are aesthetically and historically countless points of

---

20   André Previn, quoted in *Los Angeles Times* (30 April 1984), p. 16.

21   André Previn, quoted in »Almost like Bernstein,« in *TIME* (15 July 1966), http://content. time.com/time/magazine/article/0,9171,836035,00.html (accessed 22 September 2015).

22   See, e.g., Cooke, 2001, p. 797: »Film Music: Music composed, arranged, compiled or improvised to accompany moving pictures«; and p. 807: »[...] continuing primacy accorded to the visual image [...]. [...] moving pictures are the element that quintessentially distinguishes cinema from other mixed media employing music (e.g. radio, theatre and opera).«

contact between the genres.[23] Against this background, it seems reasonable to question if »film music forms a unique ontological kind« (Carroll & Moore, 2011, p. 456) at all. But this is not Previn's problem. What he does is something else, although this is related to the important discussion outlined before: that is to say that any superficial comparisons between his opera scores and the genre of film music fall short, that is, comparisons that are just grounded in the observation that his opera scores include, amongst other things, what Peter Franklin called »the typical cinematic ›love theme‹ of the 1930s and '40s, soaring violins and sobbing horns« (Franklin, 2011, p. 3)—which they do (Döhl, 2012a, pp. 92–98). Hereby, Previn adopts an argument by Noël Carroll and Margaret Moore as his own: »It is hard to see how sounding like film music would count toward a piece of music being film music as a matter of conceptual necessity« (Carroll & Moore, 2011, p. 457).

Returning to Previn's main argument, shown in the following in his handling of the character of Blanche in *A Streetcar Named Desire* and of the idea of close-up in *Brief Encounter*, that it is indeed a question of words and images that are constitutive for the relationship of his opera scores to the genre of film in general and the movies of Kazan and Lean in particular. As argued here, these two small examples allow us to draw general conclusions about this type of relationship and based hereupon about the three-step-adaptation-formula in question and the significant current trend in contemporary American opera it constitutes. First and foremost, these examples show in comparison that, even if you associate this three-step-adaptation-formula with making »movies for the stage,«[24] the spectrum of what can be done and how the relationship of the opera score to the genre of film can be defined in general as well as with regard to the specific movie referred to in particular is as far-reaching in opposing directions as it is also far-reaching beyond the musical surface of sound analogies to film music conventions. This means that comparing operas that are part of this new genre to film music aesthetics allows for the exploration of interesting insides of these works. But that real insides about the relationship of these opera adaptations to their originals can only be reached by digging deeper than the musical surface of *sounding like* film music. This is what Previn's approach stands for.

---

23   See, for an introduction to the field, Tambling, 1987; van der Lek, 1991; Kivy, 1997; Schroeder, 2002; Joe & Theresa, 2002; Duncan, 2003; Franke, 2006; Cooke, 2008, pp. 132–145; Yang, 2008; Citron, 2010; Dyer, 2010, pp. 14–18; Franklin, 2011; Joe, 2013; Citron, 2014.

24   See, for a detailed discussion, Döhl, 2012b. This wording I borrowed from Stephen Sondheim. It is part of a passage in which he describes the character of his work *Sweeney Todd* in relation to the Hitchcock soundtracks written by Bernard Herrmann, see Sondheim, 2010, p. 332.

All Eyes and Ears on Blanche: On *A Streetcar Named Desire*

A huge amount of academic and nonacademic literature has been written that deals with Williams's play and/or Kazan's movie.[25] Many different aspects have been singled out and discussed in great detail, including questions of Southern society, racial and gender equality, sexuality, language, social constraints, alcoholism, production history, textual criticism, editorial history, realism, film adaptation and film music, and censorship in Hollywood. To explore how Previn's operatic adaptation of *A Streetcar Named Desire* relates to all of these questions is an endeavour that has not been made more than cursorily so far. In such a short chapter, only one aspect could be highlighted against the background of this rich field of research, albeit it is one that is as characteristic for Previn's approach as it is for the recent trend in contemporary American opera of which his work is a prominent part. The aspect highlighted here is how Previn handled the role of Blanche to which the emphasis of his score shifted—or more precisely: shifted back to what at least from Previn's point of view is her role in Williams's original: »I looked at the film before I wrote note one and not since, because it's dangerous. The emphasis got switched when everybody's consciousness became suffused with Brando's performance. The play is really about her, and she has an absolutely enormous part in the opera« (Previn, quoted in Kolin, 2000, p. 168).

This shift in emphasis is especially evident in the many arias and quasi-aria passages that Blanche sings during the course of the opera. It is not just that most of the melodically interesting music is hers. It is that in the opera Blanche tends to monologise while in the movie Blanche's character is basically developed in dialogue. In the movie, it is through her reactions that we start to learn step-by-step what Blanche is really about, allowing us to look behind her facade and understand her earlier comments in retrospect. The harshness, honesty, and naivety of her comments gain their power from the confrontation and irritation they evoke. These are, most of the times, shorter moments contextualized within a fast interplay between the four main characters in alternating constellations. Although in the movie it is also Blanche's fortune that dominates the scenario, Kazan's version of the story enabled three of the four actresses and actors, respectively, to achieve Academy Award winning performances (Vivien Leigh, Kim Hunter, and Karl Malden), while the fourth, Marlon Brando, laid the foundation here for the legend he became. That a

---

25   See, for an introduction to the field Miller, 1971; Kolin, 1993; Londré, 1997, pp. 45–66; Kolin, 1998, pp. 51–79; Kolin, 2000; Bak, 2004; Staggs, 2005; Bloom, 2005; Smith-Howard & Heintzelman, 2005, pp. 268–279; Bloom, 2009; Bray, 2009; Clericuzio, 2012; Adler, 2013; Murphy, 2014, pp. 77–90; McConachie, 2014, pp. 181–205. Useful information also includes many books and articles about postwar American theatre and cinema in general as well as literature written by or about main contributors for the stage play and/or the film, namely the actors and the director.

movie gives a platform on such equal terms to so many actresses and actors is unusual. Here, the four main roles are very well balanced despite the fact that Blanche still is the figure around whom the story is centred.

Previn's approach is different and much more focused on Blanche. What he basically does is give her time: time to »talk« about things, to reflect and express feelings. The pace of the movie is much faster with regard to verbal interaction. Previn transforms Blanche's role to the speed of opera that is dependent on the slower moving speed of classical singing compared to spoken language (Hutcheon & O'Flynn, 2013, p. 45). This is one main reason why the common, sound-based attribution to his opera score being film music remains on the surface of the music. Here and there, its sounds seem to be informed of symphonic film music. And they obviously are not just because of Previns vita (Döhl, 2012a, pp. 92–98). So in part, his opera score for *A Streetcar Named Desire* may *sound like* film music, but it *is* not film music. Common to opera music and unusual to film music—especially when compared to Kazan's film and North's soundtrack—Previn takes much more time to let one person speak and develop the meaning and expression of the words through their musical realization as a chant. It becomes an »extension of the word,« as Previn has called it. Rather, a classic conflict can be seen here within the genre of opera at play between the tendency of the drama to move forward and the tendency of a musical realization of the words to stop the drama and express.

Previn pushes this operatic strategy even further with key arias in the third act, certifying his will to compose in an operatic way: After the rape, close to the end before Blanche is taken away, he interpolates the aria *I Can Smell the Sea Air*. It is a kind of dream sequence. We meet Blanche fantasizing about an ideal world just after her real world has been finally destroyed. The opera takes much more time to develop this state of mind into which Blanche has fallen after her nervous breakdown that was caused by her experience of being raped. Even for this traumatic experience (that is not seen explicitly in visual terms on stage), the opera invests several minutes of orchestral music while the film, not least due to obligations by the censors, limits itself to the picture of a mirror breaking as a visual symbol for what is happening.

Previn's operatic, not filmic strategy becomes even clearer when a short look is taken at his aria *I Want Magic*. In the movie, Blanche's phrase »I don't want realism. I want magic« and the few lines that follow are just a quick reply by Blanche toward Mitch when they are basically fighting about the sex life she had in her past. Like most of the important moments of the movie, it is a moment without music. But it is a crucial remark that Previn picks up here. In these few sentences, and how Vivien Leigh's Blanche verbally and facially expresses them, almost smashing them against Mitch, lies every answer to why she had decided to take this self-determined road, what she had missed in her »real life,« and that it is much more than sex she is talking about here. It is a constant struggle of self-determination and dependence on men that Blanche is caught in. That Stanley kills every self-determination soon afterward by raping her while, at the same time, imposing all the mental and physical consequences of this act on her, is the real tragedy of the story. Mitch cannot understand Blanche's point of view either. It is against the »small world« social conventions that are all he knows and that he constantly tries to justify by referring to his mother as the authority of order (as Stanley does in a similar manner in regard to the Napoleonic code he mentions several times). As outlined before, the opera takes much more time in the end than the movie to express the tragedy: Blanche's rape, her breakdown and fall into madness, and, finally, her being picked up by the psychiatric doctor. To balance this and gain at the same time further power for the tragedy that follows, Previn decided to give her some magic beforehand as well. This is what he develops from the small lines of »I don't want realism. I want magic«: out of not even 15 seconds of filmic time, he creates one of the most powerful, widely sung arias in the contemporary operatic repertoire which lasts about three-and-a-half minutes. It is not that there is much more that Blanche is saying here in these almost 200 seconds than in Kazan's 15 seconds. But she says it differently, in terms of music, exemplifying the differences between the genres and their media. Kazan's Blanche is desperately shouting with tears in her eyes. The words of Previn's Blanche are slow-moving in elaborate melodic lines, difficult to sing in their high pianissimos, while exploring different states of expression en route. Blanche, in the movie, is acting the realism that her words oppose. In the opera, she expresses the fantasy-like magic she talks about. Both solutions are very effective although they are antithetic. And both solutions rely on the strength of their respective genres and their main media: in the movie, it is close-up acting, fast cuts, and artistic lighting. In the opera, it is extending the words through music.

This example illustrates that the three-step-adaptation-formula does not aim at staging a movie as closely as possible in an opera house. It is about taking advantage of the fact that the audience will likely know the movie adaptation and not just the original play or novel, and through that the storyline; and to go from there and explore the difference and relations between the genres of novel, play, movie, and opera and their respective aesthetic and media specifics.

Longing in Close-up: On *Brief Encounter*

In *Brief Encounter*, it is also a question of time that defines the relationship between the genres of movie and opera in this score. But instead of displaying the different temporalities that characterize most works of these two genres (at least until the time structure of the movie is not also regulated by singing) as Previn does in *A Streetcar Named Desire*, he aims here at incorporating a true filmic time structure and function that is enclosed on the visual level of a close-up into the musical level of his opera score.

The libretto for the opera by John Caird is mainly based on Noël Coward's screenplay for Lean's movie version of *Brief Encounter*[26] which was premiered in late 1945. For the movie, Coward hugely extended a play of his own called *Still Life* which had been premiered in London in 1936 (Day, 2005, p. 95). Despite adding some more characters and places of action, the key difference between the play and the movie is the shift in the focus of the narration toward the main female character Laura Jessen: The story is told from her perspective.[27] We see her in action and listen to her commentary from offscreen while she tells the story in retrospect. Still, *Brief Encounter* is also in the movie version basically an intimate play and it is »the restricted range of characters [that] further simplifies and intensifies the structure« (Ellis, 2000, p. 101). Today, Coward's story is mostly known in its filmic adaptation, not in its original theatrical form.[28] In this regard, the case of Previn's *Brief Encounter* is different compared to his *A Streetcar Named Desire* where Williams's play is still staged widely. With *Brief Encounter*, the reception has become clearly focused exclusively on the movie.

In this case, Previn tried to meet the filmic challenge again head on, but this time in the opposite direction. In *Brief Encounter*, he establishes a close but not superficial relationship between the movie and opera adaptations. He spotted visual close-ups as Lean's main medium. In the movie, it is »haunting close-ups that catch the undertones of hope and worry« (Phillips, 2006, p. 97). And it is the faces of the main protagonists, as shown in the close-ups, that basically tell the story in the key scenes and rarely the words that are spoken or the action that is taken. Often, words and actions even contradict the emotions that are witnessed in the facial expressions. In fact, Lean's approach is not adoptable to the opera stage without presenting challenges with regard to the standards and conventions of the genre. Because of the distances, as Carroll has explained, the use of the medium of visual close-up one-to-one in the opera house is impossible without opting for the integration of film media directly, a strategy not uncommon in contemporary opera and that was also part, for example, of a successful recent adaptation of the same movie for the theatre

---

26   Credits onscreen call Coward the author of the play and producer. The screenplay was written in collaboration with Lean, Ronny Neame, and Anthony Havelock-Allen, who are listed as screenplay writers in the credits, although Coward even had the last word when he was abroad, see Dyer, 1993, p. 70; Phillips, 2006, pp. 86–89.

27   Phillips, 2006, p. 87. The original play, *Still Life*, is part of a series of nine one-act plays, *Tonight at 8:30*. Its new finale in the movie is adopted from another play in this series, *Shadow Play*. See Phillips, 2006, p. 95.

28   This is, for example, evident in the fact that the screenplay has been released in several editions, see, e.g., Manvell, 1950; Taylor, 1974, [2]1990.

stage by Kneehigh Theatre,[29] but a strategy which was not used by Previn and his collaborators:

> In both theater and film, lightning is an important device for guiding audience attention. But in film, the director has variable framing at her disposal as well. The filmmaker may not only enhance the illumination of the central character in order to draw our attention to him; the director can also show him in a close-up. Moreover, the hold of a close-up on the audience's attention. All things being equal, is more relentless than the use of lightning for the obvious reason that the close-up leaves the spectator with nothing else to see but that which the director mandates. Whereas in the theater, our attention might be drawn from center stage to stage right, when it comes to close-up, there *is* no stage right to divert our attention. It has been, to say, deleted. By means of devices like the close-up, the film director can assure that the spectator is looking exactly where, from the perspective of the narrative, he should be, at precisely the moment that he should be looking there. (Carroll, 2003, p. 35)

It is the last sentence that is the key to what Previn is doing here. He created small musical episodes that are not repeated or used as Leitmotifs in the course of the opera, but that are clearly distinguished from the music that surrounds them. These ephemeral episodes—»brief encounters,« if you will—work like »affection-images« (Deleuze, 1986, p. 87), to use a term coined by Gilles Deleuze. They work like a sudden filmic cut into a close-up. With these »brief encounters,« Previn »adds meaning« (Cohen, 2000, p. 361)[30] with music in a similar manner as Lean did with close-up pictures, following Béla Balázs' dictum that close-ups allow us to »see to the bottom of the soul« (Balázs, quoted in McGinn, 2005, pp. 51f.). Picking up Carroll's agenda for the close-up, Previn assures that the spectator is listening at precisely the moment that he or she should be attentive to what, from the perspective of the narrative, is happening, to recognize at all that there is something happening between the main protagonists when words or actions do not portray this or even contradict the development of the emotions that, in Lean's movie the close-up and in Previn's opera score his musical equivalents, convey to the audience.

To conclude, one final example shall illustrate this point[31]: In Act I, Scene nine of Previn's *Brief Encounter,* Laura is coming home to her husband Fred. During a light-hearted conversation in the living room about their family, having just recovered from the shock of a minor accident of the couple's son, Laura mentions that she has met a man, saying: »I had lunch today with a strange man at the Kardomah Café.« This sentence seems to be as innocent as possible and Fred seems not even to take real notice as he is doing a crossword puzzle. The couple's conversation moves

---

29 See http://www.kneehigh.co.uk/show/brief-encounter.php (accessed 8 March 2014); Georgi, 2013, pp. 66–78. See for reviews, e.g., Brantley, 2010; Spencer, 2008.

30 Hereby, Previn's »brief encounters« also fulfill a classic function of film music (Levinson, 2006, pp. 156f.).

31 For further examples, see Döhl, 2013b, pp. 327–330.

forward as if nothing has happened. In Lean's movie, Laura turns to Fred before she speaks the sentence (Example 1). From there on, we see her in close-up and it is her facial expression that strongly contradicts that the meeting she reports as superficial and as innocent as possible is anything close to meaningless.

Example 1: David Lean, Brief Encounter (1945).
Film Still, The Criterion Collection CC2123BD 2012, ca. 35:10 min.

Previn finds a musical equivalent (Example 2) that works just as fine as Lean's close-up:

Example 2: André Previn, Brief Encounter (2009).
Score. G. Schirmer: New York 2009, measures 141–142, p. 222.[32]

---

32 Music example created by the author based on the score published by G. Schirmer, New York. This was first published and used by permission in Döhl, 2012a, p. 277. On the

It is not that this passage itself, in isolation, shows something musically extra-ordinary. This is true for all of Previn's »brief encounters.« But they do not have to be true to function in the way described here; they just have to stand out from the rest of the music. Music is an art form of context. It is a typical finding for a musicologist when he or she is interested in a specific passage in a work of music, for example for its beauty, and he or she analyzes the score trying to find what makes that moment so special, that it is very seldom there in the isolated moment in question, a moment like these two measures. It is the musical context that uplifts its impact. In this example, Previn changes, for a split second, the instrumentation, pitch, texture, and level of dissonance in the chord structure, etc. It works like a sound gesture, a blink of an eye, as we see a little smile running across Laura's eyes when she speaks the sentence in question to Fred, which he cannot see as he is looking down at his crossword puzzle. He just hears what she says; and so, he misses the real meaning of her words. What the close-up of Laura's eyes achieves in the movie is exactly what the two measures in the sheet music example achieve in lieu of the close-up that the opera house does not reveal due to the distance between singers and audience.

An Opera Composer of Desire

As, on the one hand, these two examples show, the spectrum of what can be done and how the relationship can be defined of an opera score written within this three-step-adaptation-formula to the genre of movies in general and the specific movie each work refers to in particular is immense and far-reaching in opposing directions. This means that comparing operas that are part of this genre only to film music aesthetics allows for the exploration of interesting insides in these works. But that real insides about the relationship of these opera adaptations to their originals can only be reached by digging deeper than the musical surface of *sounding like* film music.

On the other hand, these two operas show that, although they are in one respect—their relation to the genre of film—antithetic in their approach, they are closely linked in another sense. As different as these two operas and their respective theatric originals and their earlier filmic adaptations are, they share the same fuel running their respective engines: desire collapsing in front of social constraints. Here and there, it is trains that function as a symbol for this purpose, although the approach toward desire is different: Here, in *A Streetcar Named Desire*, Blanche's desire for happiness is crushed by Stanley's physical desires. In *Brief Encounter*, Laura and Alex ultimately shy away from any physical and emotional fulfilment of their

---

recording of *Brief Encounter* (2011, Deutsche Grammophon 477 9351 9), the passage in question can be found on CD 1, track 13, at about 4:20 min.

desire for loving and longing. In a similar drastic manner, both dramas come to an abrupt halt about the question of desire. As an opera composer, this question is Previn's main topic. And he deals with this subject in the context of a three-step-adaptation-formula which forces him at the same time to deal with the relationship of earlier canonical filmic adaptations in particular and the genre of movies in general, on the one hand, and the operatic stage and its specifics, on the other. The antithetic solutions he developed in the process of these projects illustrate the range of possibilities that this new operatic genre possesses as a field for a specific form of adaptations of second order. And that their relationship to the genre of film brings something new to the table of the format of making an opera based on a well-known play or novel.

References

(2006). A Nathanael West Novel Gets Its Turn on the Opera Stage. *The New York Times*, April 26. http://www.nytimes.com/2006/04/28/arts/music/28juil.html?_r=0 (accessed 22 September 2015).

Abbate, C. & Parker, R. (2013). *Eine Geschichte der Oper: Die letzten 400 Jahre*. München: C. H. Beck.

Abfalter, D. (2008). *Das Unmessbare messen? Die Konstruktion von Erfolg im Musiktheater*. Wiesbaden: VS Research.

Adler, T. P. (2013). *Tennessee Williams. A Streetcar Named Desire / Cat on a Hot Tin Roof*. London: Palgrave Macmillan.

Adorno, T. W. (2004). *Aesthetic Theory*. New York: Continuum.

Agid, P. & Tarondeau, J.-C. (2010). *The Management of Opera. An International Comparative Study*. London: Palgrave Macmillan.

Ashley, T. (2011). Previn: Brief Encounter—Review. *The Guardian*, 12 May. http://www.the guardian.com/music/2011/may/12/andre-previn-brief-encounter-classical (accessed 22 September 2015).

Aspden, S. (2012). Opera and National Identity. In N. Till (Ed.), *The Cambridge Companion to Opera Studies* (pp. 276–297). Cambridge: Cambridge University Press.

Bak, J. S. (2014). Criticism on »A Streetcar Named Desire.« A Bibliographic Survey, 1947–2003. *Cercles*, 10. http://www.cercles.com/n10/bak.pdf (accessed 22 September 2015).

Belina-Johnson, A. & Scott, D. B. (Eds.). (2005). *The Business of Opera*. Aldershot: Ashgate.

Bloom, H. (Ed.). (2005). *Tennessee Williams's A Streetcar Named Desire*. New York: Chelsea.

Bloom, H. (Ed.). (2009). *Tennessee Williams's A Streetcar Named Desire*. New York: Chelsea.

Boland, M. (2007). A Streetcar Named Desire. *Variety*, 9 August. http://variety.com/2007/legit/reviews/a-streetcar-named-desire-19-1200557265/ (accessed 22 September 2015).

Bourdieu, P. (1993). *The Field of Cultural Production*. Cambridge: Cambridge University Press.

Brantley, B. (2010). Arm's-Length Soul Mates, Swooning but Stoically Chaste. *The New York Times*, 28 September. http://theater.nytimes.com/2010/09/29/theater/reviews/29brief.ht ml?pagewanted=all&_r=0 (accessed 22 September 2015).

Bray, R. (Ed.). (2009). *The Tennessee Williams Annual Review*, 10. http://www.tennessee williamsstudies.org/journal/issue.php?year=2009 (accessed 22 September 2015).

Calico, J. H. (2002). »Für eine neue deutsche Nationaloper«: Opera in the Discourse of Unification and Legitimation in the German Democratic Republic. In C. Applegate & P. Potter (Eds.), *Music and German National Identity* (pp. 190–204). Chicago: The University of Chicago Press.

Carroll, N. & Moore, M. (2011). Music and Motion Pictures. In T. Gracyk & A. Kania (Eds.), *The Routledge Companion to Philosophy and Music* (pp. 456–467). New York: Routledge.

Carroll, N. (2003). *Engaging the Moving Image*. New Haven, CT: Yale University Press.

Carroll, N. (2009). *On Criticism*. New York: Routledge.

Citron, M. J. (2010). *When Opera Meets Film*. Cambridge: Cambridge University Press.

Citron, M. J. (2014). Opera and Film. In David Neumeyer (Ed.), *The Oxford Handbook of Film Music Studies* (pp. 44–71). New York: Oxford University Press.

Clericuzio, A. (Ed.). (2012). *One Hundred Years of Desire: Tennessee Williams 1911–2011*. Perugia: Guerra.

Cohen, A. J. (2000). Film Music. Perspectives from Cognitive Psychology. In J. Buhler, C. Flinn & D. Neumeyser (Eds.), *Music and Cinema* (pp. 360–377). Hanover, NH: Wesleyan University Press.

Cooke, M. (2001). Film Music. In S. Sadie (Ed.), *The New Grove Dictionary of Music and Musicians*. 2nd Edition, vol. 8 (pp. 797–810). London: Macmillan.

Cooke, M. (2008). *A History of Film Music*. Cambridge: Cambridge University Press.

Davison, A. (2009). *Alex North's A Streetcar Named Desire: A Film Score Guide*. Lanham, MD: Scarecrow.

Day, B. (2005). *Coward on Film. The Cinema of Noël Coward*. Lanham, MD: Scarecrow Press.

Deleuze, G. (1986). *Cinema 1. The Movement Image*. Minneapolis, MN: University of Minnesota Press.

Derrida, J. (1980). The Law of Genre. *Critical Inquiry*, 7 (1), 55–81.

Döhl, F. (2012a). *André Previn. Musikalische Vielseitigkeit und ästhetischer Erfahrung*. Stuttgart: Franz Steiner Verlag.

Döhl, F. (2012b). Movie for the Stage? Zu André Previns Opern. *Archiv für Musikwissenschaft,* 69 (1), 51–64.

Döhl, F. (2013b). »Brief Encounter«: Zu David Leans Film (1945) und André Previns Oper (2009). *Archiv für Musikwissenschaft,* 70 (4), 311–332.

Döhl, F. (2013b). Book Musicals im Jazz um 1960: André Previns »Modern Jazz Performances« von *My Fair Lady* (1956) und *Porgy & Bess* (1959). *Lied und populäre Kultur / Song and Popular Culture. Jahrbuch des Deutschen Volksliedarchivs,* 58, 73–105.

Döhl, F. (2013c). André Previn. In Charles Hiroshi Garrett (Ed.), *New Grove Dictionary of American Music.* 2nd Edition, vol. 6 (pp. 597–599). New York: Oxford University Press.

Döhl, F. (2013d). André Previn. In Hanns-Werner Heister & Walter Wolfgang Sparrer (Eds.), *Komponisten der Gegenwart.* München: edition text + kritik.

Döhl, F. (2016). American Opera through American Content: Die amerikanische Metropole in der gegenwärtig florierenden Suche nach einer »Great American Opera.« *Jahrbuch für Musikwirtschafts- und Musikkulturforschung, 1* (in print).

Döhl, F. (2016). *Die Rückkehr der Great American Opera. Opernadaptionen aus Literatur, Theater und Film, 1998–2015.* Berlin: Neofelis Verlag (in print).

Duncan, D. (2003). *Charms That Soothe: Classical Music and the Narrative Film.* New York: Fordham University Press.

Dyer, R. (1993). *Brief Encounter.* London: British Film Institute.

Dyer, R. (2010). *Nino Rota. Music, Film and Feeling.* London: British Film Institute.

Ellis, J. (2000). British Cinema as Performance Art: Brief Encounter, Radio Parade of 1935 and the Circumstances of Film Exhibition. In J. Ashby & A. Higson (Eds.), *British Cinema, Past and Present* (pp. 95–109). New York: Routledge.

Fabbri, F. (1982). A Theory of Musical Genres: Two Applications. In D. Horn & P. Tagg (Eds.), *Popular Music Perspectives* (pp. 52–81). Göteberg & Exeter: IASPM.

Franke, L. (2006). The Godfather III: Film, Opera, and the Generation of Meaning. In Phil Powrie & Robynn Stilwell (Eds.), *Changing Tunes: The Use of Pre-Existing Music in Film* (pp. 31–45). Aldershot: Ashgate.

Franklin, P. (2011). *Seeing Through Music. Gender and Modernism in Classic Hollywood Film Scores.* Oxford: Oxford University Press.

Fraser, P. & Fraser, I. (2014). Creating the Opera Habit. Marketing and the Experience of Opera. In D. O'Reilly, R. Rentschler & T. Kirchner (Eds.), *The Routledge Companion to Arts Marketing* (pp. 393–402). New York: Routledge.

Frith, S. (1998). *Performing Rites. On the Value of Popular Music.* Cambridge, MA: Harvard University Press.

Frow, J. (2006). *Genre.* New York: Routledge.

Fryer, P. (2014). The Business of Opera: Opera, Advertising and the Return to Popular Culture. In P. Fryer (Ed.), *Opera in the Media Age: Essays on Art, Technology and Popular Culture* (pp. 7–31). Jefferson, NC: McFarland.

Garrett, C. H. (2013). American Opera in the Video and Digital Age. In C. H. Garrett (Ed.), *The Grove Dictionary of American Music* (pp. 225–228). New York: Oxford University Press.

Georgi, C. (2013). Kneehigh Theatre's Brief Encounter: »Live on Stage—Not the Film.« In L. Raw & D. E. Tutan (Eds.), *The Adaptation of History. Essays of Ways of Telling the Past* (pp. 66–78). Jefferson, NC: McFarland.

Glendhill, C. (2000). Rethinking Genre. In C. Gledhill & L. Williams (Eds.), *Reinventing Film Studies* (pp. 221–243). London: Arnold.

Goehr, L. (2011). »Amerikamüde/Europamüde.« The Actuality of American Opera. In L. Goehr, *Elective Affinities. Musical Essays on the History of Aesthetic Theory* (pp. 257–305). New York: Columbia University Press.

Green, J. (2008). Behold! An Operatic Miracle. *The New York Times*, 20 January. http://www.nytimes.com/2008/01/20/arts/music/20gree.html?_r=0 (accessed 22 September 2015).

Griffel, M. R. (2013). *Opera in English. A Dictionary*. Lanham, MD: Scarecrow Press.

Halliwell, M. (2005). *Opera and the Novel: The Case of Henry James*. Amsterdam: Rodopi.

Halliwell, M. (2008). From Novel into Film into Opera: Multiple Transformations of Emily Brontë's »Wuthering Heights.« In D. F. Urrows (Ed.), *Essays on World/Music Adaptation and on Surveying the Field* (pp. 29–57). Amsterdam: Rodopi.

Hamlin, J. (1998). Taking »Streetcar« to the Opera. *SFGate*, 19 July. http://articles.sfga te.com/1998-07-19/entertainment/17726955_1_new-opera-streetcar-san-francisco-opera (accessed 22 September 2015).

Henderson, S. S. (2003). *Alex North, Film Composer: A Biography, with Analyses of A Streetcar Named Desire, Spartacus, The Misfits, Under the Volcano, and Prizzi's Honor*. Jefferson, MO: McFarland.

Höhne, S., Schmidt, R.-P. & Wittmann, O. (2005). »Zwischen Kunst und Kommerz« – Fallstudien zur Institution Oper in den USA: Repertoire, Struktur, Finanzierung, aktuelle Entwicklungen. In S. Höhne (Ed.), *»Amerika, Du hast es besser?« Kulturpolitik und Kulturförderung in kontrastiver Perspektive* (pp. 159–204). Leipzig: Leipziger Universitätsverlag.

Holland, B. (1998). Pursuing the Soul of »Streetcar« in Opera. *The New York Times*, 21 September, E2. http://www.nytimes.com/1998/09/21/arts/music-review-pursuing-the-soul-ofstreetcar-in-opera.html (accessed 22 September 2015).

Holt, F. (2006). *Genre in Popular Music*. Chicago: Chicago University Press.

Hutcheon, L. & O'Flynn, S. (2013). *A Theory of Adaptation*. New York: Routledge.

Hutcheon, L. & Hutcheon, M. (2014). The Inward Turn: American Opera Revisits America's Past. *Canadian Review of American Studies*, 44 (2), 178–193.

Huwiler, E. (2010). Engaging the Ear: Teaching Radio Drama Adaptations. In D. Cutchins, L. Raw & J. M. Welsh (Eds.), *Redefining Adaptation Studies* (pp. 133–146). Lanham, MD: Scarecrow Press.

Jameson, F. (1982). Towards a New Awareness of Genre. *Science Fiction Studies*, 28, 322–324.

Joe, J. & Theresa, R. (Eds.). (2002). *Between Opera and Cinema*. New York: Routledge.

Joe, J. (2013). *Opera as Soundtrack*. Aldershot: Ashgate.

Johnson, L. A. (2013). Lyric Opera's inspired cast and artful staging can't make the case for Previn's pallid »Streetcar.« *Chicago Classical Review*, 27 March. http://chicagoclassicalre view.com/2013/03/lyric-operas-inspired-cast-and-artful-staging-cant-make-the-case-for-previns-pallid-streetcar/ (accessed 22 September 2015).

Kelly, B. L. (Ed.). (2008). *French Music, Culture, and National Identity, 1870–1939*. Rochester, NY: University of Rochester Press.

Kim, B. K. & Jensen, M. (2011). How Product Order Affects Market Identity: Repertoire Ordering in the U.S. Opera Market. *Administrative Science Quarterly*, 56 (2), 238–256.

Kirk, E. K. (2001). *American Opera*. Champaign, IL: University of Illinois Press.

Kirk, E. K. (2005). American Opera: Innovation and Tradition. In M. Cooke (Ed.), *The Cambridge Companion to Twentieth-Century Opera* (pp. 197–208). Cambridge: Cambridge University Press.

Kivy, P. (1997). Music in the Movies. A Philosophical Enquiry. In R. Allen & M. Smith (Eds.), *Film Theory and Philosophy* (pp. 308–328). Oxford: Oxford University Press.

Koch, G. R. (1999). Zur Gegenwartslage der Oper. In U. Bermbach (Ed.), *Oper im 20. Jahrhundert. Entwicklungstendenzen und Komponisten* (pp. 221–236). Stuttgart: Verlag J. B. Metzler.

Kolin, P. C. (1998). A Streetcar Named Desire. In P. C. Kolin (Ed.), *Tennessee Williams. A Guide to Research and Performance* (pp. 51–79). Westport, CT: Greenwood Press.

Kolin, P. C. (2000). *Williams: A Streetcar Named Desire*. Cambridge: Cambridge University Press.

Kolin, P. C. (Ed.). (1993). *Confronting Tennessee Williams's »A Streetcar Named Desire.«* Westport, CT: Greenwood Press.

Kramer, L. (2007a). The Great American Opera: Klinghoffer, Streetcar, and the Exception. *The Opera Quarterly*, 23 (1), 66–80.

Kramer, L. (2007b). *Why Classical Music Still Matters*, Berkeley, CA: University of California Press.

Lek, R. v. d. (1991). *Diegetic Music in Opera and Film. A Similarity between Two Genres of Drama Analyzed in Works by Erich Wolfgang Korngold*. Amsterdam: Rodopi.

Lena, J. C. & Peterson, R. A. (2008). Classification as Culture. Types and Trajectories of Music Genres. *American Sociological Review*, 73, 697–718.

Levinson, J. (2006). Film Music and Narrative Agency. In J. Levinson, *Contemplating Art. Essays in Aesthetics* (pp. 143–183). New York: Oxford University Press.

Londré, F. H. (1997). A Streetcar Running Fifty Years. In M. C. Roudané (Ed.), *The Cambridge Companion to Tennessee Williams* (pp. 45–66). Cambridge: Cambridge University Press.

Lucano, R. V. (1999). Previn: A Streetcar Named Desire. *American Record Guide*, 62 (2), 194.

Magnusson, M. (2009). Blanche Meets Stanley Anew, Reintroduced as Opera. *operatoday.com*, 11 December. http://www.operatoday.com/content/2009/12/a_streetcar_nam.php (accessed 22 September 2015).

Manvell, R. (Ed.). (1950). *Three British Screenplay*. London: Methuen.

Marino, S. (2013). A View from the Bridge. In E. Brater (Ed.), *A Student Handbook to the Plays of Arthur Miller* (pp. 157–204). New York: Bloomsbury.

McConachie, B. (2014). All in the Timing: The Meanings of »Streetcar« in 1947 and 1951. In Brenda Murphy, *The Theatre of Tennessee Williams* (pp. 181–205). New York: Bloomsbury.

McGinn, C. (2005). *The Power of Movies. How Screen and Mind Interact*. New York: Random House.

McKay, L. (2007). The Music of »Desire.« *The Vienna Review*, 2 March. http://www.viennareview.net/on-the-town/on-stage/the-music-of-desire (accessed 22 September 2015).

McKee, D. (2000). A Streetcar Named Desire. André Previn. *The Opera Quarterly*, 16 (4), 718–723.

Midgette. A. (2006). In Search for the Next Great American Opera. *The New York Times*, 19 March. http://www.nytimes.com/2006/03/19/arts/music/19midg.html?pagewanted=all&_r=0 (accessed 22 September 2015).

Midgette. A. (2007). The Voice of American Opera. *The Opera Quarterly*, 23 (1), 81–95.

Miller, J. Y. (Ed.). (1971). *Twentieth Century Interpretations of »A Streetcar Named Desire.«* Englewood Cliffs, NJ: Prentice-Hall.

Mulcahy, K. V. (2003). Entrepreneurship or Cultural Darwinism? Privatization and American Cultural Patronage. *The Journal of Arts Management, Law, and Society*, 33 (3), 165–184.

Murphy, B. (2014). *The Theatre of Tennessee Williams*. New York: Bloomsbury.

Neale, S. (1980). *Genre*. London: British Film Institute.

Negus, K. (1999). *Music Genres and Corporate Cultures*. New York: Routledge.

Opera America (Ed.). (2016). *North American Works Dictionary*. http://www.operaamerica.org/Applications/nawd/timeLine.aspx (accessed 22 September 2015).

Payne, N. (2005). Opera in the Market Place. In M. Cooke (Ed.), *The Cambridge Companion to Twentieth-Century Opera* (pp. 306–320). Cambridge: Cambridge University Press.

Payne, N. (2012). The Business of Opera. In N. Till (Ed.), *The Cambridge Companion to Opera Studies* (pp. 53–69). Cambridge: Cambridge University Press.

Peterson, R. A. & Anand, N. The Production of Cultural Perspective. *Annual Review of Sociology*, 30 (2004), 311–334.

Phillips, G. D. (2006). *Beyond the Epic. The Life & Films of David Lean*. Lexington, KY: University of Kentucky Press.

Pierce, J. L. (2000). Programmatic Risk-Taking by American Opera Companies. *Journal of Cultural Economics*, 24, 45–63.

Previn, A. & Hopkins, A. (1971). *Music Face to Face*. London: Hamilton.

Rosar, W. H. (2002). Film Music—What's in a Name? *Journal of Film Music*, 1, 1–18.

Rosmarin, L. (1999). *When Literature Becomes Opera*. Amsterdam: Rodopi.

Ross, A. (2007). Agit-Opera. »Mahagonny« and »The Grapes of Wrath.« *The New Yorker*, 5 March. http://www.newyorker.com/magazine/2007/03/05/agit-opera (accessed 22 September 2015).

Samson, J. (2001). Genre. *Grove Music Online* (accessed 22 September 2015).

Schmidgall, G. (1977). *Literature as Opera*. New York: Oxford University Press.

Schroeder, D. (2002). *Cinema's Illusions, Opera's Allure: The Operatic Impulse in Film*. New York: Continuum.

Singer, B. (2009). Encountering Previn. *Opera News*, 73 (10). http://www.operanews.com/O pera_News_Magazine/2009/4/Features/Encountering_Previn.html (accessed 22 September 2015).

Smith, T. (2004a). A Streetcar Named Desire. *Opera News*, 69 (2). http://www.operanews.co m/Opera_News_Magazine/2004/8/Review/WASHINGTON,_D_C__-A_Streetcar_Nam ed_Desire,_Washington_National_Opera,_5/15/04.html (accessed 22 September 2015).

Smith, T. (2004b). A Lush and Sultry »Streetcar.« *The Baltimore Sun*, 17 May. http://articles. baltimoresun.com/2004-05-17/features/0405170090_1_opera-house-opera-production-s treetcar-named-desire (accessed 22 September 2015).

Smith-Howard, A. & Heintzelman, G. (2005). *Critical Companion to Tennessee Williams: The Essential Reference to His Life and Work*. New York: Facts on File.

Sondheim, S. (2010). *Finishing the Hat*. New York: Alfred A. Knopf.

Speedie, P. A. (1991). *American Operas on American Themes by American Composers: A Survey of Characteristics and Influences*. Dissertation, UMI 9211987. Ann Arbor, MI: ProQuest 1991.

Spencer, C. (2008). »Brief Encounter«: A First-Class Return to Romance. *The Daily Telegraph*, 18 February. http://www.telegraph.co.uk/culture/theatre/drama/3671269/Brief-En counter-A-first-class-return-to-romance.html (accessed 22 September 2015).

Staggs, S. (2005). *When Blanche Met Brando: The Scandalous Story of »A Streetcar Named Desire.«* New York: St. Martin's Press.

Swed, M. (2009). Review: André Previn's »Brief Encounter« premieres in Houston. *Los Angeles Times*, 3 May. http://latimesblogs.latimes.com/culturemonster/2009/05/andré-previns -brief-encounter-premieres-in-houston.html (accessed 22 September 2015).

Tambling, J. (1987). *Opera, Ideology and Film*. Manchester: Manchester University Press.

Tartak, M. (1998). Opera Review: »A Streetcar Named Desire.« Just Entertaining. *San Francisco Classical Voice*, 19 September. http://www.sfcv.org/arts_revs/streetcar_9_22_98.php (accessed 22 September 2015).

Taruskin, R. (2010). *Music in the Late Twentieth-Century*. New York: Oxford University Press.

Taylor, J. R. (Ed.). (1974, ²1990). *Masterworks of the British Cinema*. London: Lorrimer, London: Faber (2nd Edition).

Ther, P. (2011). The Genre of National Opera in a European Comparative Perspective. In J. F. Fulcher (Ed.), *The Oxford Handbook of the New Cultural History of Music* (pp. 182–208). New York: Oxford University Press.

Tommasini, A. (2013). Blanche Meets Stanley Anew, Reintroduced as Opera. *The New York Times*, 15 March. http://www.nytimes.com/2013/03/16/arts/music/renee-fleming-in-stre etcar-named-desire-at-carnegie-hall.html?_r=0 (accessed 22 September 2015).

Towse, R. (2011). Opera and Ballet. In Ruth Towse (Ed.), *A Handbook of Cultural Economics* (pp. 313–319). Cheltenham: Edward Elgar.

Tuttle, R. (1999). André Previn. A Streetcar Named Desire. *Classic Net*. http://www.classical. net/music/recs/reviews/d/dgg59366a.php (accessed 22 September 2015).

Webster, D. (1998). André Previn Scores Big With His First Opera »A Streetcar Named Desire,« Premiered in San Francisco Saturday, Gave the Audience Marvelous Arias and Soprano Renée Fleming a Splendid Starring Role. *Philadelphia Inquirer*, 22 September. http://articles.philly.com/1998-09-22/entertainment/25759445_1_arias-blanche-renee-fleming (accessed 22 September 2015).

Yang, M. (2008). Moulin Rouge! And the Undoing of Opera. *Cambridge Opera Journal*, 20 (3), 269–282.

John Link

Sense and Sensibility: Music on Stage in *What Next?**

> The coexistence of human beings and puppets, without either seeming to know the difference (though the music knows), is one of the extraordinary achievements of this opera [Alban Berg's *Wozzeck*], and a source of its perturbing fascination. (Paul Griffiths)

> We always find something, eh Didi, to give us the impression we exist? (Estragon in Act II of Samuel Beckett's *Waiting for Godot*)

What Next?, a comic opera in one act with a libretto by Paul Griffiths and music by Elliott Carter, has had a mixed reception since its premiere in 1999 at the Deutsche Staatsoper, Unter den Linden, Berlin. Reviews of the early productions tended to praise Carter's music, but were hard on the libretto. »It celebrates nonsense poetry predicated on profound gibberish,« was Martin Bernheimer's conclusion (Bernheimer, 2007), and less dismissive critics expressed bafflement as often as enthusiasm. Perhaps the unkindest cut of all came from Daniel Barenboim, who had arranged the commission for *What Next?* and conducted the premiere. Asked in 2008 what he hoped Carter would write next, Barenboim replied »A big, evening-long opera with a captivating libretto.«[1] It was widely reported that the scenario of *What Next?* is based on Jacques Tati's 1971 film *Trafic*, but Carter repeatedly downplayed the film's influence on the opera, and the lack of a significant connection between the two quickly became conventional wisdom. Compounding the confusion was that, in spite of nearly universal acknowledgment of the libretto's debt to a half-century-old tradition of Absurdist theatre, most critics measured the opera's characters by a standard of theatrical naturalism descended from Wolfgang Amadeus Mozart and Giuseppe Verdi (see Schiff, 2000, p. 2; Shreffler, 2003, p. 149, n. 6; Wierzbicki, 2011, p. 91; Capuzzo, 2012, p. 8). To be sure, *What Next?* makes playful reference to a host of musical and theatrical conventions, but the »skewed fit of libretto and music«

---

*   An abridged version of this essay appeared in *The Chicago Review* 58, nos. 3 and 4 (Summer 2014), p. 198–217.

1   »Eine große, abendfüllende Oper mit einem spannenden Libretto.« Daniel Barenboim, »Musik mit Übergang: Daniel Barenboim über Elliott Carter,« (interview with Christine Mast) in the program book for the Staatskapelle Berlin concert at the Philharmonie, September 13, 2008, p. 17, http://archiv2.berlinerfestspiele.de/de/archiv/festivals2008/05_musikfest_berlin 08/mfb_08_journal/mfb_08_j_barenboim/mfb_08_j__barenboim.php.

that David Schiff has noted is a product of the opera's reception history that has obscured its estimable achievements (Schiff, 2000, p. 3).

There is no question that Carter got the libretto he wanted. He himself chose Griffiths for the project, and the two remained in frequent contact, each making essential contributions as the scenario and libretto took shape. The idea of using a scene from *Trafic* as the opera's point of departure was Carter's. In the film, Tati—playing his perennial alter ego Monsieur Hulot—works as an automobile designer for the fictitious Altra car company. Monsieur Hulot and his team are responsible for transporting the prototype of a new camper from the company's base in France to an automobile exposition in Amsterdam, and the film chronicles their exploits on the ultimately fruitless journey. The episode that Carter remembered begins with an elaborately choreographed multicar pileup. After a long sequence of cars careening out of control and auto parts flying everywhere, the energy finally dissipates and the scene becomes dramatically still and silent. Tati treats the occupants of the cars like sleepers waking up in the morning: They slowly emerge from their vehicles as though from their beds, stretch their arms and legs, test their neck muscles, and seem not too terribly aware of one another.

This episode provides the basic scenario of the opera. As the curtain rises, six characters lie amid the wreckage of an accident, then gradually disentangle themselves and begin to sing. There is the lyric soprano, Rose—a professional singer and a diva. Dressed as a bride, she seems to have been on her way to wed Harry or Larry (he says he'll answer to either name)—a baritone, bridegroom, and clown. The older generation is represented by the aging hippie and would-be guru Zen (a tenor) and Mama (a dramatic soprano) who may or may not be Zen's ex-wife and Harry or Larry's mother. Finally, there is the low contralto, Stella—an astronomer of indeterminate age who Mama thinks is Zen's current girlfriend—and a boy alto, Kid, who no one seems to recognize but everyone wants to reassure (see »Situation« quoted in Griffiths, 1997c).

Equally significant for the opera, though Carter does not say so explicitly, is the long sequence in *Trafic* that precedes the accident. When Monsieur Hulot and company drive straight through the Dutch border crossing without stopping for the required inspection, they are chased down and (with their camper) taken to a detention garage where they become ensnared in the processing of bureaucratic paperwork with a dozen or so customs officers. Amid the confusion, a tow truck arrives bringing a dented car with »Just Married« painted on the side, and a few moments later the bride walks in, still wearing her wedding dress and carrying her train (her new husband, in his tuxedo, is being held in a small cell nearby). Later, as Monsieur Hulot's team is showing off the various comical amenities afforded by the camper's high technology, an alarm sounds and the crowd of officers gathered around the camper suddenly disappears.

The unfortunate newlyweds in the customs garage seem to have inspired the opera's recurring theme of an impending wedding between Harry or Larry and Rose, which functions much like the auto show in *Trafic*: as the ostensible goal that the characters will never reach.[2] Similarly, the customs officers in Tati's film (released in 1971, when perceptions of authority—whether political, military, or civilian—were especially polarized) resemble the road workers who make a brief appearance near the end of *What Next?*. Both are manifestations of an indifferent and not terribly competent authority that abandons the main characters at a crucial moment.[3] Also notable are the opera's echoes of the Altra public relations representative, Maria. In *Trafic,* Maria seems to be everywhere at once—constantly babbling in badly accented French that often lapses into her native English, but rarely able to manage a sustained argument. Although she is forever striving to be the center of attention, and fancies herself to be the leader of the trip to Amsterdam, Maria never accomplishes a thing; instead she provides a comically inconsequential accompaniment to the actions of others. Aspects of Maria's personality find their way into two characters in the opera. Mama becomes the would-be coordinator of a collaborative effort that never materializes, while Rose inherits Maria's oblivious and self-centered flamboyance as well as her tendency to go on and on without really saying anything.

These specific correspondences reflect shared comic traditions. The characters in *Trafic*—a domineering but incompetent executive, an unflappable truck driver, and Tati's Chaplinesque Monsieur Hulot—are modern archetypes with roots in mime and vaudeville that reach back to *commedia dell'arte*. As in the films of Charlie Chaplin and Buster Keaton, the collision of these archetypes with particular details of the modern world, like traffic jams, technological gadgets, and trade shows, is the engine of the film's comedy. (For Carter, whose teenage years intersected with the great flowering of silent film comedy in the 1920s, this Modernist take on *commedia* must have been particularly appealing; placing venerable traditions and modern sensibilities on a collision course is a guiding principle of his music [see Meyer & Shreffler, 2008, p. 290]).[4] The characters in the opera—with the significant exception of Kid—are similarly familiar pop-culture archetypes: the aging hippie, the logically minded scientist, the clownish entertainer, the diva, and the flustered *mater-*

---

2   Apparently it was Carter's suggestion that two characters in the opera appear in wedding clothes (see Griffiths, 1997a, p. 303).

3   The road workers were also inspired by Carter's own experience. »In Rome one year I witnessed an auto accident and was profoundly shocked to see the police come with measuring tapes to try and find out what had happened and who was to blame—while the injured young man lay on the pavement, not being attended to or being paid attention to.« (Carter, 1997b, p. 304).

4   See also Carter's observation of »the deplorable decline in circus and vaudeville, where the musical clown was once a staple feature.« As an example, Carter cites »the concert given by Keaton and Chaplin in Limelight« (Carter, 1963, p. 34).

familias. They are a *commedia* troupe for the twenty-first century: stock characters embodying clichéd oppositions (mysticism vs. science, freedom vs. responsibility, and so on) in distinctly contemporary garb.[5]

Of course, the influence of *commedia* on comic opera is as old as the genre itself. Just as the *commedia*-derived characters in *Trafic* play against the conventions of the road movie, so the characters in *What Next?* allude in various ways to a rich operatic tradition (see Noubel, 2007, pp. 71–72). Although it is effectively continuous from beginning to end, and the vocal writing ranges seamlessly from recitative-like declamation to aria, the music for *What Next?* follows the libretto's traditional division into numbers, distinct in personnel, subject matter, and style (see Shreffler, 2003, pp. 147–148). Both halves of the opera end with dramatic (and chaotic) ensemble finales, and there is a pair of quasi-romantic duets in the second half, one (no. 27) for Mama and Zen and one (no. 30) for Rose and Harry or Larry. (In the latter, the vocal phrases of the would-be lovers increasingly overlap in the manner of »La ci darem la mano« from Mozart's *Don Giovanni*, although for much more ambiguous reasons.) Similarly, both of Stella's arias in the second half (nos. 23 and 34) resemble a cavatina and cabaletta (see Example 1), and the instrumental inter-

Example 1: Stella's Vocal Line from »What Next?,« no. 34, mm. 860–868.

---

5   Schiff also suggests a connection with *commedia dell'arte*, but attributes it to Carter's music, rather than to Griffiths's libretto (Schiff, 2000, p. 3).

lude recalls both Baroque models and later precursors, such as Richard Wagner's music dramas and Berg's *Wozzeck*.[6]

These allusions are in keeping with Carter's acknowledgment of *opera buffa* as one inspiration for the »simultaneously interacting heterogeneous character-continuities« of his divided ensemble music. In a well-known interview with Allen Edwards, Carter cites the finales of the first act of *Don Giovanni* and the second act of Verdi's *Falstaff* as specific examples.[7] Both of these scenes involve the culminating intersection of several different threads of the plot, with characters interacting at cross-purposes within the confines of a given set of location-specific social norms—those involving a dance party at an aristocrat's palace or the bedroom of a wealthy man's wife. The scene of an automobile accident is, in a sense, an ingenious modern analog—a way of bringing together a diverse cast of characters with contemporary speed and force. But in *What Next?* the accident scene is not the final convergence of events; it is the starting point, and the drama it precipitates remains both oblique and unresolved at the end.

In this respect *What Next?* departs from both the *opera buffa* tradition and from Tati's film. Like all road movies, *Trafic* is an odyssey in which a long journey is repeatedly interrupted by contrasting episodes. But in Tati's version (as the title suggests), the odyssey genre is reimagined as a kind of stop-and-go traffic jam. The episodes do not provide the characters with opportunities to attain wisdom through acts of bravery or skill, but instead make them wait passively while some unforeseen obstacle over which they have little control is cleared out of their way by indifferent forces. In his libretto for *What Next?*, Griffiths similarly suspends the dramatic action, but does so for the entire opera. (As Carter points out, the »only real event happen[s] as the curtain rises« [Carter, 2003, p. 24].) In *Trafic*, Tati uses the episodes of stasis to introduce a wide variety of secondary characters that are observed by Monsieur Hulot and his team (and by the camera) and thus framed by the larger context of the trip to Amsterdam. In *What Next?*, it is not even clear that there *is* a larger context. The secondary characters are all but eliminated, and the main characters have trouble even interacting with each other. From the moment the curtain rises, they are effectively alone.

These changes transform the opera's onstage world and introduce a very different complex of genre allusions, including dystopian fantasy, postapocalyptic story telling, and rescue opera (see Shreffler, 2003, pp. 149–150). But the strongest allusion is to the Theatre of the Absurd. By compressing Tati's odyssey into a single long scene of waiting, and depriving a group of alienated archetypal characters of any intelligi-

---

6   Schmidt (1999, p. 171) notes the connection with *Wozzeck*.
7   See Carter, quoted in Edwards (1971, pp. 101–102) and Shreffler (2003, p. 165) comparing *What Next?* to *Così fan tutte*.

ble external reality to challenge (and define) their existence, Griffiths locates *What Next?* in the tradition of plays like Beckett's *Waiting for Godot*, Eugene Ionesco's *The Bald Prima Donna*, and Tom Stoppard's *Rosencrantz and Guildenstern are Dead*. These plays parody the drawing-room comedies of an earlier era, transforming the confined setting that once epitomized insular comfort and privilege into a bleak and inescapable backdrop. The conventions of theatrical illusion—such as the fourth wall as a window onto a naturalistic world—no longer provide a reliable framework for either the characters or the audience to understand what is happening on the stage, and the resulting instability raises fundamental existential questions. Griffiths uses a similar strategy in *What Next?*, but the existential dilemma he explores is quintessentially musical. As he explains the opera's opening scenes in a letter to Carter:

> We have six characters in shock. [...] To begin with, they're dislocated, and what each of them says (sings) may make sense to that individual but doesn't to anybody else. Their concerns are immediate and personal: the bridegroom with his love, the father with his memory, the boy with his appetite, and so on. This has the wonderful advantage, in terms of musical dramaturgy, that their »conversation« is not consequential. The movement from one bit of dialogue to the next is not a question to reply or statement to response; it goes altogether more allusively. (Griffiths, 1997b)[8]

It goes, in other words, the way Carter's instrumental music does. As an analog to Carter's assignment of limited materials to each group of instruments, Griffiths gives the characters in the opera only scraps of identities—professional, philosophical, temperamental—which they divulge in enigmatic fragments not linked to those of the others semantically, but by common words or syllables, much the way the individual parts in Carter's music are connected by common pitches. Musically, each character has a repertoire of intervals and rhythmic behaviors as well as an associated instrument or instruments (see Shreffler, 2003, pp. 159–160; Noubel, 2007, pp. 75–79). As Carter points out, »Rose is a lieder singer and so is often accompanied by the piano as she attempts to recall her concert of the previous night« (Carter, 1999, p. 307). In this role, the piano often acts as a comic underling, racing frantically to keep up with Rose's peripatetic vocalizations. (When she leaves the stage without it at the end of no. 18, it seems to slink off after her.) The instrumental assignations for Stella (vibraphone and marimba) and Harry or Larry (bassoon and tuba) similarly evoke familiar roles for those instruments.[9] Mama is represented by the harp: Its wide range of timbres makes it an ideal match for her diverse moods, which range from loving to furious. Such clear-cut associations, however, would be a poor fit for the chameleon-like Zen. Rather than fixing him with specific instruments, Carter associates Zen with a kind of *Klangfarbenmelodie* between woodwinds and strings that obscures their individual timbres (e.g., see mm. 168ff. and mm. 352–

---

8   The last part of this passage is quoted in Shreffler (2003, pp. 153–154).
9   »Will a vibraphone be too corny?« Carter asked Griffiths (Griffiths, 2003, p. 29).

359). A haze of tremolos often prefigures Zen's entrances, to further emphasize the mistiness of his character. His vocal lines are as elusive as his words—moving in small intervals that often double back on themselves (see Shreffler, 2003, pp. 159–162; Noubel, 2000, pp. 249–250). They tend to intimate a sense of directed motion toward a goal, then either turn away (as at the end of his aria in no. 5) or break off unexpectedly with an abrupt dramatic gesture, typically an ascending tritone. (The latter tendency culminates with his leap into »the unknown« in no. 33.) A conception of operatic characters that are simultaneously Carterian character-continuities underlies all of these associations and behaviors and creates the Absurdist paradox at the heart of *What Next?*. The characters oscillate between realistic representations of flesh and blood human beings and abstract personifications of music with no real existence beyond what they sing on the stage.[10]

In this respect, they are carefully balanced between two modes of theatrical representation in opera—one naturalistic, one fantastical—that have coexisted since the genre's beginning. In twentieth-century criticism, the debate about naturalism versus fantasy in opera is often framed as a debate about whether music is appropriate on the theatrical stage at all. Carter articulated his own view in 1969, almost thirty years before *What Next?*, in his introduction to a poetry reading by W. H. Auden (who, among many other achievements, was the co-librettist with Chester Kallman of the 1951 opera *The Rake's Progress*, with music by Igor Stravinsky):

> The basic problem [in writing an opera libretto] is to justify art music as the central element in the stage production. This justification has to be intrinsic to the plot or to the subject matter itself, has to inform every dramatic situation and verbal text to make the enterprise convincing [...]. (Carter, 1969, p. 308, quoted in Whittall, 2008, p. 7)

To support his position, Carter quotes Auden on Wagner (»The theory of ›music-drama‹ presupposes a libretto in which there is not one sensible remark [...].«) and cites with approval Auden's dictum that »A credible situation in an opera means a situation in which it is credible that someone should sing« (Auden, 1962, p. 466, quoted in Carter, 1997a, p. 309). Both Carter's and Auden's concern for the »credibility« of music in opera echo Ferruccio Busoni, who confronted the same dilemma more than fifty years earlier in the context of a reaction against *verismo*:

> The sung word will always remain a convention on the stage, and a hindrance to any semblance of truth; to overcome this deadlock with any success a plot would have to be made in which the singers act that which is incredible, fictitious, and improbable from the very

---

10   This paradox also underlies the narrative that Griffiths uses to connect the musical numbers by Mozart in one of his earlier opera projects, *The Jewel Box* (1991). I thank Paul Griffiths for bringing *The Jewel Box* to my attention.

start, so that one impossibility supports the other and both become possible and accepta-ble.[11]

Busoni's proposed solution involves both the revival of cartoonish (as opposed to naturalistic) *commedia* characters and plots involving magic or the supernatural (Busoni, 1907/1916, pp. 58–59). In *What Next?*, Carter and Griffiths borrow some aspects of this strategy, but hedge their bets on others. The simplest explanation of the opera's scenario is the supernatural one: The characters are ghosts, trapped in a postmortem state of uncertain status and duration. In Busoni's terms, their improb-ability as ghosts supports their improbability as singing theatrical characters, thus rendering both ideas »possible and acceptable« (*möglich und annehmbar*). But the contemporary naturalism of the accident opens the possibility that the characters are not ghosts but survivors, thus maintaining an important link with the natural-istic opera tradition. As in Beckett, the severely restricted naturalism makes a degree of pathos available that an entirely cartoonish treatment of the characters could not. In the words of James Levine, who conducted the opera at Tanglewood in 2006, »If they were just ghosts we wouldn't care about them the same way« (Levine, 2008).

The dual identities of the characters—as both representations of human beings and avatars of music—play off each other throughout *What Next?*. The first nine num-bers unfold in an expanding spiral that recalls the gradually unfolding introductions of Carter's *Double Concerto* (1961) and *Concerto for Orchestra* (1969).[12] After the curtain rises, the orchestra's unpitched percussion is echoed by unvoiced sibilants—»ss« and »sh«—from the singers. Led by Kid's vowel »ah,« each one sings the same first word—»star«—in turn, but the commonality is an illusion; in the spiral's third loop, »star« becomes a syllable that points the characters in entirely different direc-tions: »starlings« for Rose, »starch« for Mama, and so on. In the fourth loop (no. 2), the star-based words begin sentences that encapsulate each character's defining at-tributes. The men are first: Zen explains why »Starts are always an embarrassment to us« (it is because »we are creatures of eternity/and each beginning is only a new illusion«), and Harry or Larry encourages us (or himself) to »Startle the stairs!/ Astonish the curtains!« and »amaze the chandelier!« The astronomer, Stella, is only slightly less poetic in the immediate disclosure of her vocation—»Starkest of nights when I look through my telescope […]«—while Mama is identified instantly with stereotypes of avid domesticity: »Starch for his handkerchiefs/pencil and paper to

11 »Immer wird das gesungene Wort auf der Bühne eine Konvention bleiben und ein Hinder-nis für alle wahrhaftige Wirkung: aus diesem Konflikt mit Anstand hervorzugehen, wird ei-ne Handlung, in welcher die Personen singend agieren, von Anfang an auf das Unglaub-hafte, Unwahre, Unwahrscheinliche gestellt sein müssen, auf daß eine Unmöglichkeit die andere stütze und so beide möglich und annehmbar werden.« (Busoni, 1907/1916, p. 58).

12 The similarity between *What Next?* and the *Double Concerto* has been widely noted (see Schmidt, 1999, pp. 167–168; Gann, 2000; Schiff, 2000, p. 4; Noubel, 2000, p. 252; Whittall, 2008, p. 5). Some differences are discussed in Capuzzo (2012, pp. 63ff.).

write down the gifts/gloves [...].«[13] As befits a diva, Rose is the most extravagantly theatrical: »Starlings entangled in my hair,/A wren warming between my breasts [...].« Her evocation of birds is characteristic as she is something of a warbler herself, grandly singing snatches of half-remembered songs and arias from her earlier performances. Later, she will transform Mama's »gloves« into »white doves« and the memory of her own »spectacular performance« into »spectacular parrots.«

That an apparent semantic connection (»star«) turns out to be inadvertent homophony is the first of the libretto's many ironies. Characters that initially seem to have a shared point of reference are in fact entirely isolated from each other (see Capuzzo, 2012, chapter 3). Faced with a dire predicament, they do not reason out their problem together (as Mama eventually insists they should), but first simply make statements one after the other, like those of the instruments at the beginning of Carter's *String Quartet No. 2* or the duos in the early stages of his *Triple Duo*.[14] Nevertheless, the isolation of the opening numbers begins to break down very early on, and the conflict between individual identity and social interaction soon becomes the opera's driving force. Griffiths specifies that, after their »star starts« in no. 1, each of the characters is »surprised and perhaps affronted to find the word they had thought their own echoed by other people« (Griffiths, 1997c, no. 1). Ironically, the sentences that result when they »begin again«—attempts at self-definition and differentiation from the others—lead directly to the opera's first interpersonal contact.[15] Stella's egregious pun (»Starkest of nights [...] my face is star-kissed«) seems to be an unintended consequence of her dualistic consideration of the ways in which »star« might apply to her, but she also has stumbled into Harry or Larry's territory without realizing it. He jumps at the opportunity to literalize and dramatically embody her words by planting a kiss on her cheek. From his first utterance, Harry or Larry tells us that he aims to startle, astonish, and amaze, so it is no surprise that he is the vehicle by which the initial isolation of the characters from each other is disrupted and dramatic conflict introduced. In no. 3, he picks up Zen's »everyone«—a word that conjoins individual and collective identity—and passes it on to Mama, who first broaches the theory that when the accident occurred »We were on our way to your wedding.« Rose, however, is not ready or willing to consider the social implications of this possibility and immediately retreats into her own world of

---

13   Noubel notes that, in No. 15, Carter underlines Mama's association with domesticity via a recurring ascending interval 11 from F4 to E5 (»fa-mi« as in »family«; see Noubel, 2007, pp. 76–77).

14   See Noubel's description of the form of *What Next?* as a »counterpoint of parallel existences« (contrapoint d'existences parallèles) as in Carter's earlier divided ensemble music (Noubel, 2000, pp. 251–252).

15   Significantly, Harry or Larry's transformation of »star« into »startle« also entails a transformation from noun to verb (see Noubel, 2000, p. 252).

performance, asking an imagined conductor to slow things down a little bit (»Più andante, maestro«).

Just as Harry or Larry's clowning represents the interaction and conflict that takes place in opera ensembles, Rose's conceited self-absorption manifests the interior world of aria. Her request for a slower tempo leads to longer, more developed solos—not only her own in no. 4, but also those that Zen, Harry or Larry, and Stella sing in the following numbers. Carter's coarse underscoring of Griffiths's joke in no. 4 about the heft of opera singers (»white doves beneath each of my feet bearing my weight«) emphasizes the fantastical nature of Rose's image of herself (and opera's image of itself)—an image also suggested by her proliferating birds.[16] It is Rose's nature to believe that she is on stage (a belief that is simultaneously false in the context of the accident scene and true in the context of the opera house).[17] When disturbed by the prospect of interpersonal communication, she turns to her aviary as a means of escape. Her »eagle opening its wings to shield me from the sun« recalls Icarus, but with the implication that her own arioso flights are more robustly protected. One could say that she uses her profession as a shield, hiding behind the words of others. Her wonderfully awkward mouthful, »hatching within my mouth a succession of kingfishers,« claims for her singing the power to bring forth halcyon days, but it also lets slip the paradox inherent in her strategy, and once again Harry or Larry is there to pounce: »Somewhere or other,« he tells her, »you'll need to find words of your own.« Rose is attempting to evade an existential danger: that her identity—her independent stratum of the Carterian divided ensemble—would dissolve if she stepped off her imagined stage to join the others.[18] But Harry or Larry has spotted the flaw in her scheme: If she stays within her isolated layer of the texture, she will find that, like one of Pirandello's *Six Characters in Search of an Author,* she exists only as an abstraction—dumped inadvertently, by extraordinary circumstance or by an absent creator, into an artificial world over which she has little control. It is left to Zen to illustrate with a pun on Harry or Larry's »words of your own« that they are all in the same boat in this regard: »But do we own words or they us?/Wherever we go words have been there first.«

Griffiths is having fun here. His playful sortie in the perennial battle over the priority of words or music in opera also evokes the familiar Absurdist paradox of characters that are verbal abstractions nonetheless engaging in self-aware rumination. And to be made out of words is not only to have an uncertain relationship to one's fellow

---

16   The extreme low register as an allusion to Rose's weight returns in m. 554.

17   Cf. Griffiths's description of Baba the Turk in *The Rake's Progress*: »She can afford to be a grotesque, and to parade herself as such without embarrassment, because she knows that she is taking part in an opera.« (Griffiths, 1982, p. 92)

18   Rose's conundrum echoes the one faced by the instrumental character-continuities in Carter's String Quartet No. 2 (see Link, 2012, p. 40).

characters; it is also to have an uncertain relationship to the outside world. This uncertainty is evidently of little consequence to Zen, who seems indifferent to the evidence of the senses, but it practically defines Stella, who grapples with the conflict between objective and subjective points of view throughout the opera. Just as Rose's soaring birds are interrupted by her memory lapses in no. 4, Stella's subjective experience in no. 14 (»all we can look at […]«) is interrupted by bursts of cold rationality (»[…] are probabilities«), which Carter sets in a contrasting beat division (see Example 2).[19]

Example 2: Stella's Vocal Line from »What Next?,« no. 14, mm. 409–17.

Similarly, in her »star echo song« (no. 9) Stella oscillates between short notes expressing numerical precision and long legato phrases that turn her recitation of the Latin names of stars into a song of rhapsodic wonder.[20]

---

19 In a sketch of this passage now in the Elliott Carter Collection of the Paul Sacher Foundation, Carter drew alternating green and purple slurs over the contrasting phrases of Stella's vocal line to highlight her dual perspective.

20 In no. 9, Carter emphasizes this tendency with a slight but telling alteration to the meaning of the words. Whereas Griffiths writes »at a distance of eight point eight eight light years« (measuring to the nearest hundredth), Carter groups the third »eight« with the words that follow, as though Stella is so struck by the enormity of the numbers that she abruptly drops the precision of »8.8« to exclaim in wonder »eight light years« (see mm. 300–303). Griffiths's concordance of the familiar names and Bayer designations of the stars mentioned in Stella's aria points to a similar dichotomy between scientific precision and fancy (see Griffiths, 1997c, no. 9, fn. 1–4).

While Stella is star-struck, Kid is hungry. His transformation of the star names »Acamar, Biham, Almach« into »A Big Mac« at the end of no. 9 is a reliably successful moment of comic bathos, but also a pivotal moment in the form. Up to that point, the others have presented their narrowly defined character traits to themselves (and to the audience). Once Kid pipes up, they immediately turn their attentions to *him* (see Capuzzo, 2012, chapter 4; also see Shreffler, 2003, p. 153). But as Mama, Zen, Rose, and Harry or Larry each do so in turn, Kid becomes increasingly indifferent to their efforts. He responds only when Stella makes one of her characteristic shifts from euphoric philosophizing (»The world now seems to be made of rainbow«) to rational analysis (»an interference of force and light,/and nothing there at all«). Griffiths's stage directions tell us that »Kid is taken with this, and expresses his allegiance to Stella by sitting down with her.« He waits to hear more, but of course there is no more. Stella's rainbow is no more conclusive than Zen's meandering kites in no. 5 as an explanation of the sky's mysteries, and she does not meet Kid's expectant gaze. But Kid nevertheless remains with Stella until she leaves the stage just before the interlude, looking for »the way to the observatory.«

Stella's dualism is the first of three very different models of the characters' relationships to each other and to their world that are presented to Kid in turn, vying for his attention and allegiance.[21] The second model argues that meaning is to be found not in the struggle between scientific inquiry and rapture, but in storytelling. Rose is the embodiment of this precept, which provides her with a different way of dealing with her existential dilemma. For Rose, telling stories is a way to join the society of the other characters without giving up her musical independence and the insular reassurance of performing the words of others. But first, as she realizes when she is deserted at the end of the first half, »There has to be an audience.« The first six numbers after the interlude are punctuated by Rose's repeated efforts to get the attention of the other characters. But they are not used to Rose trying to interact with them and they either ignore or misunderstand her.[22] Only when she appeals directly to Kid in no. 22 does Rose find the words to say what she has to say: »There will be no wedding./There never was going to be a wedding.« With this announcement, Rose not only succeeds at finally capturing the others' attention, she also abruptly dismisses the only logical explanation for any of their circumstances that has thus far been suggested. The story she offers in its place—with its »king and a queen/With hair as red as a clear sunset«—she tells for Kid's benefit.

The distancing effect of stories is partly temporal and partly geographical. For as long as they last, stories give the illusion of time suspended by superimposing their

---

21   That the three models are presented by the three female characters is not coincidental. For more on gender relationships in *What Next?*, see Capuzzo (2012, chapter 6).

22   In no. 22, they assume that her plea for them to »Listen« means that she has heard something, and they all look around to try to find its source.

own time-world on the world in which they are told. (They are »outside of time« as Zen puts it in no. 24.) Waiting—with its focus on the minutes of the outside world hastening by—is the other side of the coin. »Time is going on,« reports Mama with alarm, »and meanwhile we are stranded here.« The geographical allure of stories, as Stella realizes, is that they lead to other worlds, »serene and apart,« which provide assurances of identity and belonging. She puts her finger on it in no. 23: »I too used to believe in […] worlds beyond worlds in unlimited space […]. In being *there* they confirm that I am *here*.« But stories are also a way of looking in the mirror—of collapsing the distance between »there« and »here.« Carter suggests as much when Rose's seemingly distant vocalization crests in m. 647 on the same D5 that is prominent in Stella's vocal line. In no. 7, Harry or Larry gives Stella's »worlds beyond worlds« their familiar exotic names (»Timbuctoo,« »Atlantis,« »Eldorado,« etc.), but quickly realizes that it is only a short journey from »Shangri La« to »the Island of the Dead.« And in no. 23, Stella's awe when she thinks of the distant universe quickly changes to fear that »the stars and planets/are painted on my eyes«—as illusory as the images on the wall of Plato's cave.[23]

No such fear infects Mama's memory of domestic life as a kind of static pleasure cruise »carrying us safely nowhere else,/which is where we all wanted to be.« The »little ship« in her memory may take its circular bearings from her possible ex-husband Zen's charts, but there is an important difference. For Mama, the separateness of the onstage world from the world of her memory is not a game or an inconsequential illusion; it is real and meaningful. Once Rose's words get away from her at the end of no. 25, her hold on Kid is broken and »He walks purposefully in a curve toward Mama.«[24] Arriving at her side, he takes her hand just as she offers her most devastating critique of the artificiality of Stella's vacillation and Rose's fictive performances (and of Zen's mysticism and Harry or Larry's clowning as well): Of course words slip away from you and mean nothing, but only »if you're willing to say what you never can feel.« Mama decisively rejects both the hollowness of the stories told by the other characters and Zen's contention that »feelings are fantasies.« In the model *she* offers Kid, the true meaning of existence is to be found in human relationships.

In a more conventional drama, the third time would be the charm, and Mama's assertion would reveal itself as hard-won truth. Kid would choose Mama's love over Stella's science and Rose's art, clearing the way for the other characters to transcend their differences and find a path to rescue. But this kind of resolution is not available in *What Next?*. Mama no sooner chastises Harry or Larry and Zen for not saying

---

23   Stella makes this remark as she »leaves the others to walk to the front of the stage and look out into the auditorium,« like Estragon in Act 2 of Beckett's *Waiting for Godot*.

24   Rose's brief attempt to continue her story in no. 26 (»like a bird«) goes only »into the air, because Kid is no longer there« (Griffiths, 1997c, no. 26).

what they feel, than Zen's jokes (»If oysters were open to persuasion [...]. If Saturn's rings would take a collect call«) remind her that the conditions for doing so are beyond all of their reach. Her confrontation with Harry or Larry, which follows immediately, serves as a pivot between the generations—appealing to comedy's traditional »restoration of timeliness through [...] the marriage of young lovers« (Said, 2006, p. 6). But Harry or Larry and Rose (in no. 30) are no more able than Mama and Zen to lay a foundation of human feelings for their relationship. Their attempts to confirm the meaning of their words quickly run aground, and they are unable even to determine what it might mean to ask whether they are in love, much less than what love might feel like.

Into these scenes of confusion, the road workers arrive as a parodic *deus ex machina*. But instead of deliverance they bring only more confusion, including the thunderous return of nonpitched percussion—associated throughout the opera with the initial accident (see Capuzzo, 2012, p. 13).[25] Instead of coming to the rescue, the road workers briefly inspect the wreckage and then leave, apparently oblivious to the singing characters, whose frantic attempts to communicate only serve to underline the absurd unreality of their own state of being.[26] Just as Rose's disavowal of a wedding in no. 22 undermines one explanation of the characters' situation, the departure of the road workers marks the foundering of another: This is not an adventure in which, separated from their familiar world, the characters discover through hardship the importance of caring for each other, and are rescued when the moral lesson is learned and adversity overcome.

The collapse of the familiar rescue narrative threatens to strand the main characters indefinitely in their theatrical no-place. So, with their prospects dim, they undergo a remarkable transformation. Once again, Kid's role is pivotal. His quasi-innocent question, »How was it for only that moment/you were able to agree?,« prompts the final uproar, in which the characters abruptly drop all pretense of being isolated abstractions, unable to understand their relationships with one another. Stella suddenly knows that Rose is pregnant; Rose knowingly refers to Harry or Larry as Mama's son, and Zen bitterly accuses Stella of never having known love. What is more, after thirty-five minutes dominated by obliquely connected overlapping monologues, the characters now begin to talk to and respond to each other in sustained dialog. Stella and Zen snipe back and forth about love; Mama, Rose, and Harry or Larry argue about Rose's pregnancy; and Zen heeds Stella's mundane request that he hold her

---

25   From the moment it contradicts Mama's announcement that help has arrived in no. 32 until the departure of the road workers, percussion dominates the orchestral accompaniment, which is otherwise reduced to occasional fragments and quiet background doubling of the vocal lines.

26   The opera's formal trajectory from isolation to collaboration that ironically results only in chaos and confusion is central to the analysis in Capuzzo (2012; see, e.g., pp. 22–24).

shoes (see Capuzzo, 2012, p. 128). These ordinary exchanges are Griffiths's comic answer to the question of what would happen if the characters actually *were* able to find words of their own. The scientist needs a drink and moans about love, the guru disavows the unity of everyone, the mother becomes the whining child, and the clown says »never again« like a habitual party animal regretting his latest bender. Or perhaps they simply remove one mask to reveal another.[27] Either way, the effect is to make the entire opera up to this point seem like a play-within-a-play, from which the characters are finally released by Kid's question. Only Rose remains happily as she was, announcing that she feels sick as she continues her imagined aria, soaring toward its final high »C.«[28]

It is telling that *What Next?* ends with a character performing a »quintessentially operatic gesture« from a *different* opera (see Shreffler, 2003, 167–170, quote from p. 167). Rose's final melody—which both reenacts and *is* »a spectacular performance«—puts the end of *What Next?* in quotation marks, leaving the audience uncertain about which piece is actually supposed to be ending: the one they have been listening to or the one in Rose's memory.[29] This uncertainty about the nature of what is represented on the stage is pervasive throughout the opera. In part, it grows out of the many solos, duets, and trios (and the concomitant dearth of ensembles), and the fact that, except during the interlude, all the singing characters are on the stage all the time.[30] As Griffiths points out, »[…] those not involved as participants in an episode will probably be observers, appreciating the show put on by their companion or companions« (see »Situation,« in Griffiths, 1997c). The clear-cut distinction between observers and participants on stage creates an intermediate layer between the action and the audience. We see what happens both directly and as framed in the point of view of the nonparticipating characters. This secondary viewpoint both distances us from the action and draws our attention to the analo-

---

27 Compare Griffiths's suggestion that Tom and Anne's appearance in the Epilog of *The Rake's Progress* may imply »that all their previous honesty has been a deceit, that they knew all along that they were only characters in an opera […].« (Griffiths, 1982, p. 95).

28 Carter (1999) points out the absurdities of Rose's part: »After all, her big moment after her child-like narration [nos. 23 and 25] is when she thinks she is losing her voice! After saying she feels sick, she must burst very soon into a grand flight of intense singing! at the end.« (quoted in Meyer & Shreffler, 2008, p. 307) As a parody of the conventions of opera, these scenes echo Stravinsky's critique of »the post-stabbing coloratura in *Rigoletto*« (see Griffiths, 1982, p. 3). Also see Auden's suggestion »that Anne's aria at the end of the [first] act ought to be made to end on a high C« (Stravinsky & Craft, 1979, p. 402, quoted in Griffiths, 1982, p. 15).

29 Rose's offstage high »C« also recalls the end of Stoppard's *Rosencrantz and Guildenstern Are Dead*, in which the characters leave the stage that the audience sees and enter another stage that the audience does not see.

30 In fact, the interlude was added only after Carter expressed a desire for at least one set of entrances and exits for the characters (see Tusa, 2000).

gous relationship between the characters as observers and the audience as observers.[31]

For Bertolt Brecht, this secondary viewpoint creates a *Verfremdungseffekt* (alienation or distancing effect)—a key element of his »epic theatre.« Brecht drew on diverse sources of inspiration, including Busoni's ideas about opera, which he may have known through his work with Busoni's student Kurt Weill. As an illustration, Brecht gives the example of an eyewitness describing an accident to a group of bystanders, so that the audience is aware that what is presented on the stage is a representation of an event rather than the event itself.[32] *What Next?* creates its own kind of *Verfremdungseffekt*: The accident with which the opera begins takes place just before the curtain opens, and our only access to the events leading up to it is via the fragmentary speculations of the characters. This refracted perspective is typical of the way Griffiths's libretto places the actions of one character (or characters) within the stories told by another. Harry or Larry's and Rose's duet in no. 35 takes place in the context of Mama's and Stella's lead-in in the previous number, »These two/were going to be married,« which in turn is an action within Stella's narrative (»Someone said«), thereby creating a story, within a story, within a story. And, in no. 24, when Mama asks Rose in earnest, »How long do you expect your wedding to wait for you?,« Rose simply folds the question into her fairy tale, which thus becomes a kind of strange loop that simultaneously encloses the action of the opera and is enclosed by it.

Harry or Larry's comedy, Rose's theatricality, Mama's community, Stella's duality, and Zen's mysticism are all perspectives through which the characters (and the audience) view the onstage world and try to render it comprehensible. But the most comprehensive perspective may be Kid's (see Capuzzo, 2012, chapter 4). The scope of Kid's observations seems to extend beyond the three models of existence presented to him by Stella, Rose, and Mama, to encompass the opera's entire action, which, in this reading, becomes his imagined response to finding himself the sole survivor of the initial accident. That Kid is the only character interested in food is an important clue that he is on a separate plane of existence,[33] as is his reaction in no. 10: »[Kid] is puzzled by [Mama], as by an alien being. At some point while she is singing he raises a hand to touch her mouth« (Griffiths, 1997c, no. 10). Whereas Rose (in no. 25) is dismayed to realize that the words and music that define her are slip-

---

31   See Carter (1966/1994) for his views on the relationship between the characters and the audience in theatre.

32   See »Alienation Effects in Chinese Acting« and »The Street Scene: A Basic Model for an Epic Theatre« quoted in Brecht (1964, pp. 91–99, 121–129); also see Shum (2006).

33   Harry or Larry's »Dining we did« might be considered an exception, but the phrase is more likely the byproduct of his game of anagrams with the word »wedding« (see Capuzzo, 2012, p. 21). In the Tanglewood production, the road workers echo Kid's hunger by pounding the wreckage of the accident only briefly before breaking for lunch.

ping away, Kid is more intrigued that such sounds are emanating from such an odd source in the first place. As Dörte Schmidt reminds us, Kid's presence echoes the use of children in Arnold Schoenberg's *Von Heute auf Morgen* and Berg's *Wozzeck* (Schmidt, 1999, p. 171), but Kid's function in *What Next?* is entirely different. In *Wozzeck*, Marie's child is a powerless figure caught in the adults' distorted world. In *What Next?*, the roles may well be reversed. Kid is the first to sing at the beginning, the only character that remains on stage during the interlude, and the last character left on stage at the end. Perhaps the others are just figments of his imagination.[34]

If we are seeing *What Next?* through Kid's eyes, we may also be hearing it through his ears. Certainly the opera's music picks up the libretto's multilayered points of view. Rose's constant vocalizing »is often a comment on the parts of the other singers and actors« (Carter, 1999, p. 307), and in the orchestra, a motto of one or two »wreckage chords« recurs repeatedly, usually accompanied by unpitched percussion, as an unexpected and unwelcome reminder of the calamity that first brought the characters to their confused state (see Capuzzo, 2012, p. 44, pp. 77–79). Percussion is also the vehicle for another type of musical intermediation in *What Next?*. Early in his work on the libretto, Griffiths proposed a purely musical character, »Horn,« to be played by an onstage instrumentalist, but perceived by the others »probably [...] as horn rather than hornist« (Griffiths, 1997a, p. 159). Griffiths conceived Horn as »a unique bridge between the orchestra and the singing characters,« but by the time the libretto was completed, this function was reassigned to the road workers:

> As [the road workers] begin to make their investigation, so they begin to make sounds. At first it seems that these sounds are »natural«—that is, that they are explicable within the fiction of road workers examining, testing and measuring metallic objects. But gradually the sounds become unmistakably music, drawn from a variety of instruments concealed within and behind the wreckage. (Griffiths, 1997c, no. 19)

The episode that Griffiths describes in this stage direction involves a dual transformation: Theatrical characters become instrumental character-continuities, and the naturalistic sounds of an onstage activity shade into the abstract, absolute music of the orchestra. This sequence is the opera's *dénouement* and calls for considerable ingenuity on the part of the director, conductor, and musicians, who must overcome the problem of coordinating the onstage percussionists and the orchestra. (Too many of the opera's early productions have kept the percussionists in the pit

---

34 Kid is also the last character to speak. His final question: »What—?« (with the last word left for the orchestra) echoes the final question—»La libertà?«—in Luigi Dallapiccola's *Il Prigioniero*, which, as Dallapiccola himself pointed out in a response to his critics, had its own historical antecedent: »They had forgotten that Busoni had ended his masterpiece *Doktor Faust* (1924) on a point of interrogation put by Mephistopheles, guardian of the night: ›Shall this man be damned?‹ This marked the birth of a new dramatic form, the open opera.« (Dallapiccola, 1962, p. 27, quoted in Keller, 2013)

and left the road workers to play in pantomime, thereby considerably weakening the dramatic effect.) The idea of a character-continuity playing an onstage role also underlies the brief English horn solos that provide Kid's wordless response to the overtures of the adult characters in nos. 10–14 (see Capuzzo, 2012, chapter 4; also see Link, 2012, pp. 292–310). Then the English horn returns in the instrumental interlude to play a long and poignant lament for all the opera's inconsequential beauty. Griffiths initially called this number »The Singing Stage,« but Carter describes it only half-jokingly as »my *Swan of Tuonela*« (Schiff, 2000, p. 4).[35] Later on, the percussionists/road workers connect the characters on the stage to those in the music; when the stage characters (all but one) leave for the interlude and we are left alone with Kid, the English horn connects the music to us.

The onstage embodiment of Carter's instrumental music in *What Next?* not only revisits the problems of character and form with which he grappled earlier in his career, it also subjects the solutions he developed then to critical scrutiny by placing them in a very different context. I have mentioned Griffiths's allusion in the gradually unfolding opening numbers of the libretto to Carter's instrumental compositions of the 1960s—an allusion that Carter also takes up in the opera's music. But by 1997, Carter had begun to use the same technical innovations he rolled out to much acclaim more than thirty years earlier to create a kind of self-referential irony, and even self-parody, in his music. Unlike the *Double Concerto*, which develops from a *tabula rasa*, *What Next?* begins with a vaudeville trunk's worth of slapstick percussion. We come upon the scene of the accident as the last pieces of miscellaneous debris are falling, like the last stragglers from the back of Fibber McGee's closet. Partly, the result is to skewer the pretensions of the opera house. Whereas most nineteenth-century opera overtures inflate the sense of impending drama (and flatter the audience's sense of witnessing an event of grand importance), the overture to *What Next?* playfully subverts the expected portentousness.[36] But there is also an element of personal history at work. The percussion in *What Next?* is no longer the herald of a new world of musical possibilities (as Carter inherited it for the *Double Concerto* from Edgard Varèse, Henry Cowell, and John Cage), but a reminder of the all-too-familiar traffic, construction, and noise of the world we inhabit, intruding on the hermetic quiet of the opera house.[37] In fact, one can think of *What Next?*—in which the seedbed of organic development is a violent cataclysm—as a comic-historical reenactment of the attempts by Modernist composers in the late 1940s and 1950s to

---

35 Capuzzo suggests »that it is Kid who is ›singing‹ during the interlude, with the English horn acting as his surrogate voice« (Capuzzo, 2012, p. 96).

36 Also see the discussion of the opening of Carter's *Dialogues* in Link (2008, pp. 4–5).

37 A similar self-parody may be heard in Carter's use of percussion and polyrhythm to represent the cold mechanization of More's *Utopia* (see Noubel, 2012, pp. 253–270). Carter may have had in mind as a model the long unpitched percussion interlude in Shostakovich's *The Nose*, an opera Carter knew and admired (see Carter, 1967/1994, p. 332).

create a new expressive language »from out of the ashes of the Second World War« (Taruskin, 1993, p. 301).[38] In *What Next?*, the new musical landscape in which the principals find themselves leads them from self-identification to attempts at social interaction and collaboration that produce only confusion and cross purposes, and utterly fail to connect with the outside world. Ironically, if one hears in *What Next?* the fragmentation of the postwar search for the new, it ultimately leads back to the conventional chaotic finale of an *opera buffa*.

That Carter was an active participant in that search only deepens the irony. With the techniques of his own earlier music serving to lampoon the grand vision of postwar modernism and its ultimate disintegration, Carter's own work is pointedly within the frame of the satire. Nowhere is this irony clearer than in the character of Rose, whose identity as a professional singer, who sings almost continually through-out the opera, was one of Carter's most significant contributions to the scenario. »She just sings and sings and everything else goes on and her music is always in the background,« Carter says. »It's like what I do in my string quartets to tell the truth« (Tusa, 2000). Like the sounds made by the road worker/percussionists, Rose's sing-ing fulfills Busoni's narrow requirements for the naturalistic presence of music on the stage. But the opera's fantastical setting turns Rose's Busonian mimesis on its head, making her part the furthest removed from the artificial world in which the characters are presented to us. Rose indeed resembles the more flamboyant charac-ters in Carter's quartets, and her continuous melody takes up the lyrical thread that runs throughout his late music. Like the instruments in Carter's compositions of the 1980s, Rose's ability to spin out beautifully formed and continuously varying lines with great virtuosity is unhampered by her limited intervallic vocabulary, which is both the smallest and the most rigorously adhered to in the opera.[39] Her entire vocal part is written using only four intervals—1, 4, 7, and 11—and this restricted vocabu-lary defines a key aspect of her musical character and sets her apart from the others. By having Rose sing continuously throughout *What Next?*, Carter explores the iso-lation of his divided ensemble character-continuities from a comic perspective, even as he celebrates the seemingly indomitable ability of the lyric impulse to carry on and even fly high above the tumult. »›And of course the meaning of this,‹ Elliott

---

38 This reading is reinforced by the echo in Stella's line »It is as if designed for us,/but not we for it,« (in no. 23) of Jean Paul Sartre, who wrote in *Les Temps modernes* (October 1954): »Since the writer has no way to escape, we want him to take hold of his era firmly: it is his only chance; it was made for him and he for it […]. Our intention is to work together to produce certain changes in the society that surrounds us.« (quoted in Saunders, 1999, p. 62)

39 The other characters favor some intervals more than others, but their repertories are varia-ble—expanding and contracting to suit the dramatic situation. Occasionally the subject mat-ter will prompt one character to use intervals that are most often associated with another, as when Mama »borrows« from Rose's repertory when she sings about going to a wedding (no. 3, mm. 125–127).

says, ›is that it's like music: nobody knows what it means, but it goes on and on without stopping‹« (Griffiths, 2003, p. 33). Rose's *grande ligne* is emblematic of the opera's postmodern self-consciousness: simultaneously a wry self-parody and an affirmation, both of the persistence of music and of the aesthetic of continuous change on which Carter based his entire career.

References

Auden, W. H. (1962). Notes on Music and Opera. In *The Dyer's Hand and Other Essays* (pp. 465–74). New York: Random House.

Bernheimer, M. (2007). Elliott Carter/»What's [sic] Next?,« Miller Theatre, New York. *Financial Times*, http://www.ft.com/cms/s/0/ea902acc-a73f-11dc-a25a-0000779fd2ac.html #axzz2zvf1SgRO (accessed 10 December 2015).

Boland, M. & Link, J. (Eds.). (2012). *Elliott Carter Studies*. Cambridge: Cambridge University Press.

Brecht, B. (1964). *Brecht on Theatre*. Ed. & trans. J. Willett. New York: Hill and Wang.

Busoni, F. (1907/1916). Entwurf einer neuen Ästhetik der Tonkunst. Reprinted in F. Busoni (1983), *Von der Macht der Töne: Ausgewählte Schriften* (p. 58). Leipzig: Verlag Philipp Reclam. English translation by Rosamond Ley in F. Busoni (1957), *The Essence of Music and Other Papers* (pp. 39–40). New York: Dover.

Capuzzo, G. (2012). *Elliott Carter's »What Next?«: Communication, Cooperation, and Separation*. Rochester, NY: University of Rochester Press.

Carter, E. (1963). Letter from Europe. In J. W. Bernard (Ed.), *Elliot Carter. Collected Essays and Lectures 1937–1995* (pp. 31–40). Rochester, NY: University of Rochester Press.

Carter, E. (1966/1994). The *Gesamtkunstwerk*. In J. W. Bernard (Ed.), *Elliot Carter. Collected Essays and Lectures 1937–1995* (pp. 319–331). Rochester, NY: University of Rochester Press.

Carter, E. (1967/1994). Soviet Music. In J. W. Bernard (Ed.), *Elliot Carter. Collected Essays and Lectures 1937–1995* (pp. 331–35). Rochester, NY: University of Rochester Press.

Carter, E. (1969). Introduction to a Poetry Reading by W. H. Auden. In J. W. Bernard (Ed.), *Elliot Carter. Collected Essays and Lectures 1937–1995* (pp. 307–309). Rochester, NY: University of Rochester Press.

Carter, E. (1997a). *Collected Essays and Lectures 1937–1995*. Ed. J. W. Bernard. Rochester, NY: University of Rochester Press.

Carter, E. (1997b). Letter to Paul Griffiths, March 20. In F. Meyer & A. C. Shreffler (Eds.), *Elliot Carter: A Centennial Portrait in Letters and Documents* (pp. 303–304). Woodbridge, UK: The Boydell Press.

Carter, E. (1999). Letter to Micaela von Marcard, 29 March. In F. Meyer & A. C. Shreffler (Eds.), *Elliot Carter: A Centennial Portrait in Letters and Documents* (pp. 307–308). Woodbridge, UK: The Boydell Press.

Carter, E. (2003). *Notes to the recording Elliott Carter: »What Next?«/Asko Concerto* (CD booklet, p. 24). ECM New Series 1817.

Dallapiccola, L. (1962). What is the Answer to The Prisoner? *San Francisco Sunday Chronicle*, 2 December, 27.

Edwards, A. (1971). *Flawed Words and Stubborn Sounds: A Conversation with Elliott Carter.* New York: Norton.

Gann, K. (2000). On Life's List of Things to Do: Opera. *New York Times*, 7 March.

Griffiths, P. (1982). *Igor Stravinsky: »The Rake's Progress.«* Cambridge and New York: Cambridge University Press.

Griffiths, P. (1991). *W. A. Mozart: »The Jewel Box«* (opera libretto). London: Chatto & Windus.

Griffiths, P. (1997a). Letter to Elliott Carter, 20 March. In F. Meyer & A. C. Shreffler (Eds.), *Elliot Carter: A Centennial Portrait in Letters and Documents* (pp. 303). Woodbridge, UK: The Boydell Press.

Griffiths, P. (1997b). Letter to Elliott Carter, 27 March. Elliott Carter Collection, Paul Sacher Stiftung, Basel (quoted in Shreffler, 2003, pp. 153–154).

Griffiths, P. (1997c). »What Next?« (opera libretto). Unpublished.

Griffiths, P. (2003). What Next?—A Journal. In *Elliott Carter: »What Next?«/Asko Concerto* (CD booklet, pp. 24–33). ECM New Series 1817.

Keller, J. M. (2013). Notes on the Program. In the program book for the New York Philharmonic performances of *Il Prigioniero*, conducted by Alan Gilbert in New York City, 6 June, 8, 11.

Levine, J. (2008). Comment during a panel discussion at the Museum of Modern Art, New York City, 21 May. Video Recordings of Museum-Related Events in the Museum of Modern Art Archives, item 2008-312D.

Link, J. (2008). Elliott Carter's »Late Music«? *Tempo*, 62 (246), 2–10.

Link, J. (2012). Elliott Carter's Late Music. In M. Boland & J. Link (Eds.), *Elliott Carter Studies* (pp. 33–54). Cambridge: Cambridge University Press.

Meyer, F. & Shreffler, A. C. (2008). *Elliot Carter: A Centennial Portrait in Letters and Documents.* Woodbridge, UK: The Boydell Press.

Noubel, M. (2000). *Elliott Carter ou le temps fertile.* Geneva: Contrechamps editions.

Noubel, M. (2007). »What do I say? How do I say? Who am I to say?«: Quelques considérations sur la dramaturgie musicale dans »What Next?« d'Elliot Carter. In G. Ferrari (Ed.), *L'écriture musicale et son expression scénique au XXe siècle* (pp. 69–82). Paris: L'Harmattan.

Noubel, M. (2012). Three Illusions and Perhaps a Fourth One. In M. Boland & J. Link (Eds.), *Elliott Carter Studies* (pp. 253–70). Cambridge: Cambridge University Press.

Said, E. W. (2006). *On Late Style: Music and Literature Against the Grain.* New York: Pantheon Books.

Saunders, F. S. (1999). *The Cultural Cold War: The CIA and the World of Arts and Letters.* New York: The New Press.

Schiff, D. (2000). Keeping Up with Carter. *Tempo*, 214, 2–6.

Schmidt, D. (1999). What Next? oder: Ein Portrait des Künstlers als grand old man. In Staatsoper Unter den Linden (Ed.), *Schönberg: Von heute auf morgen. Carter: »What Next?« Zwei Einakter*. Frankfurt am Main: Insel.

Shreffler, A. C. (2003). Instrumental Dramaturgy as Humane Comedy: »What Next?« by Elliott Carter and Paul Griffiths. In H. Danuser & M. Kassel (Eds.), *Musiktheater heute* (pp. 147–171). Mainz: Schott.

Shum, A. (2006). *»Verfremdungseffekt« in Busoni's »Turandot:« A Modernist Opera*. M.A. Thesis, University of Victoria.

Stravinsky, V. & Craft, R. (1979). *Stravinsky in Pictures and Documents*. London: Hutchinson.

Taruskin, R. (1993). Back to Whom? Neoclassicism as Ideology. *19th-Century Music*, 16 (3), 286–302.

Tusa, J. (2000). Interview with Elliott Carter. http://www.bbc.co.uk/programmes/p00nc167 (accessed 10 December 2015).

Whittall, A. (2008). »A Play of Pure Forces«? Elliott Carter's Opera in Context. *The Musical Times*, 149, 3–13.

Wierzbicki, J. (2011). *Elliott Carter*. Urbana, IL: University of Illinois Press.

Sharon Mirchandani

Libby Larsen's *Barnum's Bird*
The »Great American Opera«

Introduction

The search for »The Great American Opera« is itself particularly American, originating in the desire to strengthen American cultural identity and, perhaps, in an
American drive toward identifying the best of a kind. The Great American Opera
should, then, uniquely capture the essence of America in both its subject matter and
music and, of course, be outstanding in craftsmanship. Major themes found
throughout American musical history include the conflict between art and commercialism, the tensions between religion and the secular world, the influence from
European and other cultures, and the contrast between the upper and lower classes.
Libby Larsen's chamber opera, *Barnum's Bird* (2002), contains all of these themes.
In addition, Larsen (b. 1950) is the most prolific female American opera composer
who, in addition to her extensive output of over fifteen operas, has composed a large
body (over 400) of highly regarded works in many genres: chamber, vocal, orchestral, choral, band, and multimedia. Her success in the operatic world and as a composer in general is a landmark of feminism, arguably the most important social
movement in American cultural history. Larsen marks an important point in the
steady growth trajectory in the numbers of American women composers of dramatic works and in the increasingly professional status of their work. Larsen's *Barnum's Bird*, as a well-crafted chamber opera, on an American subject, by a notable
American woman composer, with relevant dramatic themes and music, is a strong
candidate for consideration as the »Great American Opera.«

Genre

While it may seem surprising to select a chamber opera as the Great American
Opera, it is characteristic for American composers to be attracted to chamber opera.
Consider such composers as: Eleanor Freer (*Massimilliano, the Court Jester; A Leg-
end of Spain; Joan of Arc;* and *A Christmas Tale*), Amy Beach (*Cabildo*), Vivien Fine
(*Memoirs of Uliana Rooney*), Kurt Weill (*Down in the Valley*), Aaron Copland (*Sec-
ond Hurricane*), Leonard Bernstein (*Trouble in Tahiti*), Mark Bucci (*Tale for a Deaf
Ear*), Douglas Moore (*Devil and Daniel Webster*), and Gian Carlo Menotti (*The Tel-*

ephone; and *The Medium*) (Borroff, 1992, p. xv; Kirk, 2005, pp. 242–249). While Larsen's most well-known opera is the large-scale music drama *Frankenstein. The Modern Prometheus*, which was selected as one of the eight best classical music events of 1990 by USA Today, she has composed excellent chamber operas, beginning with her early *Psyke and the Pskyskraper* (1982) and continuing with the more mature chamber opera *Clair de Lune* (1985). With *Barnum's Bird*, her work in this genre shows complete mastery. The opera exploits the virtues of the small pit orchestra and in being close to the audience. Its more intimate, smaller scale allows it to be more direct and often more unique, and to place an emphasis on familiarity with the audience in the way that many American musicals do.

Subject, Structure, Origins, and Performance History

Barnum's Bird portrays the Swedish soprano Jenny Lind's historic 1850–1851 American tour, which was promoted by the American businessman P. T. Barnum.[1] Lind, known as the »Swedish Nightingale,« was considered to be one of the greatest sopranos in the nineteenth century and became one of the first cultural icons in the United States. During her extraordinarily successful American tour, she sang more than 90 concerts in 19 cities. Based only on her reputation, Barnum tried to contract her through transatlantic correspondence without having heard or seen her. She was reluctant and, perhaps thinking he would decline, asked for a large fee of $187,000 to be paid in advance.[2] Barnum had previously earned a large sum of money from Charles Sherwood Stratton, known as »General Tom Thumb,« a little person he raised and trained from the age of four and then put on exhibit (Tom Thumb was known to have danced a hornpipe and imitated Napoleon for the young Queen Victoria). Barnum had used the money from Tom Thumb's tours to buy an expensive home for himself. He mortgaged this home in order to raise the money for Lind, and the contract was signed for 150 concerts. The contract stipulated that, if after 60 or 100 concerts Lind wanted to stop, she could do so for a penalty fee of $25,000. Though Lind appeared in operas in her twenties, she retired from opera in 1849, thereafter singing only in recitals and oratorios. One explanation is that Lind was a pious Christian and was concerned that being an opera singer was not respectable. She did, however, want very much to earn money for Swedish charities, particularly orphanages, and the American tour would allow her to do this and also

---

1   A number of Larsen's other works also use strong historic female characters: the dramatic cantata *Eleanor Roosevelt*; her *Songs from Letters* (of Calamity Jane); the song cycle *Try Me, Good King: Last Words of the Wives of Henry VIII*; and the choral work *I It Am: The Shewings of Julian of Norwich*.

2   Barnum's initial offer was $150,000, $1,000 for each of the 150 concerts; and this is presented in the opera. Richard Crawford notes that the contract was settled at $187,000 (Crawford, 2001, pp. 117–120).

give to charities in the United States. Barnum promoted Lind so well that, upon her ship's arrival in New York, as many as 40,000 people came to greet her, and she continued to be greeted by crowds wherever she went. Barnum generated »Lindomania« by auctioning tickets, announcing Lind's charitable contributions, and highlighting her virtuous reputation. He also sold her endorsement for a variety of items, from face cream to tropical fish, often without her approval. After 90 concerts, Lind took the option to stop the tour with Barnum; however, she did perform for nearly a year longer in the United States under her own management before returning to Sweden. As far as it is known there was no bitterness, and Barnum and Lind parted on friendly terms (Miller, 1983, p. 78).

Larsen's *Barnum's Bird* brings to life the story of this tour, focusing on the tensions between art and entertainment, Lind's personality versus her celebrity, and the relationship between the star and the showman. The libretto was written by Bridget Carpenter and Libby Larsen. The first act (about 40 minutes long) consists of a prologue and three scenes, in which the four main characters are established: Jenny Lind (soprano); her colleague, the Italian baritone Giovanni Belletti (baritone); American showman P. T. Barnum (tenor); and his scout, the »dwarf« or little person, Tom Thumb (mezzo-soprano). There are eight dancing singers on stage and a chorus of sixteen to thirty-two people in the pit together with flute, percussion, piano, violin, viola, and cello. Some minor characters are: Mr. Dodge, a singer who would like to be promoted by Barnum; Bayard Taylor, whose »Greeting to America« won the song competition; and Taylor's daughter who sings it, very poorly, for Jenny. Singers are called upon to ballyhoo or heckle at times. The first act begins with a welcoming prologue from the chorus, followed by arias from Belletti and Lind and a minstrel chorus danced to by Tom Thumb in a London salon (sc. 1). Barnum is then introduced in his New York office and Tom Thumb proposes the idea of promoting Jenny Lind (sc. 2). Back in the salon, Tom negotiates a deal with Lind and Belletti, and the contract for her tour is signed (sc. 3).

The second act (about 50 minutes), consisting of a prologue and nine scenes, portrays Lind's tour. It is filled with much motion beginning with the Prologue, a musical automaton waltz sung by the dancing chorus in a staccato, machine-like humor. Motion is also emphasized with »The Train Ride« (sc. 1) and »Jenny's Crossing« with its humorous depiction of seasickness (sc. 3). The ever-increasing hustle and bustle of Barnum's marketing is most strongly portrayed in »Barnum's Office« (sc. 2), »The Press Conference« (sc. 4), »The Auction« (sc. 5), and »The American Tour« (sc. 7), while Jenny's beautiful vocalism is highlighted in »The Premiere« (sc. 6). »The Dressing Room« (sc. 8) is wistful as Jenny terminates her contract, and »The Farewell« (sc. 9) portrays Lind and Barnum amicably saying goodbye.

Larsen first got the idea to compose an opera about Jenny Lind in 1995 as she was composing her choral homage to heroes, *Seven Ghosts*. She came across a letter from Lind to Harriet Beecher Stowe that impressed her with Lind's compassion (this letter was set as part of her Seven Ghosts). Around the same time, Larsen was invited by conductor/organist Philip Brunelle to compose an opera in honor of the Library of Congress's Bicentennial, and she thought this would be the perfect subject. The opera was co-commissioned by Brunelle's Plymouth Music Series (now VocalEssence) and the Library of Congress. Larsen wanted to portray the person Jenny Lind more than her celebrity in her account of Lind's 1850–1851 tour. Larsen partnered with Carpenter to write the libretto. Carpenter is a younger playwright/librettist who spoke American English, was working at DreamWorks, and was living in Minnesota at the time. It was important to Larsen that she worked with someone who would write naturally in American English. The pair worked comfortably together to create the libretto, and Larsen composed the music.

After performances at the Theatre de la Jeune Lune in Minneapolis in April 20–22, 2001 (along with an earlier Larsen opera, Eric Hermannson's Soul) (Carlson, 2001; Anthony, 2001a–c), the opera was premiered by the Philip Brunelle singers on February 1 and 2, 2002, at the Coolidge Auditorium in the Library of Congress, and was later broadcast across the nation on National Public Radio's World of Opera as part of »I Hear America Singing,« a major programming initiative at the Library of Congress (LoC, 2002; Freed, 2002). A Washington Post reviewer wrote: »Virgil Thomson's quirky, ensemble-narrated operas cast obvious shadows over Barnum's Bird, but Larsen's melodic invention is more generous, her skipping polyrhythms less high-strung than Thomson's« (Washington Post, 2002). In 2004, Dr. John Pfautz directed a performance at his Opera@Augustana of Augustana College, Rock Island, Illinois, saying »Augustana has a real affection toward anything Jenny Lind« and noted the college's Jenny Lind Chorale and the Jenny Lind Chapel in Andover, Illinois (Burke, 2004). In November 2007, the UNC-Greensboro Opera Theatre also performed Barnum's Bird to acclaim (Walker, 2007).

Dramatic Themes

Larsen meticulously researched the tour, so the audience learns many details about it along the way. There are humorous comments about crab cake (»only in America«), and the tour ends acknowledging Lind's performance in a Hippodrome where cows, pigs, and chickens were present! Barnum also has some funny lines that show him as rather uncultured although he is trying to elevate his reputation by showcasing Lind. When he first hears of her and is told she is a soprano, he asks, »Soprano is her name?«

While many »Great American Plays« or »Great American Novels« are biting social critiques of some sort, Barnum's Bird does not explicitly criticize race relations. The minstrel songs selected for the opera were carefully chosen, largely for their rhythmic vitality, and do not reference ugly stereotypes. »The Bonja Song« is a lighthearted song about playing the banjo and largely uses nonsense syllables to mimic the sounds of the instrument. »Stop That Knocking At My Door« is about a girl visiting a boy, and playfully alternates between the lines »stop that knocking« and »let me in.« And only the first two phrases of the jaunty »Camptown Races« is sung, mockingly by Mr. Dodge who is trying to attract attention.

Barnum's Bird is more concerned with exploring the very American theme of the conflict between art and commercialism. Barnum wants to put Lind in a museum of sorts, to display her as an object of fascination with a mesmerizing voice. (Perhaps this is parallel to the way this very book puts a selection of operas in a museum-like display.) At the auction, to Lind's shock and dismay, frenzied people vie to be the first to get a ticket. At her premiere, Barnum, against Lind's wishes, announces to thunderous applause her intent to donate her entire fee to charity, intensifying the fervor for Lind. When she complains, he tears the contract in two and offers her a greater contract. She considers the good she can do with the money, Belletti accepts it on her behalf, and Lind and Barnum shake hands. Her art for the service to humanity has been bought. During the American tour, Lind has a brief passage where she competes vocally with Mr. Dodge's imitation of a trumpet. This disembodies her voice from her person, further dehumanizing her. While Lind eventually can no longer tolerate the commercialism and leaves the tour at the end of the opera, without Barnum's commercialism her art would not have been as well known, nor would she have been able to be as benevolent in her charitable work. The opera shows that, while there are tensions, art and commercialism can coexist successfully. Larsen states,

> There is no final resolution or answer to the tensions between art and commercialism. The opera, rather, highlights the on-going question of whether a balance between the two can be found. It does show that celebrity can eclipse the art of a person, in this case, American celebrity threatening to override Lind's artistry. (Larsen interview, 2014)

Lind's conflict between religion and career exemplifies another American theme. It is not entirely clear why Lind left operatic performance shortly before coming to America. By most accounts, she came to view opera as sinful and needed to uphold a pure image. She found concert performances a way to maintain her moral reputation and still perform. How much of this belief about opera was genuinely felt by her and how much this choice was due to social pressure is difficult to know. Without completely realizing where she was headed, she left the spectacle of the opera for the spectacle of Barnum's promotions.

The Lind–Barnum relationship embodies the American story of musical influence from Europe. Lind captivated American audiences with her combination of European arias and rather exotic »echo« and »bird« songs. She would then end her concerts singing some American favorites, particularly the beloved »Home Sweet

Home« composed by the British Henry Bishop with words by the American John Payne. After her first performance of »Casta Diva« (Act 2, sc. 6), a heckler shouts a request for »Camptown Races,« highlighting the contrast between highbrow European and lowbrow American audiences, a persistent phenomenon in American music history. Later, hecklers call for her bird song, »Home Sweet Home,« and »Happy Birthday,« and Lind accommodates to a small extent. The opera documents the changing relationship between Lind and Barnum as they move from skepticism to partnership, to distrust and annoyance, to mutual respect. Toward the end of the opera, Belletti invites Barnum to join Lind and himself in a toast to America. Barnum, a staunch American temperance advocate, chooses to drink water rather than wine, commenting on »demon rum« as »a source of great sorrow in our land.« After the toast, Lind invites Barnum to dance. He declines, citing his poor education. Lind coaxes the reluctant Barnum to dance anyway, using his catch phrase »Bah, Humbug« to everyone's surprise. These brief cross-cultural moments of connection show the positive exchange they have with each other.

The Music

The music of *Barnum's Bird* is full of rhythmic energy and excitement. When asked what might make *Barnum's Bird* »American,« Larsen commented,

> It shows the pluralistic nature of America, how any influence can be easily absorbed. American composers feel very free to introduce eclectic elements into their music. They feel free to graze among styles generating their own perception of other cultures. We can see this in works like Philip Glass's *Satyagraha*, and *Einstein on the Beach*, and in William Bolcolm's *McTeague*. (Larsen interview, 2014)

A Hybrid

This kind of hybrid, as described by Larsen, is characteristic of America, and *Barnum's Bird* has been explained as »a cross between an American musical and traditional European opera« (Siebers, 2004). The opera is a musical collage of Larsen's own contemporary music, European arias sung operatically, and American minstrel and folk songs (see Figure 1: Types of Music in Libby Larsen's *Barnum's Bird*). Larsen believes that the singing should definitely reflect the characters, with the Americans generally sounding more theatrical. Belletti initially focuses on European culture, but as he becomes more interested in the tour he tries to act American. The eight dancing singers function somewhat like a Greek chorus commenting on the action; they sing in a nonclassical American style. They are versatile, and directors have dressed them in period costumes (for the Library of Congress premiere) in red and mustard yellow in a show that emphasized minstrelsy and, in another show, all in black and white. Barnum represents rank commercialism. In the opera, his character is perhaps even more cynical than the historic person. He says the direct truth as he sees it in lines like »I create America. It's whatever I say it is.« While the historic Lind is often described as a pure, vocal oracle that the public wished »to possess and be possessed by« (Gallagher, 1995, p. 190), Larsen spotlights her human traits—her concerns, her business skill, her humanitarian motivations, and her independence of thought—in addition to showing off her vocal prowess. It was also important to Larsen to show that Lind was equally as strong as Barnum. Lind states her position on her performances forcefully when she is first contacted by Barnum, at several points along the tour, and again at the end when she decides to end the tour, with lines like »There's to be no cheap public display« and »I do not sing to satisfy curiosity, I sing for the love of God and for the Swedish children«; and Lind protests several of the arrangements Barnum makes, such as performing in a butcher's shop, saying »I do not like to sing for pigs.« Her voice never wavers from its trained operatic style. The character of Tom Thumb (a little person, referred to as a »dwarf«) is the most complex and must be versatile, at times more theatrical, at times more lyrical. While he is cast as a »trousers« role for practical reasons, the gender-bending aspect of this role is well suited to the diverse dimensions of his personality.

As in all of her vocal music, Larsen is quite sensitive to the rhythms of American English and uses it well to capture the contrast between the American and European characters. Larsen feels that American English calls for a different melodic approach. She thinks that the tessitura tends to eliminate the higher notes and the lowest of the low notes, and therefore the language tends to work best for baritone to upper mezzo roles. The rhythms and syntax have many one-syllable words, so that melismas must be treated more carefully to not sound contrived. The language is more blunt and has a narrower range of 4ths or 5ths. American English words must be separated into their own individual words more so than in bel canto singing. She observes that many American composers like Paulus, Adamo, Heggy, and Bolcolm also set American English naturally (in contrast to John Corgliano's *Ghosts of Versailles* which is more European in its setting). Larsen also had the musical style of Tom Waits, a popular singer, in mind as she was composing the work »We Tom Waits-ed Barnum!« (Larsen interview, 2014). The theatrical vocal styles and entertainment pieces have caused the opera to be referred to as a »cabaret opera« (Carlson, 2001; LoC, 2002).

Larsen's Music and Motives

Larsen's own contemporary chromatic music contrasts with the much more traditional tonal European arias and American minstrel and folk songs. Her original music uses ostinatos, intervallic manipulation, and nontraditional harmonies. Tonal melodies are interspersed in the opera and sometimes combined with Larsen's more chromatic writing. Larsen uses instruments effectively to contrast the more refined Lind with Barnum's crassness. The solo flute is frequently associated with Lind, while percussion is connected to Barnum and his circus-like promotions. Percussion is used in a number of ways: to create a circus atmosphere; for drama, especially snare drum rolls at the beginning and end of scenes; to simulate a minstrel show sound (tambourines along with banjos for minstrel numbers like the Bonja Song); to accompany dancing (woodblock for Tom Thumb) and reinforce minstrel/ragtime rhythms; and to capture the craze (mouth siren at the auction, p. 223). Barnum's character is also embodied in his nose! He has many lines where he says »I smell an audience/advertising/etc.« The character sniffs the air humorously on stage as he addresses the audience. Larsen uses at least four prominent motives in the opera, which I will name: the Circus Motive, the Train Motive, the Jenny Lind Motive, and the Marketing Motive.

Larsen derives her Circus Motive from a well-known theme associated with circuses, originally composed in 1897 by the Czech composer Julius Fučík for his *Entrance of the Gladiators* march.[3] In Fučík's piece, the march is in cut time and in a major key (Example 1a); Larsen uses rhythmic and melodic variations of it, often setting it in 5/8 and in a more chromatic context. It appears prominently in the Act I Prologue and occasionally throughout the opera to suggest the circus-like atmosphere of Barnum's promotional schemes. The Circus Motive is first sung by the singing/movement singers to the syllables »doot doot doo […]« in the Act 1 Prologue, in a 5/8 meter with a tri-tone vamp underneath (Example 1b), then it appears often in variations in the orchestra, in either case, highlighting the commercialism of the moment. The motive saturates the Act I, Prologue (mm. 23, 53, 72, 90, and 94 to name a few places) and variants of it recur throughout the opera, for example, in The Press Conference (Act 2, sc. 4) after Barnum is asked how much he will make from Lind's tour. When Barnum says »America is willing to pay,« the Circus Motive appears softly in the orchestra (Example 1c). Lind continues that she only sings for God and for children.

Example 1a: Julius Fučík: »Entrance of the Gladiators March,« mm. 1–4.

---

3   A 1910 arrangement, retitled »Thunder and Blazes,« by the Canadian composer Louis-Philippe Laurendeau helped to popularize the melody in the United States.

Example 1b: Libby Larsen: Circus Motive, p. 3, mm. 6–8.

Example 1c: Libby Larsen: Circus Motive Variant, p. 209, mm. 391–399.

In Act II, Sc. 1, »The Train Ride,« Larsen touches on a theme that is prominent in many works by American popular and classical composers. From the nineteenth century, dozens of songs and piano pieces using trains as themes can be found in collections such as the Sheet Music in the Library of Congress American Memory Project: Music for the Nation: American Sheet Music 1870–1885 Collection; and the Lester S. Levy Collection of Sheet Music at Johns Hopkins University. Examples are *Union Pacific Grand March for piano* (1870) by Henry S. Rowe and *The Railroad Conductors Song* (1881) by W. S. Mullaly. References to trains continue in American classical works of the twentieth century, such as: Charles Ives's *Concord Piano Sonata no. 2*, mvt. 2 (1910); Weill's *Railroads on Parade/Fantasia on Rail Transport* (1939); Bernstein's *Subway Ride & Imaginary Coney Island* (from *On the Town* [1944]); George Antheil's *The Golden Spike* (1945); Eric Whitacre's *Ghost Train* for wind ensemble (1993); and Steve Reich's *Different Trains* (1988).

Example 2: The Train Motive, p. 133, mm. 81–83.

At the time of Lind's tour, the transcontinental railroad had not yet been built, so the only rail travel was for shorter distances between cities on lines like the Baltimore and Ohio Railway dating from 1928. Though most of Lind's travel was by stagecoach, the excitement for rail travel was growing; and a steam locomotive built in 1847 for the London Brighton and South Coast Railway was named after Lind. Barnum later became one of the first circus owners to move his troupe by rail. In Larsen's scene, the chorus sings »The Train Motive,« an underlying rhythmic ostinato of cluster chords on neutral syllables »da doo […]« over a rolling fifths bass, while Barnum sings freely, in dialogue with the conductor about Lind's upcoming tour (Example 2). There is room for some spontaneity in the dialogue at the end of this passage.

An enormous number of products were named for Jenny Lind, and Larsen uses »The Marketing Chant« to list many of them and to show the crowd's excitement each time Lind appears in public. The chant is mostly in unison, loosely centered tonally through iteration of the tonic, in this example on E (Example 3). Some of the items are: cake, cigars, flies for trout fishing, pipes, needles, tea kettle, buggy, dahlia, pudding, truffle, stove, poker chip, paper doll, mirror, flat iron stand, chewing gum, snuff boxes, cookies, letter seal, and combs.

Example 3: The Marketing Chant, p. 159, mm. 209–210.

In the final scene of the opera, the Jenny Lind Chant, derived from the Circus Motive, is sung by the dancing singers and the chorus. The chant plays rhythmically with her name and nickname to show her as a star (Example 4).

Example 4: Jenny Lind Chant, p. 319, mm. 1119–1122.

Diagetic Music

The opera is, for the most part, historically accurate, and Larsen interpolates European arias sung by the historic Lind, who is first introduced singing »Hear Ye Israel« from Felix Mendelssohn's oratorio *Elijah* (Act 1, sc. 1). Belletti is also introduced singing a European aria, Gioachino Rossini's »Largo al factotum,« sung by Figaro in his *The Barber of Seville* (Act 1, sc. 1). Act 1 ends with a brief poignant vocal sung by

Lind. In Act 2, for the portrayal of Lind's American premiere (sc. 6) and again during her tour (sc. 7), Lind sings »Casta Diva« from Bellini's *Norma,* a piece that the historic Lind often sang in concert to much acclaim. Lind famously imitated a bird, singing her »Bird« song (Act 2, sc. 7). A highlight of the opera is when Lind sings for President Millard Fillmore during The American Tour (Act 2, sc. 7). She sings her famous Norwegian Echo Song, *The Herdsman's Song* (»Herdesänge«; published in English attributed to Ahlstrom): »Kom kjyra, kom kjyra mi!« At the end of the piece, the historic Lind adds her own coda sung in imitation of an echo, and this delighted audiences, as it does in the opera.

Music that was published using Lind's name is also used in the opera. *Jenny Lind's Favorite Polka* underlies the choral introduction to Barnum, opening the scene to Barnum's Broadway Office (Act 1, sc. 2). *Jenny Lind's Grande Valse de Caprice* by A. Dr. Galindo (1847) is sung and danced to mechanically with humor by the dancing singers who are to imitate an automaton (Act 2, Prologue). This is a nice historic touch to the opera, as there was quite a bit of fascination with, and sometimes even fear of, automatons at this time. Barnum is known, for publicity, to have held a song contest to choose a song for Lind to sing, which was won by Taylor's *Greeting to America.* In the opera, the second and third verses only are performed by Taylor's daughter Charity for Lind to hear. There is some humor when Charity butchers the song, after which Lind says, »what your song means to me I could not possibly say!« This song, in all three verses, was indeed performed by the real Lind in many concerts (Shultz, 1962, pp. 181–182).

The European music contrasts with the American popular music. The onstage chorus is, at times, used as a quartet, reminiscent of a Barbershop quartet (Act 1, Prologue and sc. 2). When Tom Thumb first comes on stage, he dances on to a minstrel tune sung by the chorus called »The Bonja Song« (Act 1, sc. 1). The humorous American parlor song »My Mustache« is sung by a solo bass in a tonal setting that contrasts with the more chromatic surrounding material in Barnum's dialogue (Act 1, sc. 2) (Mitchell, 1909). When Tom Thumb first meets Lind, he enters announced by a cowbell, mouth siren, snare, woodblock, and tambourine, dancing to a tenor solo and a rousing chorus singing the minstrel song »Stop That Knocking at My Door« (Act 1, sc. 3). In Act 2, the American folk song »Sing a Song of Sixpence« is adapted to become, at various moments, »Sing a Song of Barnum« in F Major (Act 2, sc. 2); »Sing a Song of Jenny« in F# Major (Act 2, sc. 3); and, my favorite, the humorous »Sing a Song of Seasick« (Act 2, sc. 3). With »Sing a Song of Seasick,« Belletti sings in C major accompanied by F# major, with the bitonality at a triton apart, very effectively creating the out-of-kilter feeling of motion sickness. Between »Sing a Song of Barnum« and »Sing a Song of Jenny« is a performance of the minstrel song »Josiphus Orange Blossom« by Mr. Dodge, who is trying to catch Barnum's attention throughout the show. During The American Tour, Lind is requested to sing »Happy Birthday« and »Camptown Races,« and fragments of »Camptown Races«

are sung by Mr. Dodge and the chorus (Act 2, sc. 7). Lind becomes exhausted, and Tom Thumb realizes that she will leave the tour. He honors her by singing a song to her that she often ended concerts with, the American favorite, »Home Sweet Home« (Act 2, sc. 8). It is a lovely rendition that begins with Tom Thumb alone who is then joined by Lind, the eight onstage dancing singers, and the SATB pit chorus.

Two Ensemble Scenes

The opera shines in its larger ensemble scenes, such as the »Jenny Come Along« Ensemble at the end of Act 1, sc. 3 that shows the variety of interests at play. The scene starts simply with Lind accompanying herself as she sings her only aria that is composed in Larsen's contemporary style.[4] The text is the two-stanza reflective poem »Oh World! Oh Life! Oh Time!« by Percy Bysshe Shelley, slightly adapted by Larsen. Here, using her own more dissonant music, rather than what the historic Lind sang in public, Larsen shows Lind's private, and perhaps conflicted, self as she decides to leave the operatic world. In the poem, the protagonist speaks of joy, but, addressing spring, summer, and winter, asks to be moved with grief rather than delight. Larsen's setting sets up the following dialogue between Belletti and Lind in which Lind complains of opera's »falseness and wickedness« and states her desire to sing »for people who have no voice.« Representing the common folk touches the American democratic ideal and, in the opera, links Lind's aria to the entrance of the Americans (the dancing singers) with Tom Thumb. Their lively minstrel chorus »Knocking at My Door,« danced to by Tom Thumb, leads to the entire ensemble singing »Jenny Come Along« as they persuade her to accept Barnum's proposal. The words for »Jenny Come Along« are taken from a parody published at the time of her arrival that tells how she will be welcomed in America »with speeches, and serenades, and rockets […] while P. T. will tap their pockets« (Shultz, 1962, p. 183). During this ensemble, Lind reaffirms her commitment to sing for God and charity while the Circus Motive is sung by the pit chorus, the dancing singers encourage the deal and tell Jenny to »quite these kings and queens,« Tom Thumb and Barnum revel in the anticipation of a lucrative tour, Belletti has a change of heart from reluctance to eagerness to try America, and all sing »Jenny Come Along« before the first appearance of the Jenny Lind Chant (Example 5). The ensemble is an exhilarating ending to the first half of the opera. It does wind down poignantly with Lind's brief vocal before closing.

---

4   This aria is analyzed in detail by Holly Ann Schwartz in her doctoral dissertation (Schwartz, 2008).

Example 5: Act 1, Sc. 3: »Jenny Come Along« Ensemble, p. 116, mm. 957–959.

The American Tour (Act 2, sc. 7) is another fine ensemble scene that develops from the intermingling of the musical styles. Larsen uses clever juxtapositions of both European and American songs with her own original music, culminating in a duet between Mr. Dodge singing »Camptown Races« in counterpoint with Lind's extension of »Casta Diva« and the Marketing Chant (Example 6). The mix captures the excitement and tensions of the tour quite well.

Example 6: Act 2, Sc. 7, American Tour: »Camptown Races,« extension of »Casta Diva,« and Marketing Chant, p. 277, mm. 868–869.

Summary

Barnum's Bird is a collage of original music, European arias, and American melodies, and brings together diverse elements into a cohesive whole that is accessible, creative, and well crafted. It represents the nature of America well, with its depiction of the commercialism and unfettered business practices that characterize the country's history, the interaction of European and American culture, the contrast between the cultivated and the vernacular, and the moral overtones from religion. In addition, Larsen is a standout in the long line of American women composers empowered by feminism who have forged their way into the operatic field. As a cleverly written, thoroughly researched tribute to a historic icon in the United States, *Barnum's Bird* is a strong contender for the title »Great American Opera.«

References

Anthony, M. (2001a). News & Notes; Prolific Larsen in the Spotlight with Two Operas Slated for April. *Star Tribune: Newspaper of the Twin Cities*, 4 March.

Anthony, M. (2001b). Jenny Oh!; Swedish Singer Jenny Lind's U. S. Tour Caused Pandemonium and Pioneered the Idea of Art as Commodity. It Also Inspired Libby Larsen's Newest Opera. *Star Tribune: Newspaper of the Twin Cities*, 15 April.

Anthony, M. (2001c). There's a Hint of Deeper Issues in »Barnum's Bird.« *Star Tribune: Newspaper of the Twin Cities*, 21 April.

Banno, J. (2002). The Songbird and the Huckster. *Washington Post*, February 4. https://www.washingtonpost.com/archive/lifestyle/2002/02/04/the-songbird-and-the-huckster/5d0dab17-db5b-40f9-837c-6dc6e7a320b8/ (accessed 25 February 2016).

Borroff, E. (1992). *American Operas: A Checklist*. Edited J. B. Clark. Warren, MI: Harmonie Park Press.

Burke, D. (2004). »Barnum's Bird« Brings True Story to Opera Stage. *The (IA) Quad-City Times*, 6 June.

Carlson, A. (2001). Bird Lands: Minneapolis Composer Libby Larsen Scores with 'Barnum's Bird,' a Specially Commissioned Cabaret Opera About the Time P. T. Barnum and Jenny Lind Went on a Road Trip Together. *St. Paul Pioneer Press*, 15 April.

Crawford, R. (2001). *An Introduction to America's Music*. New York: W. W. Norton & Co.

Freed, G. (2002). Delightful »Barnum's Bird« Premieres in U. S. Capital. *Star Tribune: Newspaper of the Twin Cities*, 10 February.

Gallagher, L. (1995). Jenny Lind and the Voice of America. In C. E. Blackmer & P. J. Smith (Eds.), *En Travesti: Women, Gender Subversion, Opera* (pp. 190–215). New York: Columbia University Press.

Holland, H. S. & Rockstro, W. S. (1893). *Jenny Lind the Artist, 1820–1851: A Memoir of Madame Jenny Lind Goldschmidt, Her Art-Life and Dramatic Career, from Original Doc-*

uments, Letters, MS. Diaries, &c., Collected by Mr. Otto Goldschmidt. New and Abridged Edition. New York: C. Scribner.

Kirk, E. K. (2005). *American Opera.* Urbana, IL: University of Illinois Press.

Larsen, L. (2004). *Barnum's Bird: Vocal Score.* New York; Oxford: Oxford University Press.

Larsen, L. (August 26, 2014). Phone interview by author.

Library of Congress/LoC (2002). Barnum's Bird Flies at Library of Congress. http://www.loc. gov/today/pr/2002/01-188.html (accessed 25 February 2016).

Libby Larsen. http://libbylarsen.com/ (accessed 25 February 2016).

Miller, P. L. (1983). Review of P. T. Barnum Presents Jenny Lind: The American Tour of the Swedish Nightingale by W. Porter Ware and Thaddeus C. Lockard. *American Music,* 1 (1), 78–80.

Mitchell, J. (Ed.). (1909). My Moustache. In *Heart Song, 269.* National Magazine. Boston: Chapple Publishing.

Music and Railways (2014). http://www.philpacey.pwp.blueyonder.co.uk/musrail.html (accessed 25 February 2016).

Schwartz, H. A. (2008). *Operas by Women in Twentieth Century America.* DMA diss., The University of Texas at Austin. https://repositories.lib.utexas.edu/bitstream/handle/2152/ 3949/schwartzd03881.pdf (accessed 25 February 2016).

Shultz, G. D. (1962). *Jenny Lind: The Swedish Nightingale.* Philadelphia: J. B. Lippincott Company.

Siebers, E. (2004). Barnum's Bird Doesn't Quite Fly. *Quad-City Times,* June 16. http://qc times.com/lifestyles/recreation/barnum-s-bird-doesn-t-quite-fly/article_2c95e6a6-ad2d-51b8-8d90-dd181d0c389b.html (accessed 25 February 2016).

Walker, W. T. (2007). UNCG Opera Theater: Barnum's Bird was a Hoot! *Classical Voice of North Carolina.* http://cvnc.org/reviews/2007/112007/Barnum.html (accessed 25 February 2016).

Scene page measure	Motives, keys	Prominent, newly-composed motives	European arias	American minstrel or folk tunes	Popular melodies associated with Lind
Act 1					
Prologue pp. 1-13 mm. 1-108	Circus (Ensemble)	X	–	–	–
Scene 1: The Salon pp. 13-40 mm. 109-306	"Largo al Factotum" (Belletti) C: - Eb:	–	X	–	–
	"Hear Ye Israel" (Lind) b:	–	X	–	–
	"The Bonja Song" (Tom Thumb) D:	–	–	X	–
Scene 2: The Broadway Office pp. 41-78 mm. 307-691	"Jenny Lind's Favorite Polka" (Chorus) Eb: - Bb: - Eb:	–	–	–	X
	"I Smell an Audience" (Barnum)	X	–	–	–
	"My Mustache" (Bass Solo) D: - G:	–	–	X	–
	Circus (Ensemble, Tom Thumb, Barnum)	X	–	–	–
	"Jenny Come Along" (Barnum)	X	–	–	–
Scene 3: The Salon pp. 78-124 mm. 692-124	"Oh World! Oh Life! Oh Time!" (Lind)	X	–	–	–
	"Stop That Knocking" (Tenor Solo, Chorus) D:	–	–	X	–
	"Jenny Come Along" (Ensemble)	X	–	–	–
	Circus with Jenny Lind Chant (Ensemble)	X	–	–	–
	Vocalise (Lind)	–	–	–	X
Act 2					
Prologue: The Automaton pp. 125-131 mm. 1-74	"Jenny Lind Grande Valse de Caprice" (Dancing Singers, Chorus) F:	–	–	–	X
Scene 1: The Train Ride pp. 132-147 mm. 75-145	["Whistle, steam"]				
	Train (Barnum, Chorus)	X	–	–	–
Scene 2: Barnum's Office pp. 148-170 mm. 146-243	"Sing a Song of Barnum" with Train (Dancing Singers, Chorus)	X	–	X	–
	"Josiphus Orange Blossom" (Dodge) C:	–	–	X	–
	"Sing a Song of Barnum" with Marketing Chant (Dancing Singers, Chorus) F:	X	–	X	–
Scene 3: Jenny's Crossing pp. 171-192 mm. 244-306	"Sing a Song of Jenny" with Marketing Chant (Dancing Singers, Chorus) F#:	X	–	X	–
	"Sing a Song of Seasick" (Belletti, Ensemble) C: & F#:	–	–	X	–
	Marketing Chant (Dancing Singers, Chorus) with Lind, Belletti, Tom Thumb	X	–	–	–
Scene 4: The Press Conference pp. 193-221 mm. 307-569	"It's Jenny Lind" (Dancing Singers)	X	–	–	–
	Song Contest (Ensemble)	X	–	–	–
	"Greeting to America" (Charity) G:	–	–	–	X

Figure 1: Types of Music in Libby Larsen's »Barnum's Bird.«

Act 2 cont.

Scene page measure	Motives, keys	Prominent, newly-composed motives	European arias	American minstrel or folk tunes	Popular melodies associated with Lind
Scene 5: The Auction pp. 222-236 mm. 570-656	Circus (Chorus)	X	–	–	–
	"One Ticket" (Tom Thumb, Barnum, Ensemble) G:	X	–	–	–
Scene 6: The Premiere pp. 237-252 mm. 657-759	Circus (Dancing Singers)	X	–	–	–
	"Casta Diva" (Lind) F:	–	X	–	–
	"Camptown Races" (Heckler's request)	–	–	X	–
	[Barnum: Donate Fee]				
	[Lind & Barnum argue]				
	[Settle new contract]				
Scene 7: The American Tour pp. 253-289 mm. 760-917	Circus (Dancing Singers, Chorus)	X	–	–	–
	"Camptown Races" (Chorus) C:	–	–	X	–
	"Bird Song" (Lind) B:	–	–	–	X
	"Camptown Races" (Dodge) C:	–	–	X	–
	"Casta Diva" (Lind) C:	–	X	–	–
	"Bird Song", "Home Sweet Home"	–	–	–	X
	"Happy Birthday" (Heckler's requests)	–	–	–	X
	"Bird Song" (Lind) Bb:	–	–	–	X
	"Echo Song" (Lind) D:	–	–	–	X
	"Bird Song" with Marketing Chant (Belletti, Lind, Chorus)	X	–	–	X
	"Casta Diva" with Marketing Chant (Lind, Chorus)	X	X	–	–
	"Camptown Races" with "Casta Diva" & Marketing Chant (Dodge, Lind, Ensemble)	X	X	X	–
	"One Ticket" (Tom Thumb, Barnum, Ensemble) G:	X	–	–	–
	"Bird Song" with Marketing Chant (Lind, Dodge, Dancing Singers, Chorus)	X	–	–	X
Scene 8: The Dressing Room pp. 290-305 mm.918-1059	[Jenny Lind ends tour]				
	"Home Sweet Home" (Tom Thumb, Lind, Dancing Singers, Chorus) G:	–	–	–	X
Scene 9: The Farewell pp. 306-320 mm.1060-1126	Circus, Jenny Lind Chant (Ensemble)	X	–	–	–
	["Bah Humbug!" Dance]				
	Jenny Lind Chant (Dancing Singers, Chorus)	X	–	–	–

Figure 1: Types of Music in Libby Larsen's »Barnum's Bird.«

Amy Bauer

»The Mysteries of Selma, Alabama«
Re-telling and Remembrance in David Lang's *The Difficulty of Crossing a Field*

Introduction

In his Los Angeles Times review of the Long Beach Opera's 2011 production (re-peated due to popular demand in 2014), Mark Swed declared that David Lang's *The Difficulty of Crossing a Field* was about the »difficulty of existence [...] a hybrid opera/play, unlike any other I know« (Swed, 2011).[1] Based on a one-page story by Ambrose Bierce (1842–ca. 1914), Lang's »opera« concerns a plantation owner in the antebellum south who—in full view of witnesses—disappears into thin air while crossing a field.[2] As a »hybrid opera/play,« the work's form thus matched its subject. Words, music, and drama folded into one another, mimicking the way each charac-ter's view of the opera's central mystery collapsed into the unknowable absence that drove its narrative. Although Mr. Williamson's disappearance remains ambiguous, the work's setting does not: The thoughts of his slaves, neighbors, and family reflect different existential viewpoints even as the relations between slaves and owners, and among Williamson and his wife and daughter, fix the story squarely in 1854.

I saw *Difficulty* in 2011 in that same production. Based on the anecdotal report of a man's disappearance with no immediate rational, poetic, or allegorical import, *Dif-ficulty* could glibly be said to be about nothing. Yet the entire music-theatrical expe-rience left me with a sense of profound importance and unease. Mac Wellman's li-bretto made deft use of the 700 words in Bierce's restrained account to illustrate the suspension of logic and time, while Lang's string quartet lines circled literally and figuratively around the hypnotic spoken and sung exhortations. Andreas Mitisek's novel staging for the Long Beach Opera further emphasized the gap between obser-vation and reason by putting the audience on stage, while singers and actors moved

---

1   Swed also reviewed a workshop production of the work, pleading that »this astonishing work [...] not be allowed to vanish into thin air« (Swed, 2002). Since 2010, the opera has received at least six productions.

2   The story was first published in the *San Francisco Examiner* on October 14, 1888, and was included in the collection *Can Such Things Be?* (1893). The full text can be found online at the *Ambrose Bierce Project* (http://www.ambrosebierce.org).

forward and back, and up and down, from various locations in the fog-shrouded and dimly-lit auditorium.

The opera's narrative, such as it is, is explicitly, almost didactically, structured around an absence that cannot be explained, that indeed cannot even be named. Thus Wellman's libretto proceeds as a series of seven numbered »tellings« removed from chronological time, but positioned to comment on each other through hidden repetitions and associative connections, aided by the almost subliminal effect of the subdued string quartet that accompanies most of the stage action. Each telling recounts the central event from a different viewpoint, one informed by the memories, psychology, and ideologies of those for whom Mr. Williamson's disappearance had exerted such a strange and troubling power. Here, the examination of *Difficulty* will similarly attempt to account for the opera's compelling affect through a series of seven »re-tellings,« in which the discussion moves from the libretto's source materials to the specifics of the Long Beach Opera performance that I witnessed and back toward a more abstract contemplation of the work as a whole. This global »re-telling« envisions *Difficulty* as less of an opera than a convergence of seven entwined narratives that work together in a successful production of the opera. The minimal musical score and its accompanying libretto present the most obvious strands; they offer independent, if complementary, narratives that structure the opera's surface. But the saga of Bierce and the history of America on the cusp of the Civil War cast long shadows over every production, while the libretto as a play occupies a particular place in Wellman's long career of crafting political, often confrontational, theater. Finally, the Long Beach Opera's provocative staging forced the audience to become a part of the production: The audience's perceptions of the shifting work in a sense establish a seventh narrative journey that travels beyond the production, if only to circle back to its central mysteries.

The First Re-telling: Bierce the Bitter, Quixotic Crusader

Recent scholarship has bolstered Bierce's reputation, as a minor figure of nineteenth-century American letters, and one of its most notorious investigative journalists, by acknowledging the proto-modernist strains in his fiction. As Cathy Davidson notes, Bierce was an almost postmodern »literary hippogryph,« who conjoined elements from realism and impressionism, naturalism and surrealism, while rejecting wholesale the sentimental and ideological assumptions of his contemporaries (Davidson, 1984, pp. 1–4). Bierce is popularly known for the twist in *Occurrence at Owl Creek Bridge* (1891), among other Civil War tales, and the cynical witticisms of *The Devil's Dictionary* (1911) (Bierce, 2001). Yet Bierce's stories moved far beyond standard tales of the war and the macabre. Riddled with gaps and ambiguous details, they often challenge the reader's perceptions of events and characters, exploring the limits of the narrative as a mode of expression (Griffin, 2009, p. 137). His stories influenced authors as diverse as Ernest Hemingway and William Golding, while Ryunosuke Akutagawa, Julio Cortázar, and Jorge Luis Borges have borrowed explicitly from specific stories (Davidson, 1984, p. 124; Berkove, 2002, p. 189).

Although Bierce may be best known for his Civil War narratives, his gothic and tall tales share, with the war stories, a singular obsession with time and the fallibility of human psychology. His protagonists share a faulty perception of their world, one that escalates into an often entirely preventable crisis of their own making. Thus each crisis—be it the soldier who dies outside of a sanctioned battle or the wanderer who murders a delusion—is presented as the fateful, ironic outcome of an extreme subjectivity rooted in his or her environment. Within this world, the uncanny exists to upend the blinkered assumptions of an ostensibly rational, well-read protagonist whose confusion is often mirrored in the text through the incorporation of nonlinear plot lines, the juxtaposition of multiple points of view, and precise but indeterminate language that conceals as much as it reveals. Bierce's narrative method blurs the line between perception and imagination in a way that reflects, in the words of Martin Griffin, »the profound loss of redemptive potential in the flow of memory« (Griffen, 2009, p. 153). This loss is often focused by an arrested moment, a kind of hallucinatory tableau vivant that, paradoxically, is always in motion. The stories are structured so that the act of reading recapitulates the doomed strategies that a protagonist employs to understand his or her predicament. Yet the reader is always allowed the option of escape: the luxury to misread, re-read, and adopt several conclusions, or none at all.

Difficulty is the slightest of a particular subgenre in Bierce's oeuvre, wherein an inexplicable event—here a disappearance—is left unexplained by either rational or supernatural means. Bierce provides the reader with no means by which to judge the reliability of the event's observers or to untangle subtext from text. Thus *Difficulty*, despite its brevity and presentation, could be seen as the prototypical Biercean tale. A journalistic report of the disappearance is followed by one of Bierce's favorite tropes: a trial or, in the words of *Dictionary*, »A formal inquiry designed to prove and put upon record the blameless characters of judges, advocates and jurors« (Bierce, 2001, p. 229). We could turn to Bierce's *Dictionary* for further subtext regarding every aspect of the »case,« from his satiric take on »inadmissible evidence« (i.e., that of the Wren boy and the slaves), down to the property across which Mr. Williamson strides, defined as an »object of man's brief rapacity and long indifference,« as well as a notion that »carried to its logical conclusion, [...] means that some have the right to prevent others from living« (Bierce, 2001, p. 74).

The Second Re-telling: The Theater of Subversion

Wellman, of course, greatly expanded Bierce's text in his original play through repetition and the explicit incorporation of seven »tellings« (Wellman, 2008, pp. 123–170). In this, he drew on the inspiration of Bierce's *The Moonlit Road*, a ghost story composed of three tragic narrative threads representing a bereaved son, the amnesiac father, and the ghost of a mother who speaks from the beyond despite having no more insight into her plight than the living do. More significant perhaps is that *The Moonlit Road* itself is most famous for being the source of several subsequent re-tellings: Japanese writer Ryunosuke Akutagawa explicitly rewrote it as *In a Grove*, a story later absorbed into director Akira Kurosawa's screenplay for *Rashomon*. Wellman's attraction to Bierce as a model for staged re-tellings follows from the playwright's fascination with dated language, his unease with aspects of American culture, and his highly developed ethics of theater.[3]

Wellman's obsession with language and diction stemmed initially from the concern of a loss of richness in the American vernacular, one that has led to a concomitant flattening of affect and meaning. He thus often tries to reconstruct dated oral systems in order to both preserve the physical beauty of language, like »old wood [with] a texture and grain to it,« and to establish a new speech with mythic qualities (Robinson & Wellman, 1992, p. 44). For Marc Robinson, »watching Wellman's plays is like taking a rollercoaster ride on tracks of speech,« a ride intended to evoke real feelings as opposed to the artificial emotions that rule contemporary theater (Robinson, 1992, p. 40).

The artificial emotions that Wellman derides reflect an American culture whose »demonic« lack of restrictions has led to a base political culture, commercialization, and homogenization (Savran, 1999, p. 20). Much of Wellman's work in the 1990s was overtly political and exemplified the values stated in his famous 1984 screed against the *Theatre of Good Intentions*, an epithet later shortened to »geezer theater« (Wellman, 1984). In this essay and subsequent ones, Wellman railed against the devolution of American Naturalism to stock notions of character and theatricality that exist primarily to manipulate emotion. He accused contemporary playwrights of confusing the world with »schematizations of the world,« most egregiously in their reliance on what he called the Euclidean, »rounded« character that, reduced to a formula, could never achieve the inner life of a Hamlet or Woyzeck. As Wellman notes, »a play that is a perfect and seamless summation of itself and its own intentions, and nothing else, can only be consumed once« (Wellman, 1984, p. 64). In later years, Wellman widened his critique, stating that »sentimentality is the canker on

---

3   Wellman's interest in Bierce led him to pen a further »re-telling« shortly after *Difficulty*: the monologue *Bitter Bierce or The Friction We Call Grief* (Wellman, 2008, pp. 171–226).

the bud of American art—in fiction, in poetry, in the movies« (Garrett & Wellman, 1997, p. 95).

Wellman's concerns with language and culture ultimately feed into a highly developed theatrical aesthetic, one that eschews consistent character and psychological subtext for an ethics of presence. He explicitly rejects political theater that simply reinforces one's assumptions for a kind of didactic open-endedness rooted in the »junk of the real« (Wellman & Lee, 2006, p. vii).[4] One tool of this »poetic theater« is a chaotic approach to form that employs repetition on various levels, with the aim of allowing the work to move beyond the facile journalistic accounts of an issue (Wellman, 1993). As a result, as Helen Shaw notes, many plays are practically vaudeville in their substance, with a porous structure that allows meanings »to clamber in« (Shaw, 2008, p. vii). In recent years, Wellman's ethics of openness has embraced collaborations that have further transformed his work, chiefly among those who allowed Lang great freedom in setting *Difficulty* as a libretto (Garrett & Wellman, 1997, p. 91).

Wellman's politics and aesthetics are expressed materially by his concern with the physicality of language—words such as »objects flying around the room« (Robinson & Wellman, 1992, p. 49). This embodied aesthetics may be best illustrated in *Difficulty* by those scenes in which slaves appear to spout nonsense. For instance, the first scene where the elder Virginia Creeper intones, »But I fear his true mode of locomotion, like that of Prince Zandor, was more humble: the singleton crutch, or cane. Of the tribe of Crutch, or Cane« (Wellman, 2008, p. 125). We are unsure whether the character is speaking of Mr. Williamson or of the previously cited John C. Calhoun; even less do we know whether the puzzling allusions to »locomotion,« »Prince Zandor,« or »the tribe of Crutch« reflect an underlying belief in Voudou, Christianity, or the occult, or if it simply alludes to a special knowledge that the slave chorus shares: a kind of understanding beyond sense.[5] Wellman calls these passages »moments of transcendence, moments of being absolutely spiritually naked« (Garrett & Wellman, 1997, p. 88). In the repetition of simple words and phrases (»crutch, crane«), the language transforms and interacts with the music, which has a life of its own.

---

4   Wellman's collaborators present his aesthetic in a round-table discussion on »Writing and Performance« archived in *PAJ: A Journal of Performance and Art* (Mapp et al., 2012). Paul Castagno discusses the way meaning emerges from a »linguistic force field« in Wellman's plays (Castagno, 2012, p. 118), while Ehren Fordyce discusses the social psychology of his dramas (Fordyce, 2005, pp. 538–539).

5   Calhoun was a leading American political theorist during the first half of the nineteenth century who defended slavery as a »positive good« and inspired many Southern secessionists prior to the American Civil War. Luke L. Leonard (2010) discusses the ambiguity of Wellman's libretto.

The Third Re-telling: A Fractal Journey

The seven tellings of Wellman's original script for *Difficulty* survive intact in the libretto. But whereas the play began with the first courtroom scene, Lang suggested in rehearsals that Mrs. Williamson lead the first telling (Wellman, Lang & Munk, 2000, p. 35). Allowing Mrs. Williamson's singular, troubled voice to frame the dry legal proceedings brought an intimacy and poignancy to the production that might have risked sentimentalizing it, were her character not so closely identified with the central erasure at the play's center. Mrs. Williamson is identified with the face of the moon and with the gaps in a language that cannot name what is »more than a mere disappearance.« At the very beginning of the opera, we learn that, as she has no other name than »Mrs. Williamson,« her identity has been effaced along with that of her husband. The chorus of slaves that follow her introduction exist on a different ontological plane, their proper names replaced by mundane objects and qualities such as Round, Juniper, Crabgrass, Clock, Nuisance, Doorbell, and Virginia Creeper whose double name signals his leadership status. This first scene also introduces the primary themes that distinguish the play from its terse source material. Building a nation requires the erasures of Calhoun, a defender of slavery and Southern entitlement, the Kansas-Nebraska act of 1854, and »arrangement and regularity.« Yet mysteries of Selma, Alabama, appear to extend beyond these and appear to be intimately caught up with the Fortean disappearance of a man from his field. We meet, as well, the boy Sam and the Williamson girl. The former's membership in two classes whose speech is ignored—slave hands and children—serves as a counterweight to mad Mrs. Williamson, while the Williamson girl seems to access a hidden knowledge similar to that of the slave chorus. Thus, the members of the Williamson household share affinities with the field hands and thereby stand apart from those characters who participate in the legal proceedings to come.

The presiding magistrate opens the second and fifth tellings in a closed room, where he interrogates Selma planter Armour Wren and the overseer Andrew, the first an ostensible witness to the event, the latter a biased witness to the »monstrous and grotesque fictions« of the slaves. Wren's testimony draws liberally on Bierce's richly detailed language, including the discussion of some horses that motivated Mr. Williamson's stroll. Within each telling, the events are re-told several times, highlighting the »gaps […] in the factual evidence,« but perhaps moving closer, despite the magistrate's insistence, to the truth. Andrew's testimony veers into a manifesto on slave management, but when he admits his ignorance of the matter at hand his discourse changes radically, as though he were swallowed up by the knowledge of the slave chorus. The fifth telling culminates with the central irony of Bierce's story: »It is not the purpose of this narrative« to answer the question of Williamson's disappearance, but to render a verdict that will ensure his *legal* disappearance so that his estate may be distributed.

The central third and fourth tellings are devoted to a family flashback in which we meet Mr. Williamson just prior to the event and discover that his daughter tried to warn him with a vague poem in which »Someone or something goes. Someone or something stays in the night, or in the open and visible, in broad daylight.« In the sixth telling, Mr. Williamson recapitulates on arguments with his family, the memories of other witnesses, and the motion of light and shadow across the field while narrating his own disappearance. Consonant with Wellman's interest in fractal structures (Robinson & Wellman, 1992; Wellman, 1993; Garrett & Wellman, 1997), each telling contains within it multiple re-tellings, and dialogue introduced by one character migrates to the speech of another without warning, as in the case of Andrew the overseer. This process accelerates in the final, seventh telling, an epilogue that brings together the Williamson family, Sam, and the slave chorus, as the mother sits perched on the roof where she will stay until »they tell me this is a fiction, and I am not who I am.« Robinson notes that most of Wellman's characters are obsessives, »certain that if they sustain an intense scrutiny of an idea, its importance will reveal itself and the quandary of belief will be solved« (Robinson, 1992, p. 42). But the central lack that drives Wellman's circular narrative is less of an idea than of an immutable object, no more susceptible of explanation than that of the pasture in which it takes place.

The Fourth Re-telling: A Noble Music

Carey Perloff of San Francisco's American Conservatory Theater first suggested that Lang work with Wellman; rather than begin a new project, Lang agreed to use *Difficulty* as a libretto as it already seemed to adopt »premusical strategies« (Wellman, Lang & Munk, 2000, p. 35): recycling, repetition, and permeable characters. The result was, in his own words, his »favorite piece« (personal communication, 13 April 2012). His avowed aesthetics meshed with that of Wellman: a rejection of the manipulative in favor of »art that allows multiple doorways, multiple interpretations,« aided by music with an objective, often of highly abstract quality (Wellman, Lang & Munk, 2000, p. 37; c.f. Adair & Lang, 2011). Lang calls himself a tinkerer which, not coincidentally, is one of Wellman's self-descriptions; and the intricate structures that Lang fashions to elucidate characters are constructed from the same prosaic materials as the libretto, to much the same ends. Lang speaks of the nobility of classical music in the twenty-first century as a musical experience that—in opposition to the music of definite intention that surrounds us every day—allows the listener the luxury of an unexpected emotion (Alburger & Lang, 2000, p. 3; Faires & Lang, 2010). In *Difficulty,* this includes the music's suggestion that the slave owner, Mr. Williamson, has more in common with us than we would like to believe, that the chorus knows more than any single character in the play, and that Mrs. Williamson's madness has its own peculiar lucidity.

Difficulty's score relies on two basic harmonic/vocal-leading models and their variations. The opera begins with an introduction in E minor that provides material for a series of chorale variations. A related series of four measure (or slightly longer) ostinato figures arises from a simple contrapuntal framework: a four-note descending tetrachord set against a descending step-neighbor, as shown in a harmonic reduction in Example 1.

Example 1: First Vocal-leading Model, mm. 1–4.

This pattern appears in different modes and vocals, with both the scale fragment and the neighbor motive appearing in canon (see the first variation in mm. 21–26). The chorale model is opposed to a simple two-chord progression whose root motion descends by step. This vamp figure is a familiar signifier in minimal music, but here it may conjure for the listener the D minor to C major motion that symbolizes the unknowable forest at the opening of Claude Debussy's *Pelléas et Mélisande*. The vocalist enters in Scene 1 with scale degrees ^5-^1-^b3-^2 in E minor over this vamp, introducing a horizontal (0, 1, 3) trichord as a significant motive regarding vocalists and the violin, set against the whole-tone (0, 2, 4) harmony that closes the progression, as shown in an annotated reduction in Example 2.[6] This vamp will travel through several related modes: vocalized in several octaves (mm. 172–174), with the bassline altered to produce a more emphatic i-v progression (mm. 196–199), or at times pared back to a barely perceptible harmonic tic (mm. 216–219).

---

6   Pitch-class sets follow the conventions established in Forte (1974).

Example 2: Second Vocal-leading Model, Scene 1, mm. 2–5.

Lang's polyrhythms are as restrained as his harmonic language. The first i-VII vamp establishes a rhythmic cycle in diminution, as exemplified by the pattern of attacks cited in Example 2 (where 1 = eighth note). When the slave chorus enters at A (m. 64) with an even more static pitch and rhythmic presentation, droning fifths suggest repetitive cycles within cycles, as indicated by four levels of rhythmic motion from a half-note to an eighth-note triplet (see Example 3, mm. 80–82).

Example 3: Levels of Rhythmic Motion in mm. 80–82.

As Scene 2 opens, the step-semitone motive turns in on itself and infiltrates the chorale model to produce a chromaticized neighbor that expands outward symmetrically around C, as an A minor triad blossoms into G# major, as shown in Example 4.

Example 4: Scene 2, mm. 1–7.

These hollow fifths, followed by abrupt, almost violent changes in collection and mode, herald the entrance of the law and history, as they intrude on the private mystery. The neighbor progression expands and grows more dissonant in the third, fraught scene with the family just before Mr. Williamson's disappearance. The Williamson girl complains, »I think today is the day we all should stop talking« about thickly orchestrated root position harmonies (Example 5, mm. 1–5), which shifts to the second inversion when her discourse moves from the pragmatic to the poetic (mm. 41–72; 113–116; 129–136; 281–312; 345–364; 441–466). The cycle halts only when the Williamson girl serenades the moon with her mother (mm. 101–112; mm. 117–128), although it takes a more subdued form as the scene winds down, Mr. Williamson begins his journey across the field, and Scene 4 opens.

Example 5: Scene 3, mm. 1–5.

The only exception to the choral and vamp models presented above is a gospel-tinged walking bassline in compound time during Scene 4, which accompanies the boy Sam and the slave chorus as they take center stage. Yet even here, Lang remains within a four-bar, minor framework (excerpted in Example 6); he turns this model upside down when the slave overseer Andrew takes the stand in Scene 5.

Example 6: Scene 4, mm. 98–101.

As Scene 6 begins, the neighboring figure that introduces the courtroom in Scene 2 reappears, elaborated by rising tetrachords as the Williamson girl cries plaintively, »What is the point of talking crap like that?« Scene 6 closes with the boy Sam, followed by a »wordless prayer of thanks«—sung by everyone *but* Mrs. Williamson— which expands the rising, stepwise motion to reveal a third relation from E minor to C major, as shown in a harmonic reduction in Example 7 (mm. 1–6).

Example 7: Wordless Prayer of Thanks, mm. 1–6

The final scene opens with the only true aria of *Difficulty*, an unabashed, unaccompanied ABA, compound ternary form for Mrs. Williamson, with recursive aspects that summarize the opera's themes, as indicated by a chart of the aria's form in Example 8. Two four-measure phrases centered on E minor outline a two-chord vamp (in three dotted-quarters) followed by a series of straight eighth notes (mm. 1–3).

The opening A section is followed by an 11 measure development of the (0, 1, 3) motive (shown in mm. 11–14), in which Mrs. Williamson reflects—in another circular, recursive passage—on her immediate reaction to the disappearance. This small B section, representing the recent past, ends with a cadential phrase (»what an awful thing«) on a modal dominant (A, m. 18), whereupon the A section repeats. When the aria reaches measure 32, the quasi-dominant cadential phrase is elided with a B section featuring rising scales in E minor at »more than a mere disappearance« (m. 33, marked c on the chart). Here, the solo violin answers with the entire aria in canon. At measure 52, the mezzo soprano returns to the opening A section, followed by a dotted-quarter vamp and the dotted-quarter »more than a mere disappearance« scale motive, which continues through m. 88 as the violin's canon trails off. The boy Sam, the Williamson girl, and the chorus continue, yet Mrs. Williamson interrupts with one last unaccompanied solo in straight quarters: »I am staying up here till they tell me that this is a fiction and I am not who I am.« Her daughter concludes with the quartet and the music that opened Scene 4: »Someone or something carries a candle in the night, or in the open and visible, in broad daylight.«

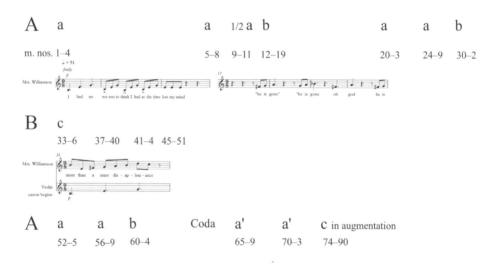

Example 8: Formal Chart of the Aria, Scene 7.

The Fifth Re-telling: A Field in Long Beach

A line of ushers at the Long Beach Opera directed the audience to the seating on the stage. Here, we faced a cavernous, dimly-lit auditorium framed by the proscenium and bisected by a metal hanamichi-like platform. The Williamson family members occupied the orchestra pit on a bed and chair; Mrs. Williamson portrayed the roof, seated atop a ladder masked by her voluminous skirts. The slave chorus tended the auditorium's empty chairs, rising up out of the blackness at various places to repeat, comment on, or take over the proceedings from the solo vocalists. The Lyris string quartet appeared to float off in the distance like a moon casting light on an empty field, while the presiding magistrate held forth from the balcony, when the same actor was not in the pit as Mr. Williamson, or heading into the gloom along the narrow platform as he »re-told« his own vanishing. The staging had the dual effect of both increasing the audience's intimacy with the performers and our distance from the material, as if we were part of the proceedings and might at any moment be asked to judge something that we never actually witnessed. Although period clothing and skillful casting rooted the narrative in mid-nineteenth century America, these touches of verisimilitude paradoxically rendered the question of the disappearance more abstractly, as though the performers functioned as avatars for earlier versions of ourselves.

The Sixth Re-telling: A History of the »Disappeared«

Bierce's politically astute, dispassionate, and succinct treatment of race, class, and history offered, in Wellman's terms, »a very elegant way of posing an enormous number of questions,« not least those that involved American politics in 1854 after the Kansas-Nebraska Act repealed the antislavery clause of the Missouri Compromise (Garrett & Wellman, 1997, p. 90). But writing about slavery directly, Wellman claims, would rob those characters »of their cunning silence, patience, their terse and succinct truth-telling. Their irony« (Garrett & Wellman, 1997, p. 90). The chorus of slaves in *Difficulty* make no more conventional sense than the—admittedly mad—character of Mrs. Williamson. As »it is not the purpose of [their] narrative,« owners and authority figures eventually depart the stage, leaving the dispossessed to »answer that question«: the slave chorus, the women, and the children, whose voices have been stricken from the official record. Yet like Mr. Williamson, those with titles and power seem more present in their absence. Neither the slaves nor the Williamson women bear Christian names that would accord them subjectivity in their community. Thus, both groups suffer a double loss: The disappearance of »Mr. Williamson« is also the loss of the signifier that knit them to their symbolic universe. Near the opera's closing stages, the Williamson girl forges a bond with the boy Sam, but Mrs. Williamson remains on the roof »till they tell me this is a fiction and I am not who I am.«

The Seventh Re-telling: Go Forth and Multiply

In the end, *Difficulty* does not so much pass the burden of truth to its audience as acknowledge that truth—that, as Bierce put it, »ingenious compound of desirability and appearance«—is a burden to be questioned (Bierce, 2001, p. 230). All who witness the series of seven numbered »tellings«—the central event recounted from different viewpoints—are implicated in a further cycle of »re-tellings« that spiral outward from each production. The opera's libretto, music, and the Long Beach Opera's particular staging all work to deny the redemptive power of narrative even as they offer repetition, remembrance, and re-reading as an ethical act. In Bierce's day, opera was »A play representing life in another world, whose inhabitants have no speech but song, no motions but gestures and no postures but attitudes,« wherein the actor took »the ape that howls« (Bierce, 2001, p. 174) for his model. Yet Lang and Wellman's opera most assuredly represents our world, a world whose inhabitants shift speech modes, postures, and sometimes identities without a clear resolution in sight. By replacing a central figure with a central lack, and a conventional plot with a circular, almost motionless narrative, *Difficulty* emphasizes the central mystery of the modern subject as a lack laid bare. Mr. Williamson has exited both the material world and the roles he played as patriarch, landholder, and overseer, a powerful figure who speculates in horses, land, and men. Yet he is not categorically dead, and thus cannot be memorialized: put to rest in his proper symbolic place. His disappearance rents the social fabric while offering an example of the unbridgeable gap that always exists between a subject and the symbolic order.

But this is only the first of the opera's many revelations. For it reminds us, as Georg Wilhelm Friedrich Hegel wrote about the Egyptians, that »the mysteries of Selma, Alabama« are mysteries for the Alabamians themselves and, by proxy, their audience. For Hegel, the Sphinx was the »objective riddle par excellence,« a work whose meaning remains obscure to all who witness it (Hegel, 1988, p. 360). So may *Difficulty* have remained an enigma for Bierce, Wellman and Lang? If Mr. Williamson's absence points to the lack that animates the social and economic disparities of the pre-Civil-War south, then perhaps the opera's marriage of hallucinatory images, cyclic repetition, and stagecraft bear witness to a lack that—in the present—drives the creation of new musical theater in a culture confused about opera's relevance in the twenty-first century.

References

Adair, M. & Lang, D. (2011). A Chat with Composer David Lang. *Los Angeles Times*, 14 June. http://latimesblogs.latimes.com/culturemonster/2011/06/disappearing-a-chat-with-david-lang.html (accessed 14 August 2014).

Alburger, M. & Lang, D. (2000). Bang on an Ear: An Interview with David Lang. *21st-century Music*, 7 (9), 1–24. http://www.21st-centurymusic.com/ML210009.pdf (accessed 14 August 2014).

Berkove, L. I. (2002). *A Prescription for Adversity: The Moral Art of Ambrose Bierce*. Columbus: Ohio State University Press.

Bierce, A. (2001). *The Unabridged Devil's Dictionary*. D. E. Schultz & S. J. Joshi (Eds.). Atlanta: University of Georgia Press.

Bierce, A. (1888). The Difficulty of Crossing a Field. *The Ambrose Bierce Project*. C. A. Warren (Ed.). http://www.ambrosebierce.org/difficulty.htm (accessed 14 August 2014).

Bierce, A. (1907). The Moonlit Road. *The Ambrose Bierce Project*. C. A. Warren (Ed.). http://www.ambrosebierce.org/moonlit.htm (accessed 14 August 2014).

Castagno, P. C. (2012). *New Playwriting Strategies: Language and Media in the 21st Century*, 2nd edition. New York: Routledge.

Davidson, Cathy N. (1984). *The Experimental Fictions of Ambrose Bierce*. Lincoln: University of Nebraska Press.

Faires, R. & Lang, D. (2010). Mystery Is Where It's At. *Austin Chronicle*, 30 April. http://www.austinchronicle.com/arts/2010-04-30/1022401/(accessed 14 August 2014)

Fordyce, E. (2005). Experimental Drama at the End of the Century. In D. Krasner, *A Companion to Twentieth-Century American Drama* (pp. 536–551). Oxford: Blackwell Publishing.

Forte, A. (1974). *The Structure of Atonal Music*. New Haven, CT: Yale University Press.

Garrett, S.-M. & Wellman, M. (1997). Werewolves, Fractals, and Forbidden Knowledge. *Theatre*, 27, 87–95.

Goho, J. (2014). *Journeys into Darkness: Critical Essays on Gothic Horror*. Lanham, MD: Rowman & Littlefield.

Griffin, M. (2009). *Ashes of the Mind: War and Memory in Northern Literature, 1865–1900*. Amherst: University of Massachusetts Press.

Hegel, G. W. F. (1988). *Lectures on Fine Art, Vol. 1*. Trans. T. M. Knox. Oxford: Oxford University Press.

Leonard, L. L. (2010). *Directing »The Difficulty of Crossing a Field«: A Symbolic and Corporeal Approach*. M.F.A. Thesis, University of Texas at Austin.

Mapp, J., Skiptares, T., Jesurun, J., Forti, S., Paxton, S., Hopkins, C., Maxwell, R., Parson, A-B., Lee, Y. J., Kalb, J., Lazar, P., Copper, K., Oswald, S., Greenberg, N., Weaver, L. & Kempson, S. (2012). Writing & Performance. *PAJ: A Journal of Performance and Art*, 34 (1), 119–140.

Swed, M. (2002). Portal to a Realm of Eerie Ambiguity: An Ambrose Bierce Tale Becomes a Haunting Musical Question in the New »The Difficulty of Crossing a Field.« *Los Angeles Times*, 25 March, F14.

Swed, M. (2011). Opera Review: David Lang's »The Difficulty of Crossing a Field« Given Southern California Premiere by Long Beach Opera. *Los Angeles Times*, 16 June. http://latimesblogs.latimes.com/culturemonster/2011/06/opera-review-david-langs-the-difficulty

-of-crossing-a-field-given-southern-california-premiere-by-lo.html (accessed 14 August 2014).

Robinson, M. (1992). Four Writers. *Theater,* 24 (1), 31–42.

Robinson, M. & Wellman, M. (1992). Figure of Speech: An Interview with Mac Wellman. *Performing Arts Journal,* 14 (1), 43–51.

Savran, D. (1999). The World According to Wellman. *American Theatre,* 16 (2), 16–21.

Shaw, H. (2008). Mac Wellman and Things of the Devil. In M. Wellman, *The Difficulty of Crossing a Field: Nine New Plays* (pp. vii–xii). Minneapolis: University of Minnesota Press.

Wellman, M. (1984). The Theatre of Good Intentions. *Performing Arts Journal,* 8 (3), 59–70.

Wellman, M. (1993). A Chrestomathy of 22 Answers to 22 Wholly Unaskable and Unrelated Questions Concerning Political and Poetic Theater. *Theater,* 24 (1), 43–51.

Wellman, M. (2008). *The Difficulty of Crossing a Field: Nine New Plays.* Minneapolis: University of Minnesota Press.

Wellman, M, Lang, D. & Munk, E. (2000). The Difficulty of Defending a Form. *Theater,* 30 (2), 34–43.

Wellman, M. & Lee, Y. J. (2006). *New Downtown Now: An Anthology of New Theater from Downtown New York.* Minneapolis: University of Minnesota Press.

Autorinnen und Autoren / Authors

Amy Bauer, Prof. PhD, lehrt Musikwissenschaft an der University of California at Irvine (US) / teaches musicology at the University of California at Irvine (US).

Mauro Fosco Bertola, Dr., lehrt Musikwissenschaft an der Ruprecht-Karls-Universität Heidelberg (Deutschland) / teaches musicology at the Ruprechts-Karls-University Heidelberg (Germany).

Frédéric Döhl, PD Dr. Ass. iur., lehrt Musikwissenschaft und Musikjournalismus an der Technischen Universität Dortmund (Deutschland) / teaches musicology and music journalism at the University of Technology Dortmund (Germany). Er ist zudem Privatdozent für Musikwissenschaft an der Freien Universität Berlin / He is also private lecturer in musicology at the Free University Berlin (Germany).

Marcus Gräser, Prof. Dr., lehrt Geschichte an der Johannes Kepler Universität Linz (Österreich) / teaches history at the Johannes Kepler University Linz (Austria).

Nils Grosch, Prof. Dr., lehrt Musikwissenschaft an der Universität Salzburg (Österreich) / teaches musicology at the University Salzburg (Austria).

Gregor Herzfeld, PD Dr., arbeitet derzeit als Dramaturg des Freiburger Barockorchesters in Freiburg (Deutschland) / works as dramaturge of the Freiburg Baroque Orchestra (Germany). Er ist zudem Privatdozent für Musikwissenschaft an der Freien Universität Berlin / He is also private lecturer in musicology at the Free University Berlin (Germany).

Marie Louise Herzfeld-Schild, Dr., ist wissenschaftliche Mitarbeiterin (postdoc) an der a.r.t.e.s. Graduate School for the Humanities an der Universität zu Köln (Deutschland) / is a post-doc research fellow at the a.r.t.e.s. Graduate School for the Humanities at the University Cologne (Germany).

John Link, Prof. PhD, lehrt Komposition und Musiktheorie an der William Paterson University (US) / teaches composition and music theory at the William Paterson University (US).

Christopher Lynch, PhD, lehrt Musikwissenschaft am Franklin & Marshall College (US) / teaches musicology at the Franklin & Marshall College (US).

Sharon Mirchandani, Prof. PhD, lehrt Musikwissenschaft an der Rider University (US) / teaches musicology at the Rider University (US).

Micah Wittmer, PhD, hat gerade ihre Promotion an der Harvard University (US) abgeschlossen / just recently gratuated with her PhD from Harvard University (US).

Aaron Ziegel, Ass. Prof. PhD, lehrt Musikwissenschaft an der Towson University (US) / teaches musicology at the Towson University (US).